BRIAN FR.
AND IRELAND'S DRAMA

Brian Friel is an enormously successful and respected Irish playwright whose reputation is growing rapidly in Britain and the
United States. This first full-length assessment of Friel and his work
identifies him as 'the Irish Chekhov' and places him in the context
of the development of Irish drama and of the European theatrical
tradition.

Richard Pine examines Friel's role as a man of the theatre and as a
political activist, and provides a framework for understanding his
origins as an Ulsterman. He follows Friel's exploration of different 'concepts of Irishness', investigates the role of drama in modern
Irish society, and locates Friel firmly in the vanguard of writers
who are exploring the emergence of a modern nation state. Pine has
discussed Friel's work with a wide range of writers, critics, and
commentators, including Friel's closest associates. Knowledge of
the private figure helps to illuminate the public writer, and a
perceptive picture emerges of the playwright and his role in the
shaping of Ireland's drama.

Richard Pine combines an international freelance lecturing and
writing schedule with a senior public affairs appointment at Radio
Telefis Eireann. Resident in Ireland since 1967, he has served as
Secretary of the Irish Writers' Union; he is co-editor of *The Irish
Literary Supplement*, a Governor of the Royal Irish Academy of
Music, and author of books on international cultural policy, Oscar
Wilde, the Dublin Gate Theatre and Lawrence Durrell.

for
EMILY PINE
face reader
who was right about Brian Friel

BRIAN FRIEL
AND
IRELAND'S DRAMA

Richard Pine

London and New York

First published 1990
by Routledge
11 New Fetter Lane, London EC4P 4EE

Simultaneously published in the USA and Canada
by Routledge
a division of Routledge, Chapman and Hall, Inc.
29 West 35th Steet, New York, NY 10001

© 1990 Richard Pine

Typeset in 10/12pt Garamond by
Ponting–Green Publishing Services, London
Printed in England by Clays Ltd, St Ives plc

British Library Cataloguing in Publication Data
Pine, Richard.
Brian Friel and Ireland's Drama.
1. Drama in English. Friel, Brian 1929–. Critical
studies
I. Title
822'.914

Library of Congress Cataloging in Publication Data
Pine, Richard.
Brian Friel and Ireland's Drama
Includes bibliographical references.
1. Friel, Brian–Criticism and interpretation. 2. National
characteristics, Irish, in literature. 3. Northern Ireland in
literature. 4. Ireland in literature. I. Title.
PR6056.R5Z86 1990
822'.914'–dc20   89-24222

ISBN 0 415 04753 6. – ISBN 0 415 04754 4 (pbk.)

CONTENTS

ACKNOWLEDGEMENTS

This book could not have been written without the active encourage-
ment and support of Seamus Deane and Richard Kearney, both of
University College, Dublin. Their constant advice and assistance
enabled the book to grow from an idea into a text; they both read
and commented very thoroughly on early drafts, but, more than
that, they believed in the book, and their reassurance, at times when
others displayed either incredulity or hostility to the project, was
vital. An early version was also read by Eilis MacCurtain Pearce
and O.Z. Whitehead, who made many helpful comments and
suggestions. I have also had the benefit of residence at the Tyrone
Guthrie Centre at Annaghmakerrig: as will be apparent, there could
have been no more appropriate rendezvous for myself and this
book, and my grateful thanks are due to the board of the Centre
and especially to the resident Director, Bernard Loughlin. At
Annaghmakerrig I have had the advantage of discussing this work
with other residents, and, in particular, I am happy to acknowledge
the valuable contributions of Crissie Poulter, Vincent Mahon and
Jim Sheridan, and also of Eugene McCabe. Ronald Mason, former
head of Radio Drama at the BBC, generously discussed the radio
plays and adaptations of Friel's work which he produced in Belfast
and London between 1958 and 1972. To my mother, who typed
three versions of the book, and to Tom McGrath, whose ability and
willingness to listen was indispensable, my heartfelt thanks. Gary
McKeone and Ulf Dantanus were able to lend me rare copies of the
radio plays. Anthony Roche (then of the University of Auburn,
Alabama), Will York, director of the graduate acting programme at
the Alabama State Theater (Montgomery), Brendan Flynn of the
Community School, Clifden and Julian Girdham of St Columba's
College, Rathfarnham, gave me the opportunity of discussing the

plays with their students. To Brian Friel (and his family) for hospitality, forbearance and, above all, honesty, I cannot properly express my thanks and appreciation. Finally, to Colm Toibin I owe an apology: I promised not to use the word 'discourse', and inevitably I broke that promise.

Richard Pine
Annaghmakerrig

ABBREVIATIONS

For ease of reference, all quotations from the published texts of plays or short stories by Brian Friel are followed by the relevant page reference. Reference to other texts and to unpublished material – mainly the typescripts of radio plays, and communications by Brian Friel to the author – are by means of superscript numbers. The following abbreviations, indicating the editions I have consulted, will be found throughout.

Ar.	*Aristocrats*, Dublin: Gallery Press, 1981
Cass	*The Loves of Cass McGuire*, Dublin: Gallery Press, 1984
CC	*The Communication Cord*, London: Faber and Faber, 1983
CF	*Crystal and Fox*, Dublin: Gallery Press, 1984
Diviner	*The Diviner, the Best Stories of Brian Friel*, with an introduction by Seamus Deane, Dublin: O'Brien Press, 1983
DL	*Dancing at Lughnasa*, London: Faber and Faber, 1990
EW	*The Enemy Within*, Dublin: Gallery Press, 1979
FH	*Faith Healer*, London: Faber and Faber, 1980
Freedom	*The Freedom of the City*, London: Faber and Faber, 1972
FS	*Fathers and Sons: after the novel by Ivan Turgenev*, London: Faber and Faber, 1987
GI	*The Gentle Island*, London: Davis Poynter, 1973
Gold	*The Gold in the Sea*, London: Faber and Faber, 1969
LQ	*Living Quarters*, London: Faber and Faber, 1978
MH	*Making History*, London: Faber and Faber, 1989
MS	*The Mundy Scheme*, in *Two Plays*, New York: Farrar Straus and Giroux, 1970

Ph.	*Philadelphia, Here I Come!*, London: Faber and Faber, 1965
Saucer	*The Saucer of Larks*, London: Gollancz, 1962
Sisters	*Three Sisters* by Anton Chekhov, a translation, Dublin: Gallery Press, 1981
Tr.	*Translations*, London: Faber and Faber, 1981
Vol.	*Volunteers*, London: Faber and Faber, 1979

CHRONOLOGY

1929   Brian Friel born in Omagh, County Tyrone.
1939   Friel family moves to Derry City.
           Friel attends St Columb's College, Derry.
1949   BA Degree, St Patrick's College, Maynooth.
           Teacher training course at St Joseph's College, Belfast.
1950   Teaches in primary and intermediate schools in Derry.
1952   Starts writing short stories; contract with *New Yorker*.
1958   *A Sort of Freedom* produced by BBC Northern Ireland Home Service; *To This Hard House* (BBC Radio).
1962   *A Doubtful Paradise* (BBC Radio); *The Enemy Within*, Abbey Theatre, Dublin (BBC Radio, 1963); *The Saucer of Larks* (Gollancz).
1963   With Tyrone Guthrie in Minneapolis, USA; *The Blind Mice*, Olympia Theatre, Dublin and BBC Radio.
1964   *Philadelphia, Here I Come!,* Gaiety Theatre, Dublin (New York; Lyric Theatre London, 1967).
1966   *The Gold in the Sea* (Gollancz); *The Loves of Cass McGuire*, Helen Hayes Theater, New York (Abbey Theatre, Dublin, 1967).
1967   *Lovers*, Gate Theatre, Dublin (Fortune Theatre, London, 1968)
1968   *Crystal and Fox*, Gaiety Theatre, Dublin.
1969   *The Mundy Scheme*, Olympia Theatre, Dublin.
1971   *The Gentle Island*, Olympia Theatre, Dublin.
1973   *The Freedom of the City*, Royal Court Theatre, London: Abbey Theatre, Dublin (New York, 1974).
1975   *Volunteers*, Abbey Theatre, Dublin.
1977   *Living Quarters*, Abbey Theatre, Dublin.
1979   *Faith Healer*, Longacre Theater, New York (Royal Court

Theatre, London. 1981; Abbey Theatre, Dublin, 1982); *Aristocrats*, Abbey Theatre, Dublin.

1980   Friel and Stephen Rea found Field Day Theatre Company; *Translations*, Guildhall, Derry (Hampstead and Lyttleton Theatres, 1981; Manhattan Theatre Club, New York, 1981).

1981   *Three Sisters*, Guildhall, Derry; Gaiety Theatre, Dublin.

1982   *The Communication Cord*, Guildhall, Derry; Gaiety Theatre, Dublin; (Hampstead Theatre, London, 1983).

1987   Friel is appointed to the Irish Senate; *Fathers and Sons*, Lyttleton Theatre, London (Long Wharf, New Haven, 1988).

1988   *Making History*, Guildhall, Derry; Gaiety Theatre, Dublin; National Theatre, London.

1989   BBC Radio devotes a six-play season to Friel: the first living playwright so to be distinguished.

1990   *Dancing at Lughnasa*, Abbey Theatre, Dublin; National Theatre, London.

INTRODUCTION

Since 1955, when he began writing professionally, Brian Friel has gained an international reputation for Irish writing in the English language. An Ulsterman who has worked in the genres of short story, radio drama and public stage, this Irish Chekhov has maintained a tradition of Irish literature by addressing local themes which have universal significance, so that plays such as *Philadelphia, Here I Come!* and *Translations* not only earn him acclaim on Broadway and in London, in Estonia and Catalonia, but also find their way into the core of the professional and amateur repertoire. He becomes increasingly the subject of serious critical attention which is tending to focus on the relationship between playwriting and other kinds of writing such as politics and history. In 1989 BBC Radio marked his achievement by devoting a season to six of his plays, the first living dramatist to be thus acknowledged. As a post-colonial writer he has much in common with his contemporaries, in particular throughout the African continent.

He is a child of a worldwide period of revaluation of the meaning and purpose of the word. Theories of evolution, relativity and psychology have provided possibilities of re-examining the basic logocentric tenet of the book: 'In the beginning was the Word.' In the theatre Friel proves himself a modern master, along with Pirandello, Beckett and Stoppard, in his reaction to this central problem of modern aesthetics.

Contemporary Irish drama begins in 1964 in *Philadelphia, Here I Come!*, with Gareth O'Donnell's bewilderment: 'I don't know. I – I – I don't know' *(Ph.* 110). Friel has plotted a course through the minefield not only of language but of personality, discrepancy, and mendacity, which creates the alternating theatre of hope and despair. His splitting of Gareth O'Donnell into the parallel

1

personae of Private Gar and Public Gar enabled him to address the interior and exterior worlds, to maintain a private conversation while conducting a public address, and his subsequent characters, in one guise or another, have continued this ploy in an attempt at reuniting the whole, integrated person in a definitive homecoming.

Thus, the location of 'Ballybeg' and its hinterland becomes the ground on which the O'Donnell family makes its various epiphanies, moving through a series of explorations which provides us with a public spectacle of growth while also charting the playwright's private odyssey. It is a world which often approximates to revelation and finality but just as easily plunges back into the inarticulate. Gar's 'I don't know' soon becomes the disorientation and ferocious indignity of *Crystal and Fox* (1968) which juxtaposes the animal and the angelic, merges hope and despair. It is not always clear to the audience (nor, one suspects, to the playwright himself) what is going to happen, or what the happening means, even though the root of this action, the psychic compulsion to leave home in order to regain it, is imprinted genetically in the collective un-conscious.

But a remarkable two-year period of writing in the late 1970s demonstrated Friel's capacity for establishing a liminality, a passage between private and public which amounts to ritual. On 28 September 1964 (the opening night of *Philadelphia, Here I Come!*) two Gareth O'Donnells, the public and the private, left home. After fifteen years in limbo, a homecoming was almost reached in the utterly Chekhovian *Aristocrats* (1979), but it was still necessary for Friel to effect two separate reunions. Then 'Private' came back in the guise of Frank Hardy in *Faith Healer* (also 1979) while 'Public' returned in 1980 as Owen O'Donnell in *Translations*. In the former case, Friel marked the recognition and quietus of the 'enemy within'; in the latter, he confronted that enemy whom he located in the public world, thus re-integrating the family he had so viciously fragmented in *Philadelphia.*

With *Faith Healer* and *Translations* Friel consolidated his position as one of the leading dramatists of our time, comparable in stature and context to Anton Chekhov. His map of Ballybeg is a portrait of modern society and its precarious lien on the verge of history: provincial, peripheral, subject to the eternal quest of individuals and communities for a homecoming, a way of reaching the hearth, an integration.

One of Friel's most compelling achievements is his

approximation, in his writing of *Translations*, to the work of George Steiner. In the master of the hedge-school we *see* the Dominus of a senescent culture, and assent to a linguistic illusion in which, without apparent translation, words spoken in one language are comprehended in another; but what we *hear* are words from the first chapter of George Steiner's *After Babel*: [1] 'it can happen that a civilisation can be imprisoned in a linguistic contour which no longer matches the landscape of fact' (*Tr.*43).

So many disturbing questions arise from the conjunction of these writers: our physical, physiological, psychological, mantic and semantic relations to landscape and to history become fragile and elusive quantities. What are we doing here at all? Are these 'privacies' (*Tr.*67) anything more than ghosts within our public personae, and is any interpretation possible between individual languages? How does one in fact establish the intimate sense of community (*communitas*) and then learn to grow into the society (*societas*) of the wider, larger, more complex world? Can there ever be a true conciliation between private language and public discourse? Is the concept of 'community' even practicable in the age of the global village?

In *Translations* Friel gives us the chance to bring to life abstract arguments and preoccupations by showing us the powerful living presence of myth in all our social actions, providing, like Synge, 'a fiction in search of belief', [2] which also shows us our own beliefs in a fictive relation to time, place and history: he thus turns drama back on itself, because he questions its relation to the 'real' world. Nothing is stable or concrete; form and content have a fluid relationship which can be alarming for an audience which finds itself moving instantaneously from the public plane to a deep connection between its own private preoccupations and those of the stage.

Friel becomes the Irish Chekhov because for him the world is not Ireland writ large but Ireland is the world writ small. A society in search of its identity must know the pathways and holy places of the mind as surely as it knows its streets, hedgerows and sheeptracks. The metaphor he employs, that of map-making, is both peculiarly Irish and peculiarly Russian. Friel's Chekhovian world combines an insistence on the importance of the everyday experience with the 'if only' of the theatre of hope. In his work, as in Beckett's, therefore, we find an acute awareness of the tragi-comic, precisely because the outsider, the deviant, the wanderer, the rebel, are central, rather than peripheral, to the way in which Irish society, like Russian society, exercises itself. This is the lesson and legacy of a colonial past, a provincialism which is still being worked through in a self-conscious search for currency. Ireland's history, in Friel's and Steiner's terms, imprisons it in a linguistic and intellectual contour which struggles to contain the past, both real and imagined, and at the same time to go out to confront its new realities. It is a prison which can project false images onto a future already apprenticed to myth. In divining this problem in his most recent plays Friel has confirmed himself as Ireland's most important contemporary writer.

If, then, Friel is close to Chekhov in what he says about locality, the significance of this fact lies not in the universal application but in the simple correspondence between the minds of the two writers. If Chekhov had been Irish, he might have written like Friel ... Why? Because the relation of culture to psychology is similar in both writers. In *The Seagull*, Chekhov's Trigorin says

> I am not a mere landscape painter, I'm also a citizen of my country, I love people. As an author I feel I'm in duty bound to write about the people, their sufferings, their future, and about science, the rights of man, and so on. [3]

Friel, too, feels a commitment to explore not only the 'landscape of fact' but also the psychological terrain, the habits, fears, and preoccupations of his locale. And because he can do so in a dramatic representation which so often takes the form of an intimate history lesson, a handing down of local experience, he fulfils Steiner's dictum that 'only genius can elaborate a vision so intense and specific that it will come across the intervening barrier of broken syntax or private meaning'. [4]

In perceiving this I have found it necessary to construct my own map of 'Ballybeg' in order to understand the 'Ballybeg' of Friel's divining mind. Thus, the examination of culture and psychology in chapter 1 is absolutely necessary in helping us to establish a view of Friel not only in relation to his own work but also in relation to Synge, Beckett, and Thomas Murphy, the only major figures of the Irish theatre with whom he shows any great affinity, and beyond Ireland with Eugene O'Neill and Chekhov. It is also the key to his method of adapting or dramatising the core arguments and central facts of sources such as Oscar Lewis's *La Vida* (in *The Freedom of the City*), Erving Goffman's *Forms of Talk* (in *The Communication*

Cord), Sean O'Faolain's *The Great O'Neill* (in *Making History*) and J.H. Andrews's *Paper Landscape* (in *Translations*).

In an early play, *The Mundy Scheme* (1969), Friel asked 'What happens to an emerging country when it has emerged?' (*MS* 157). There are many corollaries and subsidiary questions, all of them concerned with the rite of passage from provincial colonialism to sovereign state, and the psychic and cultural adjustments that take place in transition and transformation. Friel's career offers us the chance to study the personal development of an Irish writer – an Ulster writer and, moreover, a *west* Ulster writer – who is intimately concerned with his own and his people's circumstances. It allows us to explore the relation of culture to psychology, the way in which what we *mean* to say is often inaccurately conveyed or comprehended: the difference between perception and communication of what we perceive. The potent relation of myth to modern history (as discussed for example by Steiner [5]) becomes a dramatic experience in itself. If we examine not only Friel's plays, but also his short stories and his involvement with Field Day Theatre Company, we can find there, to use his own words, some 'concepts of Irishness' [6] with a wider significance. These are essential if we are to make sense of the modern world with which Friel has presented us. Such an exploration will involve us in a series of psycho-social exhumations, as we investigate this divining role: as a diviner, Friel occupies that dangerous position described by Victor Turner in referring to 'shamans, diviners, mediums, priests' as outsiders in a society's rite of passage. They precipitate 'actions and relationships which do not flow from a recognized social status but originate outside it'. [7] This sacerdotal profession is obviously most crucial in a society which seems, like the tribes which make up the sense of Ireland, or 'concepts of Irishness', to be continually experiencing a rite of passage, a transition from past to future, from mythos to logos, from becoming to being.

Friel's Ireland, if it exists at all, is a complexity of loyalties, horrors, hopes, confused time sequences, hostilities of the sacred and profane, a constant probing of its role as victim, a continual belief in the restoration of a way of living and thinking which was beneficent and provident but which has somehow turned tragic and punitive. The phenomenon of Brian Friel is made possible by the combination of two matrices: the tension between a known, secure, but receding and fading heritage, and an unknown, beckoning, tantalising future which baits and challenges.

Between these two matrices the playwright is left to work out the relative values, properties and affiliations of these 'concepts of Irishness'. He chooses to do so by imagining or containing them – he calls them religion, politics, money, position, marriage, revolts, affairs, love, loyalty, disaffection [8] – within the form of a 'family saga'. [9] None of them is mutually exclusive, nor are they necessarily inclusive: Friel's catalogue, for example, omits one of the most central of the tensions in his stories and early plays, between 'dignity' and its shadow, 'respectability'. A further tension is that between 'intellect ' and 'emotion' in almost all his folk. In each case there is a transition, a passage, for which metaphors must be found. In these crossings Friel shows us movements from one plane to another, from one time to another and also from one state of mind to another. To achieve this he has had to stand outside the 'home' which he denies himself, in order to describe it. It is in this sense that he says 'There is no home...no hearth...I acknowledge no community'. [10] The revenants who people his later plays replicate the exiles of his earlier works, but they cast their shadows in worlds vastly changed from those they once abandoned. The words are transmuted by echo.

In making that denial of home and the consequent fragmentation of experience, Friel underlines the fact that one cannot repossess that which was never possessed; that one cannot recreate that which was never whole; and that one cannot reconcile two elements which have not previously been conciliated. In this sense the present book, like *Making History*, is about modern Ireland. If I need a thesis it is the obscene affect of history as an irreconcilable problem of the human will. If I need to underline its presence in Friel's work, it is in the way he deals with the subject of fate in *The Freedom of the City*. Central to this obscene history and the problem of dispossession and violence is Friel's treatment of horror. That he mediates horror with too great a tenderness is his great quality as a man and his continual danger as an artist. But as a diviner he could not do otherwise. That tenderness, fatal to public art but essential to private survival, wrecks the precarious balance which Friel tries to maintain at the threshold between these worlds. It is of great significance to the direction his next work, *Dancing at Lughnasa*, has taken that he re-established this balance in *Fathers and Sons* as a necessary prelude to the writing of *Making History*.

This is not a book 'about' the conflicts of Northern Ireland. It is not even a book to which Northern Ireland, as a problematic political entity, is central. But it inevitably deals with the Northern, or Ulster, psyche and personality. It concerns itself with the poverty, dignity, violence, incomprehension, which Friel addresses because they are found on both sides of the physical border which divides modern Ulster. Dispossession, repossession and the returning home of the exile are of course on both sides of our mental border too. Moreover, the tendency towards melancholia, of which Friel's short stories are redolent, is not alone the product of modern Irish history, but may also result from a landscape shorn of its temporality. As Sir Tyrone Guthrie, Friel's fellow Ulsterman, friend and mentor, said of the Irish climate – he was writing particularly about Ulster – it induces 'gentle melancholy meditation...long, lazy, philosophic or reminiscent talks...anecdotage...alcoholism...a great, an overwhelming, consciousness of sin'. [11] And, perhaps for this reason, Guthrie thought, Irishmen 'suspect pity and reject patronage'. Philosophy, reminiscence, self-reproach, escapism: these are indeed one side of the equation of Irishness, but there is another which provides one of Friel's own basic creeds:

> we are still a peasant society. Peasant is an emotive word. It evokes sympathy (saint, dreamer, pure, individual, pastoral) or disgust (ignorant, vulgar, philistine, thick). But to understand anything about the history or present health of Irish drama, one must first acknowledge the peasant mind, then recognize its two dominant elements: one is a passion for the land; the other a paranoiac individualism. [12]

The conflict between these elements provides the material for the individual's struggle against authority, and also for the tribalism which runs throughout his work, beginning with *The Enemy Within* and summed up in Maire's observation in *Translations* – 'as cute as the Buncrana people' (*Tr.* 22): a tribal intuition which is divisive and full of local, familiar rivalry, rather than a nationalism which might be cohesive, unitary, and founded on common motivation.

Again, denial and fragmentation, rivalry and division, are implicit in everything Friel has written, and bitterly, but necessarily, explicit in his major plays. We can only assume allegiance or cohesion temporarily, not immemorially, and this applies equally to the artist himself as to his subject matter. All our assumptions must be temporary because (to return to Steiner's image) the landscape of fact, of perception, of inference, is constantly changing.

Friel's career also follows a natural progression from his first short stories and plays for radio (which fall together into what he calls 'private conversation' [13]) to the 'public address' of his stage plays. I have taken a thematic approach to the plays of 'love' and affiliation (chapter 3), plays of 'freedom', poverty, possession and repossession (chapter 4), and plays of 'language', meaning and ambiguity (chapter 5). In his latest work Friel has taken a public stance in exploring the difference between the private, inner land-scape and the world surrounding it and affecting it. Like Chekhov in the foundation of the Moscow Art Theatre he has become 'political' in describing 'the hidden inner psychological meaning' [14] and its significance in the agora.

In this public address it is natural that language should be the principal villain and the preordained victim. Friel's theatre stresses the fact that human behaviour burdens and importunes language in a way which bedevils meaning and the life of culture itself. As another post-colonial writer, the Kenyan Ngugi wa'Thiongo has written: 'values are the basis of a people's identity, their sense of particularity as members of the human race. All this is carried by language. Language as culture is the collective memory bank of a people's experience in history.' [15] Here is another extremely import-ant clue to the meaning of the hedge-school, as the focus of what Ngugi calls 'orature', [16] the oral transmission of culture.

Like Synge and Ngugi, Friel has provided us with a new language, an Irish–English more powerful than English–English, to express these 'concepts of Irishness', which becomes a new metaphor by means of which we can discuss both public and private sorrows, fears and even joys. And probably, just as in the case of Synge, it is the fears that stand between love and hate that have made this most necessary. It was the intention of the founders of the Irish Literary Theatre in 1899 (of whom Synge was one) to 'bring upon the stage the deeper thoughts and emotions of Ireland' [17] and the propinquity of joy and fear which they revealed has re-emerged in Friel's work.

Friel's later work stresses, like Synge's, the importance of searching within syntax, rhythm and vocabulary for the roots of difference and perception. This is especially important in distinguishing his own world-view from that of more logocentric cultures with which it comes in contact: every word counts in Friel, even though the texture differs from the density of *Faith Healer* (in which the linguistic becomes overwhelmingly visual) to the transparency of *Translations* (in which the process is reversed). Both these plays appear, one from its structure, the other from its assumptions, to be unperformable, and this serves to demonstrate the difference between a text and a dramatic experience. I have accepted that distinction. It is possible to regard Friel as text, context or pretext. I have chosen the middle path, that of context.

Friel's stories of the 1950s might at first seem to belong to another writer and another space than that occupied by today's playwright; *Faith Healer* could not have been written by the author of *The Gentle Island*. But in retrospect we can see a quite clear and deliberate progression, first from the short story *The Child* (1952) to *Philadelphia, Here I Come!* (1964); second from *The Enemy Within* (1962) to *Translations* (1980) and *Making History* (1988), and third a progress from the accumulated work of the private dramatist towards the public figure who directs Field Day Theatre Company. In particular, his most recent play, *Dancing at Lughnasa*, emphasises that the man Friel has become is the same man, translated, who began writing short stories in the 1950s, but inevitably changed, and in such a way that he begins to think of himself as (in the title of Florence Wilson's ballad about Thomas Russell) 'the man from god knows where'. [18] As Hannah Arendt says, 'Conscience is the anticipation of the fellow who awaits you if and when you come home'. [19]

Part I
PRIVATE
CONVERSATION

1

THE LANDSCAPE PAINTER

A search for images and symbols adequate to our predicament
Seamus Heaney [1]

MAN, PLACE AND TIME

Brian Friel was born in Killyclogher, close to the town of Omagh in County Tyrone, on either 9 or 10 January 1929. His father, Patrick Friel, was a schoolteacher and his mother was a postmistress; he attended the nearby National (Primary) School at Culmore, of which his father was the Principal. Friel has two sisters (also teachers) and had a younger brother who died in infancy. The figure of the schoolmaster appears in many of Friel's stories, and provides the central character for *Translations*; more importantly, perhaps, parent and mentor coalesce in two early stories, 'My Father and the Sergeant' [2] and 'The Illusionists' [3] in which Friel discusses the child's relationship with both these figures of authority.

Friel was born into a tradition of nationalism which takes its social and political hue from the context of west Ulster. This fact is also important for an understanding of both Friel's response to the cultural and political history of this part of Ireland and his sense of identity and association within his own place. So too is his consciousness of the fact that all his grandparents were Irish-speaking, and that two, his father's father and his mother's mother, were unlettered; this at times seems paradoxical to the writer working through the *English* language, one of whose principal concerns is the role of language in social communication.

Friel's father's family comes from Derry, in Northern Ireland, where the surname is common, while his mother's family is from

Glenties, in the west of County Donegal; as we shall see, this is a
crucial distinction in Friel's sense of place and in the location of his
imaginary world. A travelogue piece for *Holiday* magazine in 1963
entitled 'A Fine Day at Glenties' in fact provides a microcosm of
this world, identifying the vital elements, human, animal, topo-
graphic and meteorological, which constitute the successful operation of a finely balanced set of behaviours and contains within its
conservatism a healthy respect for disorder and deviance. [4] If Friel
is the Irish Chekhov we immediately need to know about his
'constituency', the term he prefers to the disavowed 'community', [5]
where the people of his stories and plays come from, what social
preoccupations they express and how their dilemmas are resolved.
In his portrait of Glenties he presents us with 'The Strawman
Shanaghan, the trick-o-the-loop man'; Eddie Doherty, 'farmer,
casual laborer...a practical hard-working man, not given to day-
dreams' (even though he is daydreaming as he paints this self-
portrait); Patrick Farrelly, Esq., 'but God and Glenties know him as
Pat Tom Nally, that is to say, Patrick, son of Thomas, grandson of
Eleanor'; Brigid Costigan ('Boston Biddy') who has been to, and
returned from, Boston, who is discontented: 'but that is the way she
will always be all her life because she imagines herself an unhappy
exile'; and the fair itself, 'an atmosphere, an animation, an aura of
adventure', which passes between fact and fiction: 'Glenties is the
stage, and the fairgoers are the players. This is the real thing, the
superb performance, that wonderful experience of hundreds of
people behaving naturally.' It is because performance is the real
thing, and drama is a natural condition of that social reality, that
Friel tells us: 'the events in this piece have happened at one time or
another; the people are fictitious and bear no resemblance to
anybody, living or dead'. The piece is therefore classified as 'fiction',
although there can be little room for improvement as a sociological
essay, because Friel's engagement with his 'constituency' creates
types of life sufficient to populate and encompass the largest issues
with their essential actors.

The Irish Chekhov is an Ulsterman, subject to Ulster's cultural
and political history and attempting to divine its personality. To
understand that personality the four main statements about Friel's
origins made in the preceding paragraphs must be elaborated and
qualified in order to find the values implicit within them, a task
made especially difficult since Ulster's historical and present
circumstances render improbable most attempts at definition.

Naming, for Friel as for Beckett, is the key to identity, but in his own case it presents a difficulty which typifies the position of the individual in relation to authority, and the problem of communication between two cultures: for, although he is known as *Brian* Friel, his birth certificates bear the names *Bernard* Patrick Friel. At the time of Friel's birth the Protestant bureaucracy discouraged the registration of 'Gaelic' names, and it is likely that the Anglicisation 'Bernard' was adopted for the purpose of registration in place of the intended 'Brian'. Certificates, because one exists in respect of 9 January and another for 10 January. It is not only Friel's light-heartedness but also a sense of the duality in his background and in his destiny, which makes him offer the suggestion 'Perhaps I'm twins.' [6] Self as 'otherness' is one of the basic forms of recognition for which Friel strives, and one which he initially approached in *Philadelphia* through the device of dividing the main character into two stage entities. [7]

The problem of naming can be argued by extension from Brian/Bernard Friel to the society in which he lives. For while Friel's world, the city of Derry and its hinterland, is known and real and tangible, it is almost impossible to *name* it: known to the Nationalists as Derry and to the Unionists as Londonderry, the city has only partially entered the official lexicon as 'Derry' since the Nationalist- (or Catholic-) controlled council voted to change its name; while the county surrounding it, by similarly democratic decision of the Unionist- (or Protestant-) controlled County Council, remains 'Londonderry'; BBC newsreaders, while retaining the official nomenclature of the province, now accent it as London-*derry*' whereas it was formerly pronounced '*London*-derry'. Friel's father served three terms on the council during the years of Unionist gerrymandering.

It is a divided society characterising, in its divisions, the historical evolution of western Ulster (as distinct from that of the industrialised, urbanised east). Ulster itself, one of the historical provinces of Ireland, was artificially divided by the creation in 1920 of a land boundary between the Irish Free State (later to become the Republic of Ireland) and that part of Ulster which remains within the United Kingdom, and is known as the political entity of 'Northern Ireland'. Three counties of the historical province of Ulster (Donegal, Cavan and Monaghan) became part of the Republic. Tyrone Guthrie's mother, at the time of the partition, wrote to him from their home in County Monaghan that instead of going *south* to meet strangers, they would now have to regard *northerners* as alien [8]. A new border was being drawn on the map of the mind, as well as in the atlas.

Northern Donegal, for which Derry is the natural focus, is restricted in its commerce by this boundary, and the county is itself only linked to the rest of the Republic by a narrow neck of land at its southernmost tip. At its northernmost end the peninsula of Inishowen, where Friel now lives, is, by definition, only narrowly connected to the rest of the county, and, although part of the Republic, is more northerly than almost all of 'Northern' Ireland. Moreover, as Professor Heslinga points out, 'in the course of one-and-a-half millennia "Ulster" has stood for many territories... Historically ... there is as much or as little justification for the modern Northern definition of "Ulster"... as for the pre-partition defini-tion'. [9] Without a name, a place, like a person, is incapable of fully discussing its identity, conducting its business, knowing its destiny; while it can perceive itself, it cannot celebrate itself, except by subverting simile, metaphor and analogue, by pressing imagination into mendacity.

Writing about Ulster has been problematic for 'southerners' who are largely ignorant of life in Ulster. Few residents of the Republic travel to Northern Ireland, and very few indeed have any regular contact with Ulster folk and their ways. Dervla Murphy, conscious of this lacuna, says that her 'discovery' of Northern Ireland, *A Place Apart*, was 'conceived by shame out of repentance'. [10] The mutual distrust and resentment which persists on both sides of the border is not, however, the result of that border, although its existence may have intensified the provincial rivalry already fundamental to Irish society. Indeed, Daniel O'Connell 'the Liberator' found his almost complete ignorance of Ulster a serious political disadvantage; this in itself may have helped to entrench Unionism rather than win over northern Presbyterians to the Liberal democratic alliance which O'Connell attempted to forge in the wake of Catholic emancipa-tion. [11]

The border counties in particular live in a state of bewilderment, especially Donegal which lies to the north, rather than the south, of much of Northern Ireland. In the drawing of the 1920 border Donegal lost Derry, and Derry lost Donegal. Friel locates most of his stories in Donegal and most of his plays after 1964 are set in 'Ballybeg', an imaginative realm *across the border* from Derry, the city where he has spent much of his life and of which he considers himself a citizen.

Friel's commitment to place is intense and acute. In 1939, when he was ten, his family returned from Omagh to Derry, where his father took up a new teaching post. Since then, with two important interludes, he has lived in Derry or in its hinterland. Educated at St Columb's College in the city, he then attended for over two years St Patrick's College, the national seminary at Maynooth near Dublin, a constituent college of the National University of Ireland. There he explored the vocation which he believed he had for the priesthood. He is reluctant to discuss this period of his development in which he was dismayed by the revelation of Irish Catholicism which it afforded, and which resulted in his play *The Blind Mice*. When it became evident that he was not called, he decided to follow his father's profession, and, after teacher training in St Joseph's College, Belfast, taught in Derry from 1950.

This description of Friel's background suggests a lack of fullness, or wholeness, both in himself and his 'constituency'. Such a lacuna is the greatest single factor in determining the way we see the world, and particularly the way that the 'landscape painter' represents both the zone and its people. It explains the tension between the two positions of the artist in relation to the alter ego or 'enemy within', and in relation to the public world. It also explains the sense of loss which has fractured a people's history, and the hope of reparation or restoration which gives them a sense of their future. Friel has taken this tension and this dichotomy and made them his personal style; in each of his characters who portrays the inner man in conflict with the public world, Columba (in *The Enemy Within*), Gar (Gareth O'Donnell in *Philadelphia, Here I Come!*), Fox Melarkey (in *Crystal and Fox*), Frank Hardy (in *Faith Healer*), Hugh O'Donnell (in *Translations*) and Hugh O'Neill (in *Making History*), we also see a man trying to make himself whole and to complete his vision of the world by satisfying the world's demands. And beyond these characters, a range of secondary characters act out the condition of dispossession, displacement, disintegration, the culture of poverty. Friel's activity as a writer is not merely his *response to* situations but also his *involvement in* them. He senses in himself the capacity to become a figure of authority, and to fulfil a shamanistic role, and at the same time to work out his own personal preoccupations and to coincide with the trajectory of Ballybeg.

Displacement and lack of wholeness are both spatial and temporal, physical and metaphysical. In Friel's early plays, this dilemma is expressed in the character of Columba in *The Enemy Within*, who casts out the devils of his private, tribal allegiances thus:

> Get out of my monastery! Get out of my island! Get out of my life! Go back to those damned mountains and seductive hills that have robbed me of my Christ! (*EW* 70)

But the inner man, 'the soul', remains chained to that seduction, 'to the green wooded earth of Ireland' (*EW* 21). This is both spatial, in that it tempts him away from his monastery on Iona, and temporal, in that it relies on the affective power of memory. It is a condition of internal exile in which the central image of the Irish historical imagination, the hearth, is known to be unattainable. Because the *community* cannot be collected around the hearth, therefore, Friel prefers to regard those of whom he writes, and those to whom he responds, as his 'constituency'.

Friel is very conscious of the passage of time: while it may not alter one's basic preoccupations or priorities, it subtly or rudely brings about change in the way we pursue those priorities, and in the way we perceive both ourselves and the objects of our pursuit. As Steiner says, the writer 'finds himself in constant motion, driven by time and the pressure of intervening images'. [12] This makes Friel dismissive of the past, insistent that the private details of his life are not in the public domain, that the only reality, for him, is the work-in-progress. He disregards all his work to date as 'finished...it is as it is'. [13] This lack of interest does not mean, however, that he intends to dissociate himself from what he writes. He has also said:

> You delve into a particular corner of yourself that's dark and uneasy, and you articulate the confusions and the unease of that particular period. When you do that, that's finished and you acquire other corners of unease and discontent. [14]

But the continuing exorcism of one's ghosts is also a temporal process. Even the dispossessed lost their wholeness and their place at some point in the past, and entertain hopes of repossession and restitution in time future. The desire to become whole is a project of future will. As Friel said in 1972 at the age of 43: 'I hope that between now and my death I will have acquired a religion, a philosophy, a sense of life, that will make the end less frightening than it appears to me at this moment.' [15]

There seem to be two main elements in such a hope: the idea of vocation as a lifework, an outward exploration of concern, and the idea of rationalisation or internal reconciliation of experience with belief. In this connection the mere facts of Friel's career are not as important as the attitudes which these facts represent. To quote Friel again:

> What is a fact in the context of autobiography? A fact is something that happened to me or something I experienced. It can also be something I thought happened to me, something I thought I experienced. Or indeed an autobiographical fact can be pure fiction and no less true or reliable for that. [16]

One might regard this as evasive attitudinising, but to illustrate his point Friel relates an incident central to his childhood and clear in his memory, which he now realises and acknowledges could not in fact have taken place:

> The boy I see is about nine years old and my father would have been in his early forties. We are walking home from a lake with our fishing rods across our shoulders...And there we are...singing about how my boat can safely float through the teeth of wind and weather. That's the memory. That's what happened. [17]

This affective memory, which commands the emotive side of our behaviour, is the central agent in Friel's writing. His own attempt to capture this particular memory becomes the basic ingredient in the harrowing experience at the heart of *Philadelphia*, when Gar tries to establish a line of communication with his father, to coax him into recognising that they had once shared that same experience; the mere details of the 'fact' being immaterial compared with the importance of the shared memory:

> PUBLIC (*quickly*): It doesn't matter who owned it. It doesn't even matter that it was blue. But d'you remember one afternoon in May, we were up there, the two of us, and it must have rained because you put your jacket round my shoulders and gave me your hat –
>
> S.B.: Aye?
>
> PUBLIC: And it wasn't that we were talking or anything, but suddenly, suddenly you sang 'All Round My Hat I'll Wear a Green Coloured Ribbono' –

S.B.: Me?

PUBLIC: – for no reason at all except that we, that you were happy. D'you remember? D'you remember? (*There is a pause while S.B. tries to recall*)

S.B.: No ... no, then, I don't ...

PRIVATE:(*quickly*): There! There! There!

S.B: 'All Round My Hat'? No, I don't think I ever knew that one. It wasn't 'The Flower of Sweet Strabane', was it? That was my song.

PUBLIC: It could have been. It doesn't matter.

PRIVATE: So now you know: it never happened! Ha-ha-ha-ha-ha.

(*Ph*.105)

'Private' Gar mocks his public persona not because the fishing expedition never took place, but because the affective memory has failed. Screwballs O'Donnell has failed his son by clutching at an alternative identity – 'that was my song' – and thus negating the appeal to a common time, or place, or emotion. We can individuate the common fragmented experiences, and appropriate as much of this failing memory as we can, but we also construct, in an attempt to re-integrate, those fragments which no-one else seems to acknowledge. Of his own fishing experience Friel tells us:

> for some reason this vivid memory is there in the storehouse of the mind. For some reason the mind has shuffled the pieces of verifiable truth and *composed a truth of its own*. For me it is a truth. And because I acknowledge its peculiar veracity, it becomes a layer of my subsoil; it becomes part of me. [18] (*my emphasis*)

Ultimately it is inevitable that this psychic craving for narrative wholeness will mesh with the greater political will of a people: the landscape painter must include the battle-scenes as well as the pastoral image, since they stand on the same ground. But both stem from the same simple question: ' "What is history?" Is it "the truth" or "a story"?' which makes life a drama, in Heaney's words 'a way of reshaping the consciousness of the audience in posterity...to engross the present and dominate the memory'. [19] Thus, the broken family, at home perhaps but unable to possess it either materially or metaphorically, engages in an interior drama by means of which it 'imposes a truth of its own'. On the physical plane this means

20

simply a *sense* of place; on the metaphysical, an understanding of the *culture* of the place, of the freedoms and restraints of boundaries, continuities, loyalty and betrayal, definitions, and ambiguities.

One of Friel's chief preoccupations has been the ambi-valence in both Irish and English history of the life of Hugh O'Neill, Earl of Tyrone (1550–1616); his childhood, his exogamy, his dual loyalties to the Gaelic chieftains and the English crown, his exile and the way history has fashioned him into a particular type. Having as a very young man read Sean O'Faolain's biography of O'Neill, Friel was fascinated by O'Faolain's suggestion that 'a talented dramatist might write an informative, entertaining, ironical play on the theme of the living man helplessly watching his translation into a star in the face of all the facts that had reduced him to poverty, exile and defeat'. [20] The significance of these words will not be lost to the reader as we follow Friel's exploration of those themes in Columba, Frank Hardy, and the various manifestations of the O'Donnell family, until we reach his most recent major 'creation', Hugh O'Neill himself.

It is relatively easy to state the remaining biographical facts necessary to furnish an introduction to Friel: at the same time as he began teaching he began to explore another 'vocation' (although he disavows the 'rotundity of the expression' [21]) as a writer of short stories, published mainly in *The New Yorker* with whom he had a 'first reading agreement'. He established a substantial reputation in this genre, in which he conducted a 'private conversation' exploring certain areas of his own background and of the Irish psyche. This period of his career, and the transition into the writing of radio plays, is discussed in chapters 2 and 3. From radio plays he moved into the playhouse. He discounts his first and third plays (a *Doubtful Paradise* and *The Blind Mice*), which he has refused to publish, but *The Enemy Within* (1962) marks the beginning of what can now be seen as a conscious line of exploration of the themes of self-discovery, exile, the relationship of time (and distance) to affection, and the problems of communication.

Friel attracted the attention of theatre director Tyrone Guthrie, who invited him to spend five months in America in 1962, observing his direction of *Hamlet* and *Three Sisters*, shortly before the opening of the Guthrie Theater in Minneapolis. This, says Friel, was 'my first parole from inbred, claustrophobic Ireland', [22] and it encouraged him to hear his own voice more confidently than before. Although married with a young family, he took the risk of writing full time, achieving his first international success with *Philadelphia,*

Here I Come! in 1964, first at the Dublin Theatre Festival and subsequently on Broadway. Since then he has written fourteen further plays, two short pieces for television, an adaptation or 'translation' of *Three Sisters*, a dramatisation of *Fathers and Sons* and a new version of Macklin's *The True-Born Irishman*, under the title *London Vertigo*. He continues to live close to Derry, for which he maintains a loyal affection, not least because 'it takes its animus and its ethos as much from the twenty-six counties as from the six'. [23] He built a house at Muff, just over the border in Donegal, and latterly he has moved to an old house further up the coast at Greencastle, above Moville. While writing plays remains his preoccupation, his involvement since 1980 in the daily business of the Field Day Theatre Company, which is both a touring company and a publishing house, makes a regular and heavy call on his time.

Friel describes the period in his life when he was teaching and writing stories in the evening as:

> the time when I first began to wonder what it was to be an Irish Catholic...to survey and analyse the mixed holding I had inherited, the personal, traditional and acquired knowledge that cocooned me, an Irish Catholic teacher with a nationalist background, living in a schizophrenic community...What I hope is emerging is...a faith, a feeling for life, a way of seeing life...the patient assembly of a superstructure which imposes a discipline and within which work can be performed in the light of an insight, a group of ideas, a carefully cultivated attitude; or, as Seamus Heaney puts it...there are only certain stretches of ground over which the writer's divining rod will come to life. [24]

The reference to Heaney is not fortuitous. Divining and digging are recurring images in Heaney's poems, and he has written:

> If I were asked for a figure who represents pure technique I would say a water diviner. You can't learn the craft of dowsing and divining, it is a gift for being in touch with what is there, hidden and real, a gift for mediating between the latent source and the community. [25]

In the same essay Heaney refers to the connection between the poet's 'original accent and his discovered style...the discovery of a way of writing that is natural and adequate to your sensibility'. Friel as diviner, however, has no simple task. In his own statement he refers to the 'schizophrenic community' and the 'mixed holding', and the tendency towards what has perhaps been too readily termed 'schizophrenia' is a marked condition of Irish life. 'Displacement from' one's language, land, and citizenship, and ultimately from one's history, is not synonymous with 'loss of' those properties: they continue to exist somewhere in parallel with one's destiny, untouchable but not invisible, at one remove but not finally disappeared. The splitting, or schizoid, aspect of this life is that in attempting to live one's culture one must simultaneously celebrate its strengths without offering another occasion for their loss, sing the old songs, recite the histories, while guarding against their dispersal. Thus one learns to live parallel lives, as shown in what Heaney calls Derry's 'obstinate bilingual determination to live in and through its two names'. [26]

Like Friel, Heaney (who shares much of the same background) believes that language has a life of its own, that 'the poet does not so much master a language as surrender to it'. [27] But the 'landscape painter' is obliged to create two, or perhaps many, simultaneous images, and in Friel's case this surrender has led to a main storyline on which he has worked many variations, as he makes necessary deviations in pursuit of different forms of truth. Place-names are sometimes important, sometimes immaterial, and can be subjected to ruthless action which shatters much more than the management of everyday life. As Heaney tells us, place-names 'lie deep, like some script indelibly written into the nervous system', [28] but when they are bifurcated the writer is faced with difficult choices. There has been an historical muteness of the Irish tongue which gives the writer a 'sense of belonging to a silent ancestry...with which he has embarrassed relations' [29] while there is today a corresponding, though not necessarily connected, silence which is the colonised's response to the coloniser; a need to speak but to employ forms of words which negate language and its connotations: 'whatever you say, say nothing'. [30] It is in these circumstances that Friel deploys what Heaney calls, in a brilliant phrase which identifies (and acknowledges) both sides of the problem, 'his subversive intelligence'. [31]

Friel's technique is closely allied to the 'divining' or 'digging' of Heaney's fieldwork. It is a personal construct of reality, a worldview based to a certain extent on the treasure surrendered by the strata of past experience, whether individual or collective. It is territorial, tribal, imaginative; it provides us with the tension between a society and its environment. As Friel half-mockingly said in 1975 in *Volunteers*:

> Archaeology is the scientific study of people and their culture ...What you have around you is encapsulated history, a tangible précis of the story of Irish man...the more practical our information about our ancestors, the more accurate our deductions about his attitudes, the way he thought, what his philosophy was, in other words the more comprehensive our definition of him...the more we learn about our ancestors...the more we discover about ourselves...a thrilling voyage in *self-discovery*...But the big question is: How many of us want to make that journey?
>
> (*Vol.* 31–2)

After the experience of addressing the themes of *Faith Healer* and *Translations*, Friel may very well appreciate even more grimly the distinctions between culture and civility which create the tensions of *Making History*, and which make this Irish Chekhov the fiercer and more forbidding dramatist. O'Faolain, discussing the extinction of Gaelic Ireland, says that:

> nowhere did it so obstinately persist as in the remote Ulster...it had conditioned a racial psychosis...its racial arrogance, its indiscipline, its rashness, its lack of thought, its impatience, its incogitancy, its hatred of change, its shallow opportunism, its lack of foresight.

In divining this historical experience and creating figures such as Hugh O'Donnell, Friel will have remembered that O'Faolain continues:

> there is in our respect for all such ancient ways of life much more than a veneration for something that in lasting so long seems, by its very endurance, to have established an *a priori* right to our respect. What we venerate, surely in those customs, is their intimations, as yet only half-realized, of a sensible philosophy of life, which those who practice them have no other way of expressing. [32]

In making a simultaneous voyage of self-discovery, Friel therefore finds that in his archaeology he is proving the impermanence, the provisionality, of all our assumptions, and the danger of complacency: in O'Faolain's words, 'wherever life becomes too secure, or too easy, it decays for lack of change' ;[33] in Hugh O'Donnell's, 'we fossilise' (*Tr.*66). The diviner or archaeologist stands on the threshold of both past and present, a metaphor we shall meet often in exploring Friel's work.

It becomes important therefore, not so much to research Friel's own personal circumstances as to divine his own divination, to construct a map of 'Ballybeg' in our own minds in order to find it in Friel's. The 'mixed holding' which sometimes bewilders him is the subject of the 'voyage in self-discovery'. It is also a typical ritual of transition from a state of unease and discontent and psychic disorder to one of wholeness. The following pages explore that transition, the states of mind through which it passes, and the condition of liminality which marks the passage.

DRAMA AS RITUAL

Except when (as in *Living Quarters* or *Aristocrats*) he employs stage tricks, Friel traffics in ordinary sensations: we see no ghosts, we hear no voices, we are not bewitched by faery. In examining the way in which a society receives and organises the experiences and emotions which are Friel's subject matter – the phenomena of love, courage, tenderness, *dignitas*, *gravitas*, the private landscape, and the public world, the effect of time, the 'tarot' of the community – we shall provide ourselves with a key to the sensations of the 'mixed holding'.

In order to survive, in order to 'make sense' of experience, we select, organise, classify, ordinate and stratify our knowledge, so that by creating a rationale, developing a sense out of sensation, we may control our environment. This instinct for survival is known as the *will*; it is superior to *being* and *knowing* because future projects must be *willed* in order to activate the otherwise passive memory. The will is therefore the safeguard, the gatekeeper, of intellect or 'internal vision'. [34]

If we lose that control we may once again become landless, placeless, aglossal, lose our identity, our grip on reality. As Steiner says in *After Babel*:

We speak less than the truth, we fragment in order to reconstruct desired alternatives, we select and elide. It is not 'the things which are' that we say, but those which might be, which we would bring about, which the eye and remembrance compose. [35]

The world, in other words, must be reduced to manageable proportions; we have to create *a* world out of all the *possible* worlds, even including the unpleasant, tragic or puzzling elements of life, so that they can be managed. We must allow the world to tell us that which we need to know, and must forbid it to tell us that which we should not know, even at the risk of losing what we love or crave. In this way, we can 'will' our own tragic fate, as an essential ingredient in the future project. In 1966–8 Friel gave plentiful evidence of how he intended to follow Gar's uncertain exodus with attempts at homecomings (*The Loves of Cass McGuire*, 1966), at the freedom of impetuous flight (*Lovers*, 1967) and at the nature of betrayal (*Crystal and Fox*, 1968). In Fox Melarkey he gives us a crucial portrait of one kind of desperate passion triumphing over, and destroying, a more tender but subservient love. Friel explored this dichotomy with supreme maturity in 1979 in *Faith Healer* and has returned to it in the post-language plays (1987–8) *Fathers and Sons*, *Making History* and *Dancing at Lughnasa*.

The dichotomy illustrates an important and salutary collision between the intellectual and the romantic traditions. Ulf Dantanus refers to 'Friel's basically tragic creative imagination...[his] philosophic and artistic stance which is founded on the essential irony of life'. [36] This irony, that man exercises his freedom in obeying the dictates of fate, that a homecoming is essential and yet impossible, that the successful act of love is also one of betrayal, is what most allies Friel to Chekhov. And it exemplifies the chief characteristic of both writers – comparing, for example, *Aristocrats* with *The Cherry Orchard*, or *Translations* with *The Seagull* – that they discover, within the intellectual quest for the 'dark and private places of individual souls', [37] a means of decoding the condition of despair in which the romantic artist, on the outside of society, finds himself.

Steiner states that, in order to survive the weight of experience, we 'live lives based on selected fictions', [38] yet there is a distinction to be made between the capacity for truth and the capacity for fiction, and that distinction is based on the special condition of madness, the inclination to stand outside (*ekstasis*) rather than inside the institutes. Hugh O'Donnell in *Translations* echoes Steiner: [39] 'to remember everything is a form of madness' (*Tr.* 67); but Columba has told us 'I remember everything' (*EW* 18). Some are prepared to set boundaries to the known world, to give it shape, to name their perceptions, to *nominate*, from all the possible ideas, those by which their daily lives can be governed. But others have to jump over the fence, to become barbarians, because that is the only way they can find to embrace their otherness.

A civilisation is a community which has drawn a circle around its identity in order to civilise (to make civil) some barbarians, and yet to exclude more than it embraces. There is a fundamental relationship between culture and *communitas*. But even here we need to distinguish between 'truths immemorially posited' (*Tr.*42) and the laws by which our society is actually governed, and which give us our boundaries and the rules to play within them. This is clearly established by Friel in *The Gentle Island* in which the biblical device of the two sons is used to show that the role of one in the community is hearth-based and poetic, replacing the lost mother, while the other is outward and manly, deputising for the discommoded father.

Communication translates discrete psychologies into a public culture. This is one of Friel's public tasks. Private psychology provides, public culture authorises. That which is excluded is ignored – (unknown, *ignotus*): *Barbarus hic ego sum quia non intelligor ulli*:[40] I am a barbarian here because no one understands me' (*Tr.* 64).

Naming, the *consuetudo nominationum*[41] or, as Friel calls it, the *caerimonia nominationis* (*Tr.* 23), is central to place and also to time. Places are named *through* time; it is a sensual as well as a temporal process. A thing, a person, or a place initially has no name. Perceiving it, we compare its properties with similar objects, identify its points of congruence and divergence, and name it. *It* can then utter its own name, a catechetic identity, and thus become a subject:

> OWEN: We name a thing and – bang! it leaps into existence!
> YOLLAND: Each name a perfect equation with its roots!
> (*Tr.* 45)[42]

(Already some of the mocking humour of *The Communication Cord* can be detected here.)

Without a name I cannot function, because I cannot say 'I', I cannot express a psychology, I cannot perceive. To announce one's name is to offer one's most secret life. As Steiner says:

To falsify or withhold one's real name...is to guard one's life from pillage or alien procurement. To pretend to be another, to oneself or at large, is to employ the 'alternative' powers of language in the most thorough, ontologically liberating way... Through the 'make-up' of language, man is able, in part at least, to exit from his own skin, and, where the compulsion to 'otherness' becomes pathological, to splinter his own identity into unrelated or contrastive voices. The speech of schizophrenia is that of extreme 'alternity'. [43]

Similarly, to be given another name is to receive a new identity, something of which we may be justifiably afraid. It affects us superficially, but it also questions our deeper understanding of our identity. It makes that identity provisional, turns 'who we are' into 'who we may be'. It interferes quintessentially with our ability to decide on courses of action. Thus Cass is seduced by the following exchange:

TRILBE: By the way, m'dear, what *is* your Christian name?
CASS: Cass.
TRILBE: Cass? Cass? It's certainly not Cass.

(*Cass* 24)

The statement is uncompromising, but it causes the equivocation in Cass's subsequent conduct and relations with both her family and cognate members of 'Eden House'. Cass becomes 'Catherine', and she in her turn renames Mr Ingram (who already has the shadow identity of 'Meurice') as 'Buster'. When she adopts her new identity, accepting Trilbe's re-naming, she con-fuses her past per-sonae, both real and imagined:

CASS: My name is Olsen by the way. My late husband, mebbe you heard of him, General Cornelius Olsen; he made quite a name for himself in the last war, but you just call me Catherine.

(*Cass* 67)

And to be given a nickname, or alternative name, is to be denied one's real existence. Officially, as we have seen, 'Brian Friel' does not exist. Although we cannot penetrate his privacy, we can speculate on the effect that the denial and imposition of names can have had on his view of personality. It is another recipe for Steiner's schizophrenic 'alternity'. Not only people: within the extended family, places, people, and things (shipwrecked objects in *The*

Gentle Island, or those with personal associations, such as the pieces of furniture in *Aristocrats*) take on special names according to their role: patronymics, nicknames (according to job, idiosyncrasy or distinguishing features), size or achievement. In *Making History* Hugh O'Neill is known as Hugh, as The O'Neill, and as the Earl of Tyrone, or simply Tyrone. [44] The name as a persona, therefore, is a function of time, an intricate association of history and secrecy.

Ireland, like Russia, suffers from such schizophrenia. It is recognisable in R.D. Laing's statement, 'the experience and behaviour that gets labelled schizophrenia is a special strategy that a person invents in order to live in an unlivable situation'. [45] Both these peoples suffer from the inability to say 'I am': there is no expression in the Irish or Russian language for the present tense of the verb *to be*. Self is perceived as otherness, as someone else to whom things happen, to whom experience accrues. It comes naturally to writers like Friel and Beckett in putting on the stage images and symbols of their own predicament.

In this context the 'images for the affection' are also closely felt, although other, and they can therefore be devalued as easily as they can be elevated and mystified. We must remember that *Philadelphia* and Friel's other early plays are the product of his early thirties, and of a period when Ireland's 'oppressive atmosphere' made many young men unequivocally and bitterly angry. 'Let me communicate with someone, that's what they all advise, communicate, pour out your pent-up feelings into a sympathetic ear' (*Ph.* 42–3). However, the 'Master', the archetypal pedagogue, becomes a 'sorry wreck ...arrogant and pathetic' (*Ph.* 44) and the 'Canon' Mick O'Byrne, that other 'moulder of the mind', is upbraided for his inability to mediate:

> There's an affinity between Screwballs and me that no one, literally, no one could understand except you Canon (*deadly serious*), because you're warm, and kind and soft and sympathetic, all things to all men; because you could translate all this loneliness, this groping, this dreadful bloody buffoonery into Christian terms that will make life bearable for us all. And yet you don't say a word. Why Canon? Why arid Canon? Isn't it your job, to translate?
>
> (*Ph.* 96)

The outburst that Friel puts into Gar's mouth is surely a loosing of his own frustration:

29

Look around you for God's sake! Look at Master Boyle!
Look at my father! Look at the Canon! Look at the boys!
Asylum cases, the whole bloody lot of them!...it's a bloody
quagmire, a backwater, a dead-end! And everybody in it goes
crazy sooner or later! Everybody!

(*Ph.* 80–1)

(In *The Enemy Within* Grillaan asks Columba: 'A priest or a
politician – which?' [*EW* 33] Within this degraded tarot, the difference hardly seems relevant.)

Within the known permissible world we organise the qualities of
life; types of space, of direction, of belief, of sensation, are at first
confused and held together in a single aesthetic: *aistheta*, that which
is perceived. I perceive a tree, I perceive motion, I perceive a god,
are, at first, ideas of equal validity and meaning. But in order to
avoid a metaphysical chaos we soon discover the need to codify, to
establish both lateral and vertical hierarchies: the concept of time, as
a result of observing motion; the concept of change, as a result of
observing the process of time; ultimately, awareness of one's own
awareness, and the realisation of self, persuade us that to explore
self we must understand otherness and embarrassment. Communication, we discover, is shared, unembarrassed meaning, the social
construction of reality. Structures of knowledge, structures of belief,
structures of society, are the result of this communication or con-
sensus.

We select that which we *need* to know (*logos*). But, if the will
functions badly as gatekeeper, we also allow ourselves to select that
which we *want* to know (*mythos*). The confusion of the two results
in embarrassment and psychic disorder. Existence, or being, is
therefore a membrane or metaphor between myth and logic. This is
a mytho-logical present where past and future, known and unknown,
seen and unseen meet. As Ernest Fenollosa says, 'metaphor is ...the
very substance of poetry...the bridge whereby to cross from the
minor truth of the seen to the major truth of the unseen'. [46]

Vision, because it is the quickest sense, is the paradigm of all
experience. The way we appear, our epiphany (*epiphanein*), is our
first identity. Once we understand what vision is, we realise that that
which can see can also be seen. Thus we establish the reciprocity of
vision, and therefore of existence. *To know* means *to have seen*
(*eidenai* is the past tense of *idein*). All meaning comes from
imaging, that is, from picturing to oneself, so that we can think

within on that which we have seen without. But the discrepancy between what we see (imagine) and what we think (know) is that while our public world is primarily visual, our interior world is aural. We see ideas, but they are interpreted, controlled and marshalled by voices. This distinction is essential in considering the difference between the world presented to the audience in *Faith Healer* and the interior world of its characters. The medium of reception and transmission is the same: I am the threshold, the membrane of cultural exchange. Another potential embarrassment, another source of psychic disorder, arises when we continue to use the visual imperative: demanding that you comprehend, I cry: 'Can't you *see!*'

Map-making becomes a metaphor of the visual and the literal. We explain the world with words, we re-present it with pictures. Our maps, whether they are images of the interior landscape or of the public world, are our way of expressing more than the merely superficial contours. As André Brink puts it in his essay 'Map-makers':

> The writer is not concerned only with 'reproducing' the real. What he does is to perceive, below the line of the map he draws, the contours of another world. And from the inter-action between the land as he *perceives* it to be and the land as he knows it *can* be, someone from outside, the 'reader' of the map, watches and aids the emergence of the meaning of the map. [47]

Or as one of Ireland's current cartographers says: 'to fasten my experience of the territory to my expression of it on paper...a map will be faithful to more than the measurable'. [48]

A map, like an icon, puts before us a paradigm, something which mediates between an *absolute* and that which we can comprehend. Through maps, icons and myths, the unrealistic concepts of un-controlled space, being and time are made real. Words, particularly written words, are secondary to all this. As Brink says, truth, 'which is...vast and non-verbal, has to assume the form of language', socially acceptable, codified, but also subjectively uttered by 'a relative, uncertain, undependable, disreputable man' who is 'con-stantly humbled by his encounters with truth and with the world'. [49]

Words themselves become relative, uncertain, undependable, dis-reputable, and it may be necessary for the writer to dispense with the prevailing conventions, either by inventing new languages, or by abandoning words themselves in favour of new media. The aesthetic world and its security system might therefore be posited in this way:

ABSOLUTE PHENOMENA

	SPACE	TIME	BEING	OTHERNESS
PARADIGM	World	History	God	Kin
MEDIATION	Place	Myth	Identity	Tarot
PERCEPTION	Vision	Motion	Thinking	Distance
KNOWLEDGE	Omphalos	Present	Persona	Affection
EXPRESSION	Digging	Word	Nomination	Love
INSTITUTE	Boundary	Text	Icon	Tribe

The absolute phenomena, which we cannot perceive or conceive, are represented to us by means of 'paradigms' which make them conceivable but not yet perceptible: world for space, history for absolute time, god for absolute being, kin for 'otherness'. To become the subject of 'perception', however, these paradigmatic concepts must be 'mediated': world by place, which is thus perceived by vision; history by myth which is perceived by temporal motion; God by identity, which is perceived by thought; the paradigm of kin by the tarot, perceived by distance and difference. Perceptions are turned into 'knowledge' and knowledge is thus capable of being 'expressed'. The 'institutes', or boundaries, enable us to distinguish between the permitted and the impermissible, between that which enables life to be lived and that which kills life.

WITHIN	WITHOUT
Communitas	Societas
Simplex	Complex
Ballybeg	Ballymore
Country	Town
Stability	Chaos
Ordered Speech	Babel
Name	Anonymity
Security	Challenge
Religion of Control	Religion of Ecstasy
Mythos	Logos
Unconscious	Conscious
Lived	Learned
Illiterate	Literate
Intuitive	Analytic

Of course, because it is logocentric, such a schema does not sufficiently explain how we become aware of our own existence. Consciousness, or perception of self, depends on being perceived by others. The central importance of the 'esse est percipi' theory is not that *one* is perceived, but that *both* are mutually perceived in a symbiotic relationship.

In such a way we can understand our communal interactions and our relationship, as people, with the real and surreal landscape. It is by becoming conscious of the movement from one condition to another that society, or an individual, can take account not only of the passage of time, but also of the psychic motion which is being undertaken, a carrying across of the psyche from illness to health, from ignorance to knowledge, from incompleteness to fulfilment, from relative barbarism to relative civility. As V.W. Turner remarks,

> Practically all rituals of any length and complexity represent a passage from one position to another. In this regard they may be said to possess temporal structure and to be dominated by the notion of time. But in passing from structure to structure many rituals pass through communitas. Communitas is almost always thought of as portrayed by actors as a timeless condition, an eternal now, as 'a moment in and not of time', or as a state to which the structural view of time is not applicable. [50]

It is when such a state of *liminality* is achieved – standing on the threshold, signifying both arrival and departure – that the artist, or shaman or diviner is at his most vulnerable, and the experience is most painful. To conduct the tribe, or even one's own incomplete self, from one side of the membrane to the other, demands that the artist become membrane himself, establish the threshold, or medium, by which each world can address the other. The *sacerdos liminalis* is therefore a polyglot, able to translate both worlds, but a citizen in neither. As Hegel says, 'Ich bin der Kampf. Ich bin nicht Einer der im Kampf Begriffenen, sondern Ich bin Kampfende und der Kampf selbst' (I am the conflict. I am not one of the combatants. I am both combatants and the conflict itself). [51] Turner's work provides almost a commentary on this stance:

> In this gap between ordered worlds almost anything can happen. In this interim of liminality the possibility exists of standing aside not only from one's own social position but

from all social positions and of formulating a potentially unlimited series of alternative social arrangements. [52]

We shall see in *Making History* the especial tragedy that can occur in this 'gap'.

That Turner's theories, based on observation of African tribes, are applicable to Irish drama is clear from his basic theory that drama is the root of all ritual, and that participants are 'released from structure into communitas only to return to structures revitalised by the experience of communitas'. [53] We shall see particularly in the case of *The Freedom of the City* and *Translations* how essential this condition of liminality can be, and how in *Living Quarters* and *Aristocrats* 'almost anything can happen'. As Friel himself said, 'Ritual is part of all drama. Drama without ritual is poetry without rhythm – hence not poetry, not drama...Drama is a RITE, and always religious in the purest sense.' [54]

There is a clear indication here of the influence of Tyrone Guthrie, who wrote in 1966:

> The most important rites...centred upon human sacrifice... Gradually...instead of an actual sacrifice, the offering took symbolic form. A *story* of sacrifice was enacted in honour of the God: a tragedy. All theatrical performances, from *Oedipus* to striptease, are conducted, like war dances, like rain dances, according to age-old formulae...The theatre relates itself to God by means of ritual. It does so more consistently than any other activity, except prayer because, like organized prayer, it is the direct descendant of primitive religious ceremonies. [55]

Also, of course, ritual theatre serves as a therapy through role-playing, a psychic release of physical tensions (between man and man) and metaphysical problems (between man and God). But this brings us back to the fact that we must, whether consciously or 'subliminally', achieve some awareness of the fact that the passage-ritual is affecting us, that the therapy is in fact taking effect. And that requires that we are conscious of passage through time *and* space.

To comprehend time *and* place we need to understand place *as* time. This may seem somewhat abstract until we consult the world of writers like Eliot, Heaney, Durrell and Beckett, who in some way mediate in their own work between the myths of sacred history and our everyday cultures. The five senses do not of themselves enable us to understand what 'sense' of place, or 'sense' of time are. Beckett's introduction to *Film* helps to illustrate not only his own concern with his particular brand of metaphysics: it also expressly tackles the problem of what we mean by perception, if 'to be' means 'to be perceived':

> *Esse est percipi.* All extraneous perception suppressed, animal, human, divine, self-perception maintains in being. Search of non-being in flight from extraneous perception breaking down in inescapability of self-perception ... In order to be figured in this situation the protagonist is sundered into object (O) and eye (E), the former in flight, the latter in pursuit. It will not be clear until end of film that pursuing perception is not extraneous, but self. [56]

Not extraneous, but self. Therein lies the absolute problem of knowing where *I* ends and the rest of the world, other worlds, begin. Although I am created by the eye of another, that other must be me or an affect of me. This is the essence of *communitas*, the ego, the id, the relationship with others, the extension of self into family, into world. In this world, the faces of the tarot are manifestations of my own existence, tribal affects.

Not only do we establish boundaries to our own total civilisation to keep certain things in and certain things out, we also establish boundaries to our personae to make them readily identifiable, since otherwise our personalities would spill over into one another, a situation which can only be accommodated briefly by physical or intellectual intercourse. We therefore develop prototypes or icons of the Tarot whom we invest with unique inherent powers: the father, the mother, the priest, the slave, the farmer, the scholar ... or as Yeats said,

> A country which has no national institutions must show its young men *images for the affections*, although they be but diagrams of which it should be or maybe. He [Thomas Davis] and his school *imagined* the Soldier, the Orator, the Patriot, the Poet, the Chieftain, and above all, the Peasant. [57] (*my emphasis*)

What then is the relationship between the Irish landscape and the Irish mind? Is there a specifically Irish psychology which results in a specifically Irish culture? Is there a specially Irish quality of vision, an Irish theory of vision? Heaney says:

although it has long been fashionable to smile indulgently at the Celtic twilight, it has to be remembered that the movement was the beginning of a discovery of confidence in our own ground, in our place, in our speech, English and Irish. And it seems to me undeniable that Yeats's sense of the otherness of his Sligo places led him to seek for a language and an imagery other than the ones which were available to him in the aesthetic modes of literary London.

The result, he affirms, was Synge's expression of 'the life of Aran, in the language of the tribe': 'A new country of the mind was conceived in English, the west that the poets imagined'. [58]

But that new country has not been pursued since Synge's time. The idea that the Irish landscape and its peoples could furnish a dramatic representation of inner states of being still requires the sort of analysis which Friel is mapping. The Irish intellectual tradition, long dismissed or devalued as a twilit irresponsible reverie upon misfortune, has, however, recently received serious critical attention. For example Richard Kearney writes:

Could it be that the Irish mind, in its various expressions often flew in the face of logocentrism by showing that meaning is not only determined by a logic that centralises and censors but also by a logic which disseminates: a structured dispersal exploring what is *other*, what is irreducibly diverse. In contra-distinction to the orthodox dualist logic of *either/or*, the Irish mind may be seen to favour a more didactical logic of *both/and*, an intellectual ability to hold the traditional oppositions of classical reason held together in creative confluence. [59]

There has also been a sustained critical attempt to locate this synchronicity within a 'middle ground' or 'fifth province': Brendan Purcell observes: 'the old Irish name for Meath, *An Mhidhe*...meant "the centre" or "central area"...The provinces were known as "fifths", *coicead*, as if they were a fifth province... Possibly this "fifth" was less a political area than a symbol of cosmic order'. [60] Mark Patrick Hederman also writes, 'Uisneach, the secret centre, was the place where all oppositions were resolved. The constitution of such a place would require that each person discover it for himself within himself.' [61] Friel, perhaps with unconscious irony, allows the 'fictitious' biography of Hugh O'Neill to begin with the statement 'his name and fame spread throughout the five provinces of Ireland' (*MH* 70).

Such discovery is, in any case, a tribal as well as a personal knowledge. Heaney refers to:

My *patria*, my deep design
To be at home
In my own place and dwell within
Its proper name. [62]

And the 'proper' name here implies temporal as well as spiritual connotations – a name, whether it is 'Ulster' or 'Mossbawn', or 'Ballybeg', which has evolved through time, represents the layering of experience. Landscape, Heaney says, is, or was, 'sacramental, instinct with signs, implying a system of reality beyond the visible realities'. And in the same essay he refers to 'that temperate understanding of the relationship between a person and his place, of the way the surface of the earth can be accepted into, and be a steadying influence upon, the quiet depths of the mind'. [63] This, like a textual authority, represents a constant reaffirmation of known points, the known centre. In his essay 'Mossbawn' Heaney says:

I would begin with the Greek word, *omphalos*, meaning the navel, and hence the stone that marked the centre of the world, and repeat it, *omphalos*, *omphalos*, *omphalos*, until its blunt and falling music becomes the music of somebody pumping water at the pump outside our back door. [64]

But while that *omphalos* is being repeated, incanted into a certainty, other certainties with which it bears an apparent affinity may crumble and carry away with them the society which has made one of them its pillars.

Searching for the stable centre, the *omphalos*, the Irish mind casts its imagination back through perhaps four centuries, to rediscover a world such as that evoked by O'Faolain, one which is radically, psychically, different to that which displaced it – medieval as opposed to renaissance, mythopoeic rather than logocentric, observing the 'sacred wood' of its imagination eroded by the exponential growth of the empire of knowledge and logic. We are also asked, as O'Faolain puts it, to place beside 'the Patriot myth': 'each new Hero rising against the ancient Tyrant', an *alternative myth*: 'the ancient Hero rising against the new Tyrant'. On O'Neill's recognition of this alternative myth O'Faolain comments that it was

> quite clear to Tyrone. It was beyond the understanding of his
> Gaelic followers because it was outside their experience. And
> it was equally outside the experience of all the native annalists
> who therefore recorded Tyrone's life in terms of the Patriot
> Myth without reference to that other myth which is at the
> core of so many of Shakespeare's historical and patriotic plays
> and about which they knew nothing. [65]

'To remember that', O'Faolain admonishes us, 'is of paramount
importance.' It must have seemed so to Friel when he read it, since
the marrying of those two worlds has so far concerned him that he
has abandoned many of the developed conventions of the stage (as
Synge did before him) in elucidating the passage from certainty to
doubt, from high ground to low, from 'quiet depths of the mind' to
those charged with maddening questions and more clamouring
answers than can be accommodated into one familiar pattern. As an
example of this he draws our attention to the fact that the artist
John Behan's work, which has previously been rooted in strength,
certainty and security has now come to reflect in its 'flights of birds,
makers of music and uncertain heroes' a complex world of vague
possibilities, in which 'man's mind is on the point of despair', and
that Behan displays 'a new wisdom and a new conviction that the
world is one of necessary doubts'. [66] Friel sees this as clearly in the
Ireland of the late twentieth century as in that of the sixteenth.

Words, and all our logocentric thought, are unreliable because, as
Steiner says, 'that which we call fact may well be a veil spun by
language to shroud the mind from reality', [67] from the weight of
time. But as he says also, we are trapped within this unreliability:
'Man is a language animal...What access we have to the life of the
mind, to the dynamics of consciousness, to the metamorphic and
innovative capacities of the imagination, is linguistic.' We might be
led to suppose that this imagination is therefore totally strictured by
language, but this is not so. As Steiner also notes, from the example
of other forms of non-verbal communication such as mathematics,
'the experience and perception of reality [have been divided] into
separate domains'. [68]

It thus becomes possible to regard the distance between the self
that experiences and the self that describes experience, as the
distance also between experience itself and the description of experience. There is a fundamental implication here for much of Friel's

work, especially *The Loves of Cass McGuire*, *Crystal and Fox*, and *Translations*, as he moves from a problematic relationship between characters and audience to one where audiences no longer observe action but sense themselves participating in it. This conjuring of perception of a different order becomes a national drama in its relocation of the Irishman at the centre of history rather than on its sidelines. We will now examine the application of such a schema as I have outlined, logocentric though it may be, to Friel's work.

THE PLAYWRIGHT'S COMMITMENT

The city of Derry and its natural hinterland in Donegal constitute a total environment from which Friel draws not just his inspiration but his messages. He sets his stories and plays in 'Ballybeg' (Baile Beag, small town) or in 'Ballymore' (Baile Mor, big town) but the experiences he relates, whether they are fact-as-experience or emotion-as-experience, are translations, into words and images, of 'real' places he has sensed: Glen-na-Fuiseog (the valley, or 'saucer', of larks), Coradinna, Mullaghduff, are composites, extractions and recreations of Glenties, Kincasslagh, Urris; likewise the surnames of people, O'Donnell, Boyle, Sweeney, and their first names, Manus, Sarah, Philly, Nora Dan.

But even within this world there is a tension, epitomised by Derry itself, the last walled city built in Europe, and, even in this, an anachronism, a mediaeval idiom to serve the needs of a modern colonial power. In 1848 Mrs Alexander, wife of the Bishop of Derry, glimpsed 'a green hill far away, without a city wall': it is now the (largely) Catholic Creggan estate, part of the electoral ward represented by Patrick Friel. This hill outside the city was excluded from the world of the apprentices' protected guilds, for whom Derry was built, and it is almost as if, in this social experiment, each element of an equation, town and country, which should have been reciprocally interactive and interdependent, became mutually polarised and exclusive. Perhaps there has always been an implicit failure in the Derry formula, an apprenticeship to the tensions of historical myth. This divorce is another motive force in Friel's psychology, and conditions much of his subject matter.

If, as Professor Estyn Evans argues, the Ulster landscape is representative of the geography of Ireland, then it is in the Ulster mind, representative, in its turn, of that landscape, that the events of history, both *mythos* and *logos*, are best worked out. 'Topographically, Ulster displays the characteristic fragmentation even better than the other three provinces: indeed, when one looks at the full record of habitat, heritage and history, one begins to think of Ulster as the most Irish of all the regions'. [69] Ulster has been called a 'narrow ground': 'the war in Ulster', says A.T.G Stewart, 'is being fought out on a narrower ground than even the most patient observer might imagine, a ground every inch of which has its own associations and special meaning...locality and history are welded together'. [70] And, as F.S.L. Lyons has pointed out:

> both sides constantly appeal to history and continue to use sectarian terminology which the world has long discarded ...The history and terminology are unavoidable because they relate to unfinished business. They are alive today – and this is pre-eminently the sense in which the seventeenth century lives on in Ulster – because the sequence of events over more than three hundred years has ensured that the issues raised when the different cultures first mingled on that 'narrow ground' should still be crucial issues. The context changes but the issues remain identical. [71]

The issues are those of possession and dispossession, mastery and servility, alienation and exile, crystallised in the stereotypes of the 'Planter' and the 'Gael'. The dispossession of the last Gaelic society by the seventeenth-century plantation was more than a displacement of people from the land. It created a labile people in whose cultural disintegration one can see the original tensions which ultimately led to the civic disturbances, riots and civil war. This is by no means unique to Ireland or even to the colonised peoples of the imperial West. Indeed, we can legitimately take an anthropological perspective, as Friel himself does in *The Freedom of the City* through the character of Dodds, and state the ubiquity of this form of dispossession and its consequences. As has been written of the Ndembu of Northern Rhodesia, who were the particular subject of Victor Turner:

> Most of the Ndembu's neighbours were suffering in their contact with the white man, with his copper mines and his railways, but the Ndembu ... seemed to have retained rich cultural and religious traditions. They were obviously a stubborn people. They were also a jealous, individualistic, strife-ridden people, troubled by mischievous spirits, witches and

ancestral ghosts who were quick to punish Ndembu who failed to 'remember' them. Symptomatically the weak and powerless were often afflicted with illness and then subjected to elaborate curing rites that gave symbolic expression to their conflicts and incorporated them into curing cults. Turner says that what little unity existed among the Ndembu was enforced by these rituals ... The 'thudding of ritual drums' gave Turner his key to Ndembu society. [72]

If we substitute for the name Ndembu the term 'the people of Ballybeg' we will be able to hear, in most of Friel's work, 'the thudding of ritual drums'. In the curing cult of death in *The Freedom of the City* and *Faith Healer*, in the observance of a ritual of *communitas* in the schoolroom of *Translations* and the confusion of *Aristocrats*, in the hurt of Sarah's muteness as it becomes the catalyst of *Translations*, and in the individual stubbornness of Lily, Columba, Cass and Keeney, we see Friel almost inevitably fulfilling a liminal, shamanistic role as he sets about his task of divining the elements of ritual and translating them into drama.

The tensions which have been concentrated in Ulster have ironically only been contained in 'Northern Ireland' by the artificial boundary of the 1920 partition. It has led to the mutation of the *aisling* (dream, vision) culture of loss and poverty of the Gaelic seventeenth-century kingdoms into a Chekhovian dream of national hope focussed on tomorrow, an introspection on the part of the dispossessed, a second-class citizenry, on the glory and wealth of that which they once held, and which they dream of regaining: language, identity, self-respect. That such a demeanour should be servile, and yet eloquent, is a characteristic of depression. As Hugh O'Donnell explains:

> certain cultures expend on their vocabularies and syntax acquisitive energies and ostentations entirely lacking in their material lives...A rich language...full of the mythologies of fantasy and hope and self-deception, a syntax opulent with tomorrows. It is our response to mud cabins and a diet of potatoes: our only method of replying to ... inevitabilities.
>
> (*Tr.* 42)

Beyond the division of a society which is predominantly agrarian and where largely planter and Gael, Catholic and Protestant (that is, Anglican, Presbyterian, Methodist) live in close and mutual suspicion, there is the specific division of urban sectarian segregation with its own opposing cultures of possession and poverty. Friel's single unequivocal treatment of contemporary disorder and the urban *déclassé* is *The Freedom of the City* (1973). As his sociologist Dodds (whose arguments are derived from Oscar Lewis's *La Vida*) explains in that play:

> The subculture of poverty...transmitted from generation to generation...is the way the poor adapt to their marginal position in society which is capitalistic, stratified into classes and highly individuated; and it is also their method of reacting against society. In other words it is the method they have devised to cope with the hopelessness and despair they experience because they know they'll never be successful in terms of values and goals of the dominant society...They (the poor of the Western world) share a critical attitude to many of the values and institutions of the dominant class; they share a suspicion of government, a detestation of the police, and very often a cynicism to the church ... any movement, trade union, religious, civil rights, pacifist, revolutionary – any movement which gives them this objectivity, organizes them, gives them real hope, promotes solidarity. Such a movement inevitably smashes the rigid caste which encases their minds and bodies.
>
> (*Freedom* 19–21)

On to this global screen Friel projects, particularly in the character of Lily, the concrete poverty of Derry in the time of the transition from civil rights activities to rioting and death. That in the heat of the moment the incidents of 'Bloody Sunday' (30 January 1972) and the subsequent Widgery Report should have given rise to this play and to Thomas Kinsella's poem 'Butcher's Dozen' is natural; [73] but that nothing else of this literary quality should have followed until the work of Graham Reid as an aesthetic challenge to this or other poignant tragedies is surprising until one realises that in general terms the Irish writer, whether rooted in Ulster or elsewhere, has refused to become engaged in the actual fighting of a war which is taking place today on that narrow ground; preferring (or perhaps finding it impossible not to engage in a dialogue with the past) to rehearse a war in the mind, contrition rather than attrition, imprisoned in its own wordiness.

Only two years before writing *The Freedom of the City*, Friel said that he did not expect a play on the Northern troubles to emerge for some time. [74] He has insisted that he is a spectator, not involved; that this is the appropriate position for the artist, [75] but it is difficult to see his response to those troubles, as shown in *The Freedom*, as a detached view; however much he may wish to remain a cold commentator, no one in Derry, whatever his provenance, could remain uninvolved in the events of the 'war', untouched by the culture of dispossession. One of those injured on Bloody Sunday was Joseph Friel: apparently not a relation of the playwright, but one bearing his name. But Friel argues that while there is 'no Irish writer who is not passionately engaged in our current problems ... he must maintain a perspective as a writer'. [76]

His strongest plea for the detachment of the artist came in fact in 1972:

> In each of us the line between the Irish mind and the creative mind is much too fine ... There must be a far greater distinction between the Irishman who suffers and the artist's mind which creates ... The intensity of emotion we all feel for our country (and in the present climate, that emotion is heightened) is not of itself the surest foundation for the best drama which, as Eliot says comes from the 'intensity of the artistic process, the pressure, so to speak, under which the fusion takes place'. [77]

Friel here adopts a difficult position, one which will become his most painful, because putting such a distance between himself and the world – *his* world – allows his constituents to accuse him of neglect and betrayal. It makes the writer's own choices that much more painful. It is indeed difficult to make the distinction between the artist-as-citizen and the citizen-as-artist. The difficulty lies in seeing the Irish mind as creative and reflective, expressing *both* thought-as-experience *and* experience-as-thought. Columba, for example, answers the affective call of memory: 'he went because he loved them all ... every native instinct and inclination tore at him to go to the aid of his friends' (*EW* 27–8); and André Brink, in a very similar society, says 'literature and art are forced back to their very roots, to elemental and rudimentary beginnings. Anything but not silence. *I can't keep silent, because I have lived it*'. [78]

Friel has said that involvement 'means pigmentation and perhaps contamination', [79] but life can also be painful on the sidelines especially because not to obey the affective rules would amount to an act of betrayal. Writing *Faith Healer* was a betrayal because it concentrated on the privacy of the artist-as-performer rather than the public role of the artist-as-spokesman or saviour. In the same sense, *Making History* betrays the course of Irish history because it asks that the Hero or Saviour described in *The Annals of The Four Masters* be rewritten, re-imagined as a man of private parts, a man whose conscience can be governed by interior as well as communal forces.

Since 1982, when Friel took the drastic step of writing a farce (*The Communication Cord*) to accompany, defuse and subvert the success of *Translations*, he had been exploring, in a number of draft texts, the question of betrayal, something with which he finally came to terms in *Fathers and Sons*. He enters the difficult area which, as Thomas Kilroy says, lies in 'the web of secondary circumstances that lie below the writing ...where the essentially private activity of writing comes into contact with the shared experience of human beings living in the one culture'. [80] Friel would certainly like to be free to write plays on other themes, but while troubles persist, whether social, intellectual or moral, there remains this Chekhovian compulsion to write about them in terms where the everyday meets the apocalyptic. To take a holiday from Ireland (as he did in writing *Fathers and Sons*) is to betray it by keeping silence. The nearest he can come without frivolity is the catastrophic events of earlier days: the 'Flight of the Earls' which he rubbishes with equal effect in *The Gentle Island* and in *Making History*, or the silencing of the poets. But in doing so he acknowledges the impossibility of keeping silent. Just as André Brink, under censorship, must fictionalise his argument, thus making in *An Instant in the Wind* one of the most beautiful love stories, of the meeting of black and white, finding the gap between cultures, so Friel also 'fictionalises' episodes in Irish history in order to approximate to the intercourse which may have occurred between Hugh O'Neill and Mabel Bagenal, between Maire Chatach and George Yolland: 'Never more than an instant. Perhaps we can't bear more than an instant at a time... This terrible space surrounding us creates the silence in which, so rarely, preciously, I dare to recognise you and be recognised by you'. [81]

An inescapable part of existence is not only perception and consciousness, but also the breaking of silence: to be is to utter. In Friel's context, therefore, that which *matters*, that which is perceived or experienced, must be uttered. Even his 'time out' in the adaptation of *Three Sisters* relates to his concern for wholeness, the integrity of the family as an extension of the self. When writing *Aristocrats* he noticed that

> its true direction is being thwarted by irrelevant 'politics', social issues, class. And an intuition that implicit in their language, attitudes, style, will be all the 'politics' I need...The play – this must be remembered – is about *family life*, its quality, its cohesion, its stultifying aspects, its affording of opportunities for what we designate 'love' and 'affection' and 'loyalty'. Class, politics, social aspiration are the qualifying decor but not the core. [82]

His 'loyalty' to the tribe and to the particular relationships within the web of affections, is in some ways, therefore, his response to the larger spectacle of the public world.

As we shall see in chapter 4, the problems of serving one's community and of serving oneself as an artist are equally subject to violence. In order to be engaged, one must be engaged with the past *and* with the future, interpreting each to each. If silence represents privacy, and language approximates to the world, then the paths to silence, to regaining the wholeness of the inner world, lead inevitably through the minefield of language. Privacies have no right to remain privacies. To be the diviner or shaman of a culture exposes the artist not only to the adulation but also the calumny of the tribe.

But there is another more particular sense in which Friel's world is a paradox, and where, as a citizen of that world, he has found it necessary to speak out. This concerns language as a medium of communication and as a metaphor of culture, where it is intimately connected with the provinciality of Ulster both historically and in present politics.

Other northern poets, including John Montague, for example in *The Rough Field* and *The Dead Kingdom*, and Seamus Deane in *Gradual Wars*, *Rumours* and *History Lessons*, have explored this. Among southerners, also involved in the dilemma of seeking restoration, Thomas Kinsella, in his essay 'The Divided Mind', sets out the problem of writing in one language while culturally pursuing an ideal best asserted in another. [83] Friel is acutely conscious of the fact that 'the language which we speak in Ireland' is English. but not English as it is spoken or understood by English people. It is a language adopted by Irish people which 'forms us and shapes us in a way that is neither healthy nor valuable to us'. As a result the Irish theatre has barely developed, because 'it is a new and young discipline for us and apart from Synge, all our dramatists have pitched their voice for English acceptance and recognition'. The error of assuming that Ireland and England had a language in common has therefore led both nations into the mantic *and* semantic errors of thinking that they could provide the metaphor to interpret between privacies. Accordingly, Friel believes 'we must continually look at ourselves, recognize and identify ourselves. We must make English identifiably our own language': [84] this is the realisation which, ultimately, makes Hugh O'Donnell the hero and central character of *Translations*.

Friel's most recent contribution to this debate has been his 'language plays', particularly *Faith Healer* (1979) and *Translations* (1980). In the latter he examines the problem of a civilisation confronted by its own language as a barrier to progress and an instrument of change. He had earlier given us a humorous glimpse into this in 'Mr Sing My Heart's Delight': 'a constant source of fun was Granny's English. Gaelic was her first tongue and she never felt at ease in English which she shouted and spat out as if it were getting in her way' (*Saucer*, 60). [85]

Translations is in fact a paradox in that it presents us with a neo-colonial project: to regain its cultural integrity, Ballybeg must not reject, but embrace, the dominant, incursive language in order to make it 'identifiably our own language'. In Genet's *Les Nègres* the blacks, in attempting to reject white civilisation, have to reject white language. Two black lovers find it impossible to communicate without using the language of the whites. In *Translations* the 'blacks' wish neither to reject nor embrace white civilisation. Whichever course they take they will be living a lie; but a lie of great and possibly liberating power. Two lovers, one black one white, demonstrate to us much more than the impossibility of communication, or of translating between privacies: they tell us that the problem of using one language for utterance and another for cultural existentialism is a problem of revolt from both yesterday and tomorrow and that the only real solution lies in silence.

Ultimately the two problems – place and language – merge, because place means who you are and where you come from, and language is the facility by which you express that identity and provenance. A place requires a name, and a tongue to pronounce it. So as Eavan Boland says of 'the northern writers' crisis of conscience', they cannot continue to accept the confusion of childhood. They must somehow shape it, order it. The attempt to coax order out of the chaotic experience of lost community and childhood *could* have produced an inner crisis, in which either bewilderment is burned away or talent is burned out. [86]

Since that was written, the inner crisis has intensified, and has not been resolved, because it has not been possible to find the proper way to dramatise the drama. Tom MacIntyre's almost wordless, balletic drama has offered one possibility; Friel's antithesis is to pursue words relentlessly, because he believes that he can thus more satisfactorily approach both the private and the public – precisely because we cannot abandon that weapon which has so deeply incised our consciousness. In his most recent play, *Dancing at Lughnasa*, however, he turns the knife in a different fashion. A play which is poised between music and vertigo, between the two elements that make of dance itself the seduction and the ritual that expresses life as it is both lived and imagined, *Dancing at Lughnasa* attempts to eschew words in favour of gesture – the logic overtaken by the mythic: 'Dancing as if language had surrendered to movement... Dancing as if language no longer existed, because words were no longer necessary' (*DL* 71). Friel does not in fact make that surrender in the same way that MacIntyre has done so in his gestural theatre – the repetition of the words 'as if' is salutary – simply because he is not prepared to fumble in the dramatic interstices, and yet he comes close to acknowledging the claim not only of silence on the spoken word but also that of movement on thought.

NAMING THINGS

Irish engagement in the present has been conducted as a congruence between culture and nationalism. This led to the ideological foundation of the Irish Free State through agencies so apparently disparate as the Land League, the Irish Literary (later the National) Theatre, the Gaelic League, the Gaelic Athletic Association, the Irish Republican Brotherhood and the Irish Volunteers. This congruence was based on the assumption that there was, in some golden age, a Gaelic race of poet-kings, the regaining of which has been the cultural and political quest of the republic.

But the question of identity, of meaning, is the same as that asked by Shakespeare's MacMorris – 'What ish my nation?' [87] – questions that appeal not only to kinship and loyalty but which ask what cultural, social and economic properties are necessary before a community becomes viable. It is obviously more acute in Ulster, a client province of two nations, than elsewhere. Declan Kiberd has described the tendency towards introspection in search of an identity as 'Inventing Irelands', [88] a discovery within, but one which, in my reading of his essay, has led to falsification, or a false glorification of an Ireland which could not be reinvented because it had never existed. In this the chief actors in modern times, according to Kiberd, were Yeats, Douglas Hyde and Eamon de Valera. Yeats certainly celebrated a bardic tradition based on 'the oral poetry of unlettered singers'. [89] Yeats claimed:

> In Ireland today the old world that sang and listened is, it may be for the last time in Europe, face to face with the world that reads and writes, and their antagonism is always present under some name or other in Irish imagination and intellect. [90]

The concept of the 'Western Isle', a noble peasant civilisation, is in fact an artificial response to the challenge of change, of which Friel is healthily sceptical: writing *Translations* he noted: 'one aspect that keeps eluding me; the wholeness, the integrity of that Gaelic past. Maybe because I don't believe in it'. [91] The distinctions I have drawn up to this point have been in the field of definitions, the hazards of making statements about situations which, though perhaps perfectly understood, can be only imperfectly expressed, because these all stem from the 'confusions of childhood' of writers like Friel. But a qualitative difference needs to be understood here, between the life we lead, the life we think we lead, and the life we would like to lead. This distinction is vital to the survival of writers and their nations and cultures, both political and aesthetic. In this sense, the reaction to *The Playboy of the Western World* in 1908 is a continuing reaction: as a contemporary newspaper commented: 'we looked into a mirror for the first time and found ourselves hideous. We fear to face the thing', on which Seamus Deane observes: 'Ireland would have been extraordinary had it produced literature less intimate with its political fate.' [92]

Literature was therefore certain to be obsessed with identity, to confuse form and content, to approach the question of viability by turning, Janus-like, towards both the past which imprisoned it, and the future which contained its best hopes. It is a literature which, however 'opulent with tomorrows', remains wary of the 'nation-

48

once-again' theory, knowing that anthropologists, geographers and historians – those distinguished scientists of the mind – have said that the Irish are a tribal people, not a nation.

In these circumstances, meaning becomes vacuous, and emotion is betrayed when it relies on 'false feeling, false sympathy, and false use of language'. [93] The heart grows brutal in its need to find new means of survival. In the meantime Irish writers feel ambiguously 'lost, unhappy and at home'. [94] But overriding this internal debate is what Beckett calls 'the mythological present', a stoical shrinking from the present, from the moment of decision. Beckett might seem a strange bedfellow with Friel, but in discussing the trap of the mythological present he reveals, perhaps because of the spareness of his language, a sensitivity to the imprecision of language and cognition:

> It, say it, not knowing what...The fact would seem to be, if in my situation one may speak of facts, not only that I shall have to speak of things of which I cannot speak, but also that I shall have to, I forget, no matter. And at the same time I am obliged to speak. I shall never be silent. Never. [95]

Echoes, or predictions, of Gareth O'Donnell's 'It doesn't matter'; an immaterialism and an agony of doubt and silence, the man who can not exist because he cannot utter: 'Screwballs, say something! Say something father!' (*Ph.* 83). Silence offers security, but it is also an open prison.

2

THE SHORT STORIES

Silence once broken will never again be whole

Samuel Beckett[1]

DIVINATION

Friel conveys the immediacy of 'our' world. It is not just the quotidian, workaday continuity of people's actions, but, as Seamus Deane observes, 'that local intimate detail which emerges out of the author's knowledge of his society's moral code'. [2] Deane says that 'each story is social in its setting, moral in its implications' but this takes us only part of the way in understanding Friel's intentions. Beyond morality, beyond the social boundaries which the moral code dictates, there is a 'quality of mercy' which takes the form of a tenderness mediating between the wry and the grotesque. In the sense that Friel's stories have two dimensions, the actual and the metaphysical, the important factor is the way in which he translates each to the other: here he is most Chekhovian because he unites the reader with his intentions, and *his intention is the subject itself*, the simple relation of self and society.

Friel's main themes in the stories are: illusion; expectation (and the disillusion which comes with the failure of expectation), and the various types of dignity which interweave among the social and moral dimensions of our lives. His technique in drawing us into his world is to live vicariously through us in the illusion, disillusion, and attempts at dignity, so that when he resolves whatever crisis has been posed – loss of faith, disintegration of the family, failure of memory, displacement of affection – *we* become responsible for that resolution.

Friel's device, therefore, is to make us the medium of our own

50

culture by translating us into the *id* of his world; we thus id-entify
with the people and psyche of Ballybeg. In this he is divining not
only himself and Ballybeg, but also the other participant in this
private conversation, the reader. The technique is also applied in the
radio plays, which possess the same intimacy of the word spoken
directly into the ear. No other Irish writer is so adept at this form
of divination except Heaney, whose gift of mediation is as great as
Friel's; if Heaney wrote short stories and plays, one feels they
would have the same texture and *gravitas* as Friel's.

The Swedish critic Ulf Dantanus refers on several occasions to
Friel's 'defining': 'his efforts to define and interpret the Irish psyche';
'to define its main characteristics'; 'to unearth essential qualities of
Irishness and to define the nature of the Irish past'; 'to express and
define the Irish identity'; 'an effort to understand and define history
and especially the spiritual past and various attitudes to it'; 'these
concepts are finally tested and defined'. [3] This is of course the result
of a mis-hearing which turns 'divine' into 'define', and which Friel
would absolutely disown. The Irish psyche, and the nature of the
Irish past, are subject to – and demand – divination, but not
definition. Both Friel and Heaney divine and dig below the everyday
surface to show us, like a cubist dissecting the inner frames of
reference of planes hidden to ordinary view, the tensions which
hold some parts of people, and society, together and keep others
apart. Eventually, however, they return us to the surface in a
closure which often resembles the coda of an archaeologist's exposition.

Friel refers to this as 'the successful invention'. Discussing the
accumulation of memory, such as that of the 'fictional' fishing trip
already referred to, he says, 'perhaps the important thing is not the
accurate memory but the successful invention. And at this stage of
my life I no longer know what is invention and what "authentic".
The two have merged into one truth for me'. And 'Ballybeg' 'is a
village of the mind, more a depository for remembered or invented
experience than a geographical location'. [4]

This accounts for the private conception of Ballybeg. The 'public'
reason for its existence is, perhaps, more significant, and will become
clearer when we turn to the later plays. His emphasis on the
parochial has developed,

> perhaps because whatever literary tradition we have here – in
> the English language – doesn't derive from the confidence of

an integrated nation. English authors work from an achieved, complete and continuous tradition. Maybe in lieu of a nation we place our faith in the only alternative we have; the parish. [5]

This helps us to understand why the Irish short story so often strikes English readers as being written in a foreign tongue; although the language is ostensibly the same it is being used in the service of a quite different set of perceptions, a series of 'successful inventions' predominating over the 'authentic'. As Friel recounts in 'Kelly's Hall':

> I heard the story so often from my mother and I grew so close to the man himself...that I can scarcely convince myself that I do not remember the scene although the baptismal water must still have been damp on my head that evening.
>
> (*Saucer* 91)

In the fiction, we notice, *the child* is ushered into the family and extended family, the private and the public culture of the tribe, in order to become both a participant in, and a means of relaying, that culture. There are two sides to this awareness of fact, and rejection of its tyranny: one is what Ulf Dantanus calls 'the essentially private nature of truth'. [6] The other is the essentially *public* nature of truth. The difference between them is the difference between language and silence, since private truth is unspoken whilst public truth is a text which must be uttered in order to have existence. One is thought, representing a paradigm of being, the other moves through the paradigm of absolute time, an affect of history.

Between these two, the characters, their author and, by the subtlety of his extension, his audience, move towards a discovery of their faith. Because there are no longer any certainties, either in the secret garden of Irish memory or in the wide world, that movement is bedevilled not only by the unreliability of words and other signals, but by dichotomies in the nature of the world itself, which we are seeking to make sense of by description.

'The world of the senses was liable always to sidestep into sinister territories of the mind' says A.N. Jeffares. [7] It is a world which, however much we may resent it, may ultimately expel us into a much more painful and violent exile, the rite of passage in search of home. We feel this insecurity because 'home' can project itself not just as place but as character. This is distinctly Irish as it is essentially Chekhovian, because, in Patrick Kavanagh's words, 'Parochialism is universal; it deals with the fundamentals.' [8] Columba's exclamation, 'what more do you demand of me, damned Ireland? My soul?' (*EW* 71) takes on an extra significance as we see Ireland as a character in the fiction. Friel's 'romantic ideal that we call Cathleen'[9] is not simply a state of mind, but an epiphany of place. The 'mother Ireland', the poor old woman (*shan van vocht*), seeking the restitution of her four green fields, who dominates Yeats's 'Cathleen Ni Houlihan' and who haunts modern Irish literature, places Irish men and women at her disposal. The attempt to re-unite the modern political states of Ireland is a fictive approach to the greater and deeper mythic needs of the Irish psyche.

If place can have personality, then our response to it cannot be impersonal, it signs to us and we sign to it, in a mythopoeic, rather than a logocentric, language. If we find fault with a place, the fault is similar to that we would detect in another person. In 'The Diviner' this is the essence of Nelly Devenny's resentment of the lake where her husband has drowned; the attraction of the place is the magnetism of a person, as in the silent virginal beauty of 'The Wee Lake Beyond', and the jealousy it engenders between father and son. If we resent place, it is because place to an overwhelming extent gives essence and meaning, forms our perceptions like a teacher, under-writes our earliest sensations like a parent, provides us with name, identity and purpose.

Friel's response in art began in 1952 with the publication in *The Bell* of his first story, 'The Child'.[10] It was an act of courageous faith for a young writer. Friel, however, neither wishes nor permits this story to be republished, so despite the fact that it is the seminal work from which flow all his insights into the question of love, language and freedom, I can only summarise it, no doubt quite inadequately.

A boy ('the child') lies awake at night. He hears the reassuring sounds of his mother at work in the kitchen below. The comfortable world is shattered by the one event which obviously lurks in the child's abiding dread: the entry of the father, a drunkard who can communicate only in the language of familiar hostility. The boy is startled into customary terror. He begs God not to let them fight. But God lets them fight: a ritual, symbiotic captivity of caged animals. He goes almost automatically to the head of the stairs to witness the spectacle: 'the child knew the routine by heart...it was the scene he knew so well'. God is implored once more as the intermediary: promise God you will be good if only the beasts below can be separated. 'Down below they were roaring at each other. Quietly he rose, and, blinded with tears, groped his way back to his room.'

This is not 'the reality of rural Ireland' as Dantanus suggests but it is *a* reality. [11] It suggests the personality of a thing called 'home' which, we know, Friel denies. It sets 'pleasant memories of the day' – the Arcadian vision – against the 'waiting black void' of the night, the exit into sleep and our other, subliminal, self. It contrasts the outdoor freedoms with the ferocious domination of the indoors by the father, the fight between mother and father for control of the kitchen, the hearth. The child is outlawed from the adult world in which the tensions of village life are worked out privately; he is blinded both by his own tears and by the darkness.

No clearer proof need be furnished that Friel, by concentrating his vision on rural society and 'Ballybeg', is singing an Arcadian eclogue, to the exclusion of 'reality'. 'Reality' in fact is a mixture of arcadian and infernal, of white and black, dexter and sinister. Friel records:

> One's life in retrospect seems to be defined by precise contours and primary colours: all summers were arcadian, all winters were arctic, pleasures were unqualified, disappointments were total. This remembering, I imagine, is a conscious and deliberate attempt to invest mediocrity with passion and drama. [12]

The art of reconstructing reality lies in qualifying and reducing the absolutes in which children (and some adults) see the world in the light of retrospect, while maintaining the passion and drama of the situation being described. But the description is of course fiction, because it no longer exists. The return to one's past, whether it is purely through time or, as in the case of the revenant exile, also through space, is a recherche of a paradise or hell which, because it is no longer real, might never have been real.

Therefore, Friel is at liberty in these stories to construct representations of a reality which may never have been 'authentic'. His travellers carry cardboard suitcases; his father-figures carry authority, usually schoolmasters or those in other positions of guardianship, reaching across *space* to admonish; and grandfathers, irresponsible and attractive, reaching out across *time* to subvert and amaze and reveal; all the stock population of a town like Glenties (Ballybeg) or Omagh (Ballymore). 'Home' is the hearth – literally the *focus* – around which they gather for their rituals. But in the stories and radio plays there is also the wife and mother, fretful, tense, warm, resourceful, beautiful, whose absence in the later plays is a continual reproach to Friel's ability to make life whole again.

In reviewing Friel's stories Robert Lacy commented on 'the touching sense of loss, a clearly communicated feeling that something magical and grand has slipped away'. [13] The dangers of such recollection are obvious, but, as I hope I have shown, Friel is not pursuing an arcadian vision. The reconstruction, which places the relation of time and memory at the centre of Friel's stories, is much more than the restitution to the disappointed child of his shattered paradise. Friel knows that the child also numbers hell among his realities, and that he voluntarily throws away the crown of ecstasy. Therefore he seeks to reconstruct not so much what was as *what might have been.*

In this the grandfathers are the perpetrators of a vicious and irresponsible hoax on the boys. In fact there is the suspicion throughout the stories that because of the effective elision of the father-figure where the grandfather is concerned, Friel is describing a world where all the boys are encouraged to grow old and already have an aged psychology. Boys, as if they were old men, are searching back into their own boyhood because they cannot recognise and grasp it as *now*, and are all the time sitting in the waiting room for death.

HOMECOMINGS

One slips back into one's place by the power of memory. 'Baile' means home *and* town. And yet the Irish have never been 'at home' in towns as the English understand them. 'We have always feared towns' says Sean O'Faolain. [14] Yet the search for that powerful focal hearth goes on as surely in the private mind as that for the four green fields occupies, and persists in, the public conscience. In *The Great O'Neill* O'Faolain makes the point more strongly: 'each centre is the centre only of its own *locus*. No hierarchy or predominance has been established. History is still a complete gamble.' Once again the temperament is Chekhovian: Ulster was 'practically bare of town life'; O'Neill and his folk were 'men for whom the outer world existed only as a remote and practically irrelevant detail. Their interests were personal and local.' [15] And they continue to be so when we start to explore the unease we feel with the encroachment of the outer world. Heaney becomes 'Unhappy and at home'; Friel denies the existence of 'home' itself, but he encourages sons and fathers to explore what this particular avenue of memory has to offer. Of course they find that memory is only effective if they maintain their faith in history.

Thus in 'Among the Ruins', because his own childhood dream of innocence has been lost rather than confirmed, Joe *wills* his son to be a man, because, he now knows, the future at least holds no illusions: 'It's a good thing for a man to cry like that sometimes.' Joe wants the boy to 'grow up', to rush through the misery and disillusion of adolescence, so that he can join his father in a common bond:

> Generations of fathers stretching back and back, all finding magic and sustenance in the brief, quickly destroyed happiness of their children. The past did not have meaning. It was neither reality nor dreams, neither today's patchy oaks nor the great woods of his boyhood. It was simply continuance, life repeating itself and surviving.
>
> (*Diviner* 136)

If such a Lawrentian resolution appears trite, it is due to the need to reaffirm a life-force in the face of the disintegration Friel sees in the familiar world, a need which endangers the first act of *Translations* in its apparent complacency. (Triteness, encouraged by the *New Yorker* formula, is also a reason for Friel's eventual dissatisfaction with the limiting conventions of the short story in favour of the more open possibilities of the play.) This is particularly evident in the conclusion of 'Everything Neat and Tidy':

> Chilled by the sudden personal disaster, he drove faster and faster, as if he could escape the moment when he would take up the lonely burden of recollection that the dead had fled from and the living had forgotten.
>
> (*Diviner* 155)

This fear of taking up 'the lonely burden of recollection' is precisely that fear which persuades the Irish to remember their future rather than their past. [16] And it is one which Friel accosts only imperfectly in his stories. He has not been influenced by Chekhov in story-writing (unlike his play-writing) and this possibly accounts for the fact that his mercy, unlike Chekhov's, is too great, his tenderness mediates too far, in displacing horror with dignity. As a result they ultimately address themselves to the problem of individuation, which, as Seamus Deane notes, 'with its emphasis on internal freedom... most often makes a virtue of alienation and a fetish of integrity'. [17] Where Chekhov faced such a challenge by embracing fear, for example in 'A Boring Story', Friel prefers to resolve his crises by rushing into the arms of fate. Seldom in the stories is this technique fully successful, partly because Friel falls into the trap of triteness, and partly because he seems afraid to call the bluff of fate. His greatest success in meeting the challenge is an unjustly neglected story, 'The Flower of Kiltymore', which in many ways announces the ultimate resolution which he achieves in *Faith Healer*. In this story, Sergeant Burke, regarded by his late wife as lacking professional dignity ('she had been a sergeant's daughter herself, and anybody below the rank of superintendent was a nobody'), finds that the 'calm and peace' brought by his wife's death conveys nothing so much as a sense of his own unease, perhaps impending death. He is mocked by his assistant guard, 'a Kerryman, young and keen and cunning', who has outmanoeuvred him socially by his alliance with the Canon; he is taunted by the local pranksters ('the Blue Boys'), bewildered by the clean bill of health from the doctor, which is contradicted by his 'unnatural tranquillity'. Thus excluded from peace, from social position, from professional authority, he asks in a Gethsemane-like appeal, for the 'unnatural tranquillity' to pass:

> So this was peace, this terrible emptiness. So this was what in those odd moments of treachery, when Lily flogged him with her tongue, he had dreamed of, this vacuity that was a pain within him. Sweet God, he prayed, sweet God, if this is what I wanted, take it away from me.
>
> (*Gold* 138)

Finally he calls the bluff of 'the Blue Boys' who allege that they have found a mine on the beach. The message is no bluff, the mine explodes and the youngsters, 'the flower of Kiltymore', are killed. [18] Now ruined and hated by the community, he faces a commissioner's inquiry which can only restore to him the natural tranquillity he seeks. The events of the tragedy, by making him an outcast, 'assured him that he was still the centre of the pushing stream of life, and not floating, as he had been since Lily's death, in the peace and calm of some stagnant backwater'. Like Frank Hardy, he can face the firing squad of self-betrayal:

> He got up from the bed, put on his Sunday uniform and his good boots, combed his hair, and straightened his tie. As he

went down the stairs to meet his judges, the wretchedness of the last four weeks was forgotten, and he knew again the only joy he had ever known. The month of ghostly isolation was over. His prayer in the garden had been answered. Let the Superintendent and the Commissioner do their damnedest to him! He knew now he had the capacity to survive it, because his life had suddenly happily slipped back into its old groove.

(*Gold* 144–5)

Perhaps Friel succeeds in this conclusion because he is not afraid of pieties, he does not embrace them simply because they represent some Lawrentian life-force. There comes a point, which becomes clear, particularly in his later plays, where 'piety', in seeking to remain within the borders of the moral code, becomes absurd and grotesque. Here, however, Friel knows, more maturely than elsewhere in the stories, that the 'enemy within' is a devil, and that homecoming necessitates a death: it predicts the fate of Yolland, the alter ego revenant of *Translations*, and of Bazarov in *Fathers and Sons*, because otherwise the story could not continue.

DIGNITY AND RESPECTABILITY

Friel is at his most suggestive, and his writing exhibits the finest quality, when he combines the descriptive with the emotive. Thus in 'Foundry House' his characterisation of Mrs Hogan: 'She was a tall, ungraceful woman, with a man's shoulders and a wasted body and long thin feet. When she spoke, her mouth and lips worked in excessive movement' (*Diviner* 78).

In fact, Friel's stories reveal a skill not only at characterisation, but also gesture and emphasis, which present quite different challenges in drama, and at which his stage directions are often less successful. Thus his 'private conversation' (confabulation) with the reader sometimes achieves a more affective result than the 'public address' which denies such finesse. In the passage quoted above, the words 'ungraceful', 'worked' and 'excessive' convey a personality and a neurosis which no actor could easily effect. At first the combination of 'long' and 'thin' seems *de trop*, but taken together with the woman's shoulders and her mouth-motion, it suggests a mediaeval effigy which Friel has manipulated into an uneasy recovery, a devilish creation. Similarly with the cadences in which he describes or recreates movement: as Nelly Devenny goes towards her particular Calvary, the divining of her second drunken husband's body in the lake, she 'left the priest's car for the first time that day, and ran to join the watchers. The women gathered protectively around her' (*Diviner* 28–9). *Left, ran, gathered*: a flight towards the fold, in this case the elusive dignity denied to Nelly by a fate she has not found the courage to confront. Another example of Friel's ability to combine the descriptive with the emotive is in the opening pages of 'The Illusionists':

> Once a month Father Shiels, the manager, drove out the twisted five miles from the town, in one breath asked us were we good and told us to say our prayers, shook father's hand firmly, and scuttled away again as if there were someone chasing him.
>
> (*Diviner* 91)

Not only is this a comical, clockwork-like figure but we can see how distastefully, almost fearfully, the priest performs his automatic, perfunctory and indifferent task.

It is by means of this emotive descriptiveness that Friel achieves a suggestion of what Seamus Deane calls 'the co-existence of two realms, one clearly stated and social, the other amorphous and imaginative', in which he says 'the author's insistence on the actuality of event and on the reality of imagination is quite impartial'.[19] I would add that the same assumption of the reader's common knowledge and intimacy that greets us in Chekhov's stories is taken a stage further by Friel in inducing a complicity in the moral code and, in his most successful stories, in the transgression of that code in the working out of individual salvation. This was Friel's reply to the situation of displacement of people within a fixed locale. The realisation that it did not go far enough was the reason for eventually abandoning the short story.

We can find that reason clearly spelt out in his approach to the problem of authority. As Deane says, 'Authority in its most basic form grows out of a sense of mystery but in its more quotidian form out of awareness of status.'[20] That degeneracy is best expressed through differing attitudes to, or differing attempts to express, the idea of 'dignity'; those who are 'dignified', who possess dignity, or whose internal explorations result in the repossession of a lost dignity, emerge from the stories as the 'winners', while those who scramble for dignity, for the acquisition of a quality which they imagine can be achieved through an appeal to some external authority, 'respectability', are the 'losers'. Dantanus makes the valuable distinction between *respectability*, an acceptance of agreed communal values, and *dignity*, the individual's response. [21] Tribal pressure to conform is exerted by means of respectability, whereas the divination of the individual seeking dignity can only be achieved by rejecting the collective insistence. Nelly Devenny, through her public humiliation, becomes 'skilled in reticence and fanatically jealous of her dignity' (*Diviner* 20), but in fact she was fanatically jealous of the 'dignity' she sees in others; her second attempt to achieve it, by marrying a second husband (and thus acquiring a new identity in her new name, Nelly Doherty) leaves her the ultimate appeal, to the external authority of her peers – 'the women gathered protectively around her'. The *diviner* discloses more in the waters of the lake than the body of Mr Doherty who has no other name, and comes simply from 'the West': he draws up another way of confronting reality, another set of perceptions by which to test our received and time-worn responses to the climate, to land and our 'community'.

It is remarkable that Friel is not especially aware of the pursuit of dignity, or the condition of being dignified in either his stories or plays. [22] Yet Seamus Deane insists that Friel 'never forsakes the notion that human need, however artificially expressed, is rooted in the natural inclination towards dignity'. [23] As we shall see in examining the plays, Friel often explicitly presents us with the fear which inhabits people when that natural inclination is thwarted. Thus in 'Everything Neat and Tidy' Mrs MacMenamin suffers 'anguish and indignity' at her husband's death; to live with her married daughter is 'the final, crushing indignity'. But her eventual achievement – not acquisition – of peace is in some way a redemption of dignity of a different order (*Diviner* 146–55). This is very effectively expressed in 'The First of My Sins' which also looks at dignity in two ways: 'a slap on the face merely pricks one's pride, but cow-dung on new shoes shatters one's dignity' (*Gold* 157). It would be easy to confuse a superficial tenure on *respectability* with the idea that one must act out the community's perception of oneself. In 'The First of My Sins' that 'slap on the face' is something we all endure every day in social exchange; that which shatters dignity is a breach of the family integer. We are told not of the narrator's boyish 'sins' but of his uncle's petty thieving, a 'crime' which hardly offends the criminal code but inflicts a moral disorder within the family.

Friel is also content to dismiss the search for respectability with wry and disdainful humour, in 'The Queen of Troy Close' (*Gold:* 'We'll put manners on them!') or 'The Fawn Pup' (*Saucer:* 'he managed to carry himself with a shabby dignity, like a down-at-heel military man') or the 'grandfather' whose 'sufficient charity' puts a name to a fatherless child in 'Mr Sing My Heart's Delight' (*Saucer*).

The status of dignity as a *tribal* quality clearly vexes Friel: in *The Enemy Within* there is a distinct relationship between Eoghan's 'gauche dignity' and his 'quiet power' (*EW* 58). There is also a connection between dignity and the exotic as if the ultimate test of dignity is whether or not it can survive the challenge of the external. In 'Kelly's Hall' the debacle of Grandfather's wondrous gramophone as a source of income places his family at the hands of charity:

> This new method of living, 'charity' she called it, imposed a great strain on Grandmother's virtue. She longed for the old days again when he went on binges and when her vanity had to weather only short, well-spaced storms...'God be with the days when he used to be carried home drunk to me'.
>
> (*Saucer* 95–6)

Like Synge, Friel bows to the need for illusion, in Deane's words 'in a society which so severely distorts the psychic life'. [24] This may be the illusion which is simply destroyed by the force of 'reality' as in 'The Illusionists' or an illusion which is reinforced in the flight from reality, as in 'Foundry House': Joe, having realised that the real Mr Hogan 'was not the image' he carried in his memory, insists on relating to his wife an evasive version of the encounter, in which he claims Mr Hogan is 'the same as ever...no different' (*Diviner* 89–90). The exotic, in 'Kelly's Hall', in the form of Grandfather Kelly's gramophone, leads him into the lie or illusion in which the exotic becomes bizarre: 'He never played a disk without first prefacing the performance with an entirely fictitious history of the composer and the music' (*Saucer* 94). In 'The Gold in the Sea' illusion is used as a tool of social engineering: Con, having admitted that the shipwrecked gold has already been salvaged, maintains, in front of the younger fishermen, the pretence that it has *not*: 'It is better for them to think it is still there. They're young men...You see, friend, they never got much out of life, not like me' (*Diviner* 44).

Pigeon fanciers and breeders of fighting cocks are typical, and natural, victims of their own illusions, as in 'The Widowhood System' and 'Ginger Hero' (in *The Diviner*), but Friel's most immediate experience, as the pupil of his own father's national school, provides a most powerful example in the eponymous 'The Illusionists'. In this story there are three illusionists: M. L'Estrange, Prince of the Occult (in reality Barney O'Reilly); the narrator's father, who is refusing to come to terms with the difference between his present circumstances and the image of his former self which he espouses; and the narrator, who expects by becoming an apprentice illusionist to reach some Chekhovian Moscow, and who is eventually forced not only to admit the illusionary nature of M. L'Estrange's past and therefore his own future, but also to embrace, or reclaim, a known, but equally illusory world, offered to him through the affective authority of his mother.

The exotic (in this case M. L'Estrange) is also used as an alternative to familiar disappointment. Friel, and much modern Irish fiction, turns accepted critical theory on its head, since he shows the wisdom of age and authority as a synonym for buffoonery and drunkenness. 'In the analogy of innocence', writes Northrop Frye, 'the divine or spiritual figures are usually paternal wise old men with magical powers'. [25] Irish society tends to smile on, if not to extol, the alchoholic, that genetically disappointed result of psychological and environmental tragedy, in the same way as it invests the associated deficiencies of insanity or mental aberration with healing and magical powers: an illusion – a lie – that guarantees a tender, forgiving smile and recognises those affects in oneself. But the exotic, even though he is also master, and creature, of illusion, can dispel that atmosphere of tolerance and open a door into a more exciting darkness. In 'Segova, The Savage Turk' it is Segova's strength which attracts the child, in contrast to his father's weakness. Segova's thick dark hair symbolises his strength, 'the supreme in manhood...the crystallisation of every hope and ambition I would ever have'. Even when he is beaten for trying to be like Segova, the child realises that 'every stroke [was] alienating me more and more from the puny and the feeble and strengthening me in my resolve to join forces with the brawny and the mighty' (*Saucer* 121).

In their treatment of expectation destroyed, or hope deferred, or the assessment of dignity, Friel's stories are more important in a modern reading than his attention to illusion *per se*, which is not in itself as central to his later work as these other elements. The psychic disorders of Irish society are not only served by illusion or illusionism; visually and verbally Irish people are being asked to reassess what they see and what they hear and thus to re-examine the architecture of their minds. Friel's contribution to this process – the German 'Prozess' seems appropriate here – has been characterised by a concern for tenderness evident in even his overtly violent play, *The Freedom of the City*, and the most covertly fierce, *Crystal and Fox*; while in *The Loves of Cass McGuire* Cass's outbursts are counterpointed by a poignant series of rhapsodies, culminating in Cass's own entry into a dream world. An illusion, yes, but more than that, a way of dealing with time and place rediscovered which reveals the sensibility more attuned to nicety, to tension, to heartache, to panic in the face of the grotesque or bizarre, than to the problems of self-deceit, however disturbing those may be. Friel, particularly in the stories, divines within us the frightened child. With his mixture of strictness and compassion, he exposes the near-brutality to which our psychic disorder has reduced us, and then shows us how to become whole. Through the private conversation of his stories and radio plays, he does this on an intimate level; since the appearance of *The Enemy Within* he has been working out how to achieve this through the public address system. There is a good deal of Eliot's intellectuality and spirituality in Friel's plays, because of his attention to the psyche. These are the stories Eliot might have written.

Friel's psychological techniques are those of recurring visions and appeals to past time. Chekhov's frightened children express the problem thus: Carlotta: 'Where I come from and who I am I don't know'; Yepihodov: 'I can't seem to make out where I'm going, what it is I really want...to live or to shoot myself, so to speak'; Liubov Andreeyevna: 'What truth? *You* can see where the truth is, and where it isn't, but I seem to have lost my power of vision.' [26] Friel's characters, particularly in the stories, experience the same problem – If I can't speak my name, I can't be a person, so I can't go anywhere among men; if I can't see, I have no moral or aesthetic vision, so I can't find my way in the world; if I can't tell the real from the unreal, I can't discriminate, I lose the power of choice, so I am immobolised. Ordinarily Friel's people have names which delineate their role in society on both its physical and metaphysical levels: Flames Flaherty 'who used to run before the fire brigade in the old days, clearing the street' (*Gold* 80) – we can *see* him *and* his job; 'Mr Sing My Heart's Delight' for the packman Singh, because he fills the lonely woman's fading memories with an exotic richness; and the qualifying names which we meet in 'Sarah Johnny Sally' (*Tr.*28) telling us seed, breed and generation. Then there are the nicknames – of description: Lobster O'Brien with the injured eye (in 'The Fawn Pup'); of moral value: Anna na mBreag, Anna of the Lies, maker of bad poteen (*Tr.* 27) – and the series of names by which a single body has many personae in the family and extended family: 'at home I was Joe or "Joey boy" or even in his softer moments "Plumb" but in school I was plain Hargan' ('My Father and the Sergeant'). Finally, there are the names that mislead, which give us a mistaken identity: Owen/Roland in *Translations* being the most poignant as well as the most treacherous. Beyond ourselves there are the objective/subjective names we give to places. Once again *Translations* provides us with the mental and physical problem of map-making, but a neglected story, 'The Wee Lake Beyond', tells us not only of the lake whose map-names translate that meaning into topography (*'Lough Fada*, the long lake; *Lough Na Noilean*, the lake with the islands; *Lough Gorm*, the blue lake; *Lough Rower*, the fat lake' *Gold* 69–70) but also of those lakes which 'were nameless and inaccessible'. Nameless and *therefore* inaccessible: naming them would make them accessible, would add to their definition on the map, would open them up for discussion. Ordinarily we locate ourselves by means of *vision*, and only secondarily by other senses. In 'The Gold in the Sea' 'the blackness was so dense that the three fishermen had identity only by their voices' (*Diviner* 37). Their identity, it is suggested, is diminished by their invisibility; in 'The Widowhood System' the bird 'suffered from mental blackouts, like blown fuses, so that it had to fly blind for periods until the psyche righted itself' (*Diviner* 55), in other words it had to relocate itself by reference to the inner, not the outer, world. At the opening of 'The Barney Game' Barney Cole sat on an upturned box in the yard behind the poultry shop, killing chickens with his eyes closed. 'It's the feel of them I know', he explained...'If I looked at what I was doing, I'd only be all thumbs' (*Gold* 103). More than an index to physical contact, vision can also act as a trigger to memory and imagination:

> 'Very poor', she said quietly, adding the detail to the picture she was composing in her mind. 'And the oranges and bananas grow there on trees and there are all classes of fruit and flowers with all the colours of the rainbow on them.'
>
> 'Yes', he said simply, for he was remembering his own picture. 'It is very beautiful, good lady. Very beau-ti-ful'.
>
> (*Saucer* 68)

Finally, there is the use of time as an ordinary technique of story-writing. Friel's stories usually open with a statement of time, rather than of place or person. 'The very day his mother was buried' (*Diviner* 45); 'November frost had starched the flat countryside into silent rigidity' (*Diviner* 65); 'When his father and mother died' (*Diviner* 75); 'I can recall the precise moment in my childhood' (*Gold* 157). This last opening creates a flashback of the kind which triggers memory in the narrator, and imagination of time past in the reader/spectator. It is particularly effective cinematically in its combination of the visual and the temporal dimensions. The appeal is to a 'state that was', *in illo tempore*, as in 'Among the Ruins': 'We're going to see where Daddy used to play when he was a little boy' (*Diviner* 127); or 'The Wee Lake Beyond' in which the timeless landscape of mountains and lakes holds simultaneously the events of the holiday now and those of the holiday forty-five years earlier. This is partly 'emotion recollected in tranquillity' and partly an attempt to solve the 'crisis recollected from childhood' in the crucible of memory and thus isolate it from contemporary events.

It is of course noticeable that Friel's stories are non-eclectic. As D.E.S. Maxwell comments, 'Friel rarely writes about the city, he writes about Catholics but not Protestants' (even his 'aristocrats' in 'Foundry House' and of course in *Aristocrats* itself, are Catholics); most of his people are poor, they carry cardboard suitcases. Maxwell says quite rightly that 'he is not an artist of the whole community' and that he could not be, since neither of the two traditions of Ulster 'has any real and natural intimacy with the other'. [27] But while Friel is not a spokesman for Catholic or nationalist viewpoints, and does not attempt to portray anything other than his own folk, the more serious imbalance in his stories is the lack of that intimacy which comes from mutual commerce between town and country. As Raymond Williams says:

> The common image of the country is now an image of the past, and the common image of the city an image of the future. That leaves, if we isolate them, an undefined present. The pull of the idea of the country is towards old ways, human ways, natural ways. [28]

To translate this into the Derry/Donegal context, we can quite distinctly see Friel in his stories addressing one side of the equation in his concentration on the past, on a traditional, Gaelic world, and therefore leaving the 'undefined present' dangerously unresolved.

Conscious of writing in a genre that owed too much to the influence of a master like Frank O'Connor, and of being too easily seduced by the demands of the American market, once Friel had begun to extend the private voice with his radio plays he abandoned the short story form. But at the same time we cannot dismiss the elements of the stories simply because they tend towards the elegiac. (The danger of elegy has been underlined in *The Gentle Island*: 'My God it's beautiful up there, Shane: the sun and the fresh wind from the sea and the sky alive with larks and the smell of heather' *GI* 36.) The strengths of the pastoral are present in all his plays, even *Volunteers* and *The Freedom of the City*: the extension lies in the fact that he is now prepared to add into the equation the dynamic of the city, and the future tense. His tone continues to be lyric, but it now looks for external, as well as interior, freedom.

Part II
PUBLIC ADDRESS

3

PLAYS OF LOVE

My heart expanded with an immense remembered love for
her, and then at once shrank in terror of her

Living Quarters [1]

RADIO DRAMA

With two plays written specifically for radio in 1958, *A Sort of
Freedom* and *To This Hard House*, and a stage play, *A Doubtful
Paradise* (1960), Friel began the progression from the private conversation of the short stories to the public address of the stage presenta-
tion. The Northern Ireland Home Service, as the BBC's station in
Ulster was then called, had a long and fruitful history of fostering
radio drama, initiated by Tyrone Guthrie himself at the inception of
the service in 1924, and continued at that time by Ronald Mason,
who encouraged Friel and commissioned his first two plays. Radio
drama offered a method of developing the technique of the short
story by voicing its various personalities and making explicit the
main preoccupations. MacNeice had found that the device of
'splitting a mind into different voices' could assist in taking 'the
listener directly into the mind of a complex man', [2] a device which
Friel himself would succeed in putting on the stage in *Philadelphia,
Here I Come!* In his early plays he moves towards that position by
experimenting with the basic short-story form, while (in the radio
version of *The Loves of Cass McGuire*) developing the role of the
narrator by aligning it with the main character in the play.

Friel's plays, from 1958 up to the present time, represent the
classical dramatic cycle, in the four phases of *agon*, *pathos*,
sparagmos, and *anagnorisis*. *Agon*, or place of romantic conflict, in
which Friel sets out his main themes of contention and

examination, is found in *A Sort of Freedom* (1958), *To This Hard House* (1958), *A Doubtful Paradise* (stage and radio, 1960), *The Enemy Within* (1962), *The Blind Mice* (1963), *Philadelphia, Here I Come!* (1964), two playlets, *The Founder Members* (for radio, 1964) and *Three Fathers,Three Sons* (for television, 1964), *The Loves of Cass McGuire* (1966), *Lovers* ('Winners' and 'Losers', 1967), *Crystal and Fox* (1968), *The Gentle Island* (1971) and re–emerges in *Dancing at Lughnasa.* The *pathos* in which the conflict themes are tragically worked out comes for Friel in the plays concerned with liberation and its consequences, *The Mundy Scheme* (1969), *The Freedom of the City* (1973), *Volunteers* (1975), *Living Quarters* (1977) and *Aristocrats* (1979). The *sparagmos*, or ironic tearing apart of the hero, is found in two plays, *Faith Healer* (1979) and *Making History* (1988), while the *anagnorisis*, the comic recognition or resolution of his work to date, consists of the twin plays *Translations* (1980) and *The Communication Cord* (1982), the playlet *American Welcome* (1980), his translation of *Three Sisters* (1981), the dramatisation of *Fathers and Sons* (1987) and, once again, *Making History*. In 1976 there were also the television plays, *Farewell to Ardstraw* and *The Next Parish*.

This may seem too rigid a classification; and it is of course possible to classify or categorise them quite differently. For example, all Friel's plays seem to fall into two cycles, one beginning with the radio plays, passing through the 'love' plays, and culminating in a 'black' comedy, *The Mundy Scheme*; another beginning then with another 'love' theme, passing through the probing and experimental works related to 'freedom', and culminating in another comedy, this time a 'white' one, in *The Communication Cord*.

I prefer to concentrate on three groups: the 'love' plays in which the author's main concern is the examination of family and community ties and allegiances; the 'freedom' plays in which the consequences which the author has discovered about love are examined; and the 'language' plays in which our means of communicating about love, politics, culture, are rigorously inspected and largely set aside. *Making History* goes beyond many of these questions, in particular in focussing on the nature of fiction and in questioning the idea of a family. Of course here too there are overlappings: *family* for example, runs throughout Friel's work as a major theme, especially in *The Enemy Within, Philadelphia, Living Quarters, Aristocrats, Translations, Three Sisters, Fathers and Sons* and *Dancing at Lughnasa*; while the 'political' element in *The Mundy Scheme*, *The Freedom*, and *Volunteers* is also to be found in *Translations* and again in *Fathers and Sons*. It is also tempting to follow the classical formula and to see *Faith Healer* entirely in its own right as a unique statement about the hero and the artist.

All the problems, dichotomies, anxieties latent in Irish society as they are discussed or implied in Friel's short stories are present, and made more explicit, in his first attempts at drama. At first Friel remains in what Northrop Frye calls 'the low mimetic area', [3] using ordinary images of experience to create a set of ideas in, initially, the listener's mind. The transition into drama is thus gradual: the author is extending, rather than exchanging, his original voice, while the reader, who has to create his own voices in the inner ear, becomes the listener for whom the sounds (now external) are provided.

It is perhaps surprising that although Guthrie contributed significantly to the development of radio drama with his own plays *Squirrel's Cage* (1929), *The Flowers Are Not for You to Pick* (1930) and *Matrimonial News* (1932), his influence in this area did not extend particularly to Friel. (Friel's approach to the development of *The Loves of Cass McGuire* from radio to stage is, however, reminiscent of Guthrie's work, and at the time of his death in 1971 Guthrie was preparing to produce *Cass*.) Guthrie regarded the actor's irresistible temptation to create effects as an opportunity to dispense with realism and naturalism and to produce social archetypes – through which to introduce to the listener's ear a series of social and political problems. As in Greek drama, his characters remained masked and 'were wholly dependent upon the word'. [4] In Guthrie's *Matrimonial News* we are introduced to the stream of consciousness of a frustrated and disheartened woman. [5] 'Remember', says the announcer, 'you are overhearing her thoughts. She is alone.' We might easily adopt the same approach to a radio version of *Cass*, but by the time he wrote *Cass* Friel had already moved significantly away from radio, a medium in which he seems to have encountered considerable difficulties, principally because he was approaching it as literature rather than drama. Ronald Mason, however, believes that Friel remains pre-eminently a radio writer, in the sense that not only do his stage plays 'translate' easily and naturally into radio, but also because in those of his plays which are 'short' in action – *Lovers*, *Faith Healer* and *Making History* in particular – Friel still uses the style and techniques of the radio medium, the 'Come here till I whisper in your ear'. [6]

The stilted language and rhythm of speech in *To This Hard House* indicate that Friel was not yet at ease with the new medium, that he could not confidently convey all the short-story narrator's sense either of the personality of place or of the observations permitted to the narrator himself. Both *A Sort of Freedom* and *To This Hard House* have relatively weak closures because the author has so far failed to adapt the literary closure of the story into a dramatic conclusion: *A Sort of Freedom* closes with Joe Reddin, the recipient of a form of redundancy payment or conscience money from his former employer, Jack Frazer, talking to himself: 'The decentest man in town, in the whole country... that's what Joe Frazer is' [7] – a moral statement, resonant of story telling, such as we find in all the dignity-related stories. In *To This Hard House* a runaway daughter returns to an ineffectual welcome: 'I knew she would be welcome. I'll call her in, Daniel. (*calls off*) Fiona, come on in child; come on in to the room'. [8] Similarly the radio version of *A Doubtful Paradise* (also entitled *The Francophile*) ends in an anticlimax, because the story-writer cannot carry the characters beyond the final 'curtain' and yet end the play from the audience/listener's point of view. Here the ineffectual father, disillusioned by his failure to acquire a cosmopolitan culture by taking evening classes in French, fantasises on the 'expression of the brotherhood of man, the one-ness, the family one-ness of creation', and the play ends with his announcement 'Next month I'm going to take up... Esperanto!' [9] Short story endings occur within the dialogue also: in *A Sort of Freedom* the doctor tries to persuade Jack Frazer that the death of his adopted child was not due to neglect: 'It was one of those tragic accidents that happen now and again'. [10] That whole sentence could easily, and satisfactorily, provide the 'fateful' conclusion to a story with similar import to 'The Diviner'. But Friel is obviously moving closer to the point where tragic events do take place within the context of, if not necessarily upon, the dramatic stage, and, like a Greek dramatist, he must therefore find a dramatic, rather than a narrative, method. So too he must find ways of expressing emotional conviction. Jack Frazer remonstrates with the doctor, insisting that the dead baby would have grown up in his own image. He has already commissioned new boards for his works' gates – 'Frazer & Son, Haulage Contractors' (the baby is eight months old) – and now

72

he insists 'He was called Jack Frazer after me. He would have been me.' [11] That, too, suits the father in a narrative such as 'Among the Ruins', but is unconvincing as a bald statement which the storyteller has not supported by creating a dramatic emotional context.

Beside the technical problems Friel encountered in these plays, between the stories and the later 'love' plays, they supply one distinctive transitional feature: they are plays in which the hopeful children are a disappointment to their fathers, and in which the mothers mediate the hopes and disappointments. Mary Reddin in *A Sort of Freedom*, Lily Stone in *To This Hard House*, Maggie Logue in *A Doubtful Paradise*, all supply a degree of tenderness and compassion lacking in, for example, *Living Quarters* or *Aristocrats*, in which the children have to work out their own salvation, and their parental relationships, practically unaided. In that sense Friel is still writing in the same frame of mind as in 'The Illusionists' (with which *A Doubtful Paradise*, especially because it is also known as *The Francophile*, has obvious affinities). But he is also changing gear for the bitterness of *Philadelphia*: the mother's intervention, which will be possible in *Philadelphia* only through the surrogate role of the housekeeper, Madge, and impossible thereafter, is here inconclusive and, implicitly, ineffectual.

In another sense Friel is clarifying the elements in his 'family' discussions. The grandfather, who in the stories has been a key figure standing slightly outside the main family circle, but one of 'the child's' key points of reference (as in 'My True Kinsman'), also disappears. Thus the elision of the father, by means of the child–grandfather liaison, is no longer possible and the confrontation so feared in the stories has to begin in *Philadelphia* (*agon*) and to be worked through (*pathos*) until it finds a kind of resolution (*anagnorisis*) in *Translations*.

At the age of thirty Friel was strongly aware of the 'traditional' problems of rural Ireland. He had not yet had the 'first parole from inbred, claustrophobic Ireland', and he presents those problems conceptually, almost symbolically, rather than engagingly. He continues to do this until the transitional *Philadelphia*, where the principal contestants in the *agon*, Private/Public Gar and his father, begin to move from their cardboard effigies into three dimensions. Then in *To This Hard House* Lily Stone mediates not only for her children but between her husband and that other authoritarian figure, the Inspector (who recedes with the stories until he is re-admitted obliquely as the offstage Mr George Alexander, Justice of the Peace, and directly in the English sapper Captain Lancey, both in *Translations*). Daniel Stone is 'proud perhaps, and cock-of-the-walk in a transparent sort of way, but for all that, a simple man...a good man'. [12] But both fathers and children have feet of clay. Once again in *A Doubtful Paradise*, the mother–wife, Maggie Logue, breaks off from conversation, or remonstration, with her husband to address *us*, the reader/listener, in the third person:

> (*Inexorably*) And when the family was growing up, I hoped that it would be like the father they would turn out... When he said 'Chris is destined for a business career' it sounded the grandest thing in the world...And Kevin, he was to 'grace the legal profession' and Una was to 'care for the sick'. That's what he said, those were his very words. But they were my children as well as his and although I never said it to myself, I knew what was happening all along and I done nothing. [13]

The children, like their father, fail to realise their pipe-dreams, and another traditional Irish theme is born. It is left to the mothers to hope. Jack Frazer's wife tells him 'a woman never gives up hope, Jack, never despairs...You will be content to have the vision of what might have been and you will be safe with that. Even you can't destroy a vision'. [14]

There is in these plays, though, a new note unrelated to the themes of the stories: not only do we know that 'this is not a world of ideals', [15] but we are made aware for the first time of the consequences of trying to hold to false or unrealistic ideals, of trying to act retrospectively. All at once the search for identity in memory and past time is ruled out of order.

Those who are clearly being left behind are those whose visual impairment is due to a split perspective between the past (which appears clear and certain) and the future (which is turbulent and threatening). In *To This Hard House* Daniel Stone typifies this refusal to accept the 'consequences' of an irreversible demographic trend. His lack of visual acuity is translated into an inability to deal with physical properties, a natural difficulty in coping with one sensual deficiency, given a clever metaphysical twist: 'his eyesight is not as good as it was...Somehow he seems to be losing his grip...He doesn't seem to have the same clear grasp of things.' [16] We encounter the same negative properties in Manus Sweeney in *The Gentle Island* and in Andy Tracey in 'Losers'. 'Losers' is a play with little dramatic content in the conventional sense. Its monologal scheme derives, of course, from its origins as a short story ('The Highwayman and the Saint'). In this sense it has more in common with Beckett's work than anything else Friel has written, except *Faith Healer*, particularly in the nihilistic visual imagery which he employs in the opening scene: 'He is staring fixedly through a pair of binoculars at the grey stone wall, which is only a few yards from where he is sitting. It becomes obvious that he is watching nothing: there is nothing to watch' (*Lovers* 93).

When Andy begins his monologue, he makes four statements each fixing his position in relation to the wall:

- I see damn all through these things.
- Well, I mean there's damn all to see.
- Anyway, most of the time I sit with my eyes closed ...
- These are his glasses. And this is where he was found dead.

(*Lovers* 93)

First, Andy perceives nothing, a situation he rapidly rationalises by shifting the initiative for perception, or lack of it, onto an empty backyard; then the lack of perception shifts back to him again, when he makes another attempt to explain his 'blindness', and finally he appeals to his initiation into a tradition of blindness, in which he refers to his father-in-law, his predecessor in the chair. The sightlessness, the lack of any transaction between Andy and his environment, is described as 'a gesture', but it is obviously an empty gesture, a despairing surrender which negates his previous existence as a lively and inventive suitor.

But vision is double, two-faced. The seventeenth-century Irish philosopher William Molyneux suggested that we see things differently by each eye, and that it is the task of the brain to rationalise these two into a single vision. [17] Double vision implies the ability to live by the power of a truth and, simultaneously, by the power of its opposite, a lie. We see Friel hinting at this in *A Sort of Freedom*, when Jack Frazer tries to exercise the individual's rights in the face of authority by persuading the doctor to falsify a certificate of innoculation for his adopted son: 'it's only a matter of signing your name', [18] and in *Making History* Hugh O'Neill offers to verify his biography on the grounds: 'one of the advantages of fading eyesight is that it gives the imagination the edge over reality' (*MH* 66).

THE STRUGGLE OF LOVE

With *Philadelphia* the mothers and wives disappear. Suddenly Friel introduces a series of experiments to replace the mother and to create discussion between fathers and sons, between brother and sister: discussion of the mother's role, her relationship with the father, and of the other relationships, mostly between father and son, in which she had previously mediated. The mothers of the stories, pursed, drawn, anxious, determined, grey, real, have become golden-haired memories, more sinned against than sinning.

By this drastic device, and the recession of other characters (grandfathers, inspectors), Friel literally clears the stage for the expression of his main themes. That the greatest and most pervasive of these themes is 'love' requires some explanation at this point. In the 'love' plays, which correspond closely to the *agon* in Friel's development, he uses the themes and techniques of his stories and radio plays in order to explore the relationships of the ego, the self and the world, to discover for himself, for the hero at the centre of the play, the system of checks and balances which holds the world together, whether it is the family unit, the whole tribe, or the wide world. This is an emotional rather than an intellectual process. Friel takes the psychologies of his zone and translates them into a personal culture: this is what we receive from him as gatekeeper in the texts of these plays, whereas in his next phase we see him attempting to rationalise those emotional findings, a venture which can be equally catastrophic.

These first plays are 'love' plays because they show very clearly not only the relationships of love between fathers and sons, between siblings, within families, but also the 'images for the affection' which transcend direct relationships and represent a 'culture of communitas', or, as Friel might prefer to put it, a culture of constituency. Within this culture we experience the love which affects, and the love by which we affect others. But it need not be the familiar love known as *eros* or *agape*: it may be equally affective in the whole community through the expression of courage, dignity, memory, nomination or the experience of embarrassment – that is, through 'affiliation'. In this sense all Friel's plays are 'love' plays, but the themes he explores explicitly in the earlier plays are tidied (although not put away) in his later writing, in favour of a more clinical approach to language itself. In fact his latest play, *Dancing at Lughnasa*, revisits these questions in exploring the relationships

PLAYS OF LOVE

between five sisters and their separate and collective existences.

In *The Enemy Within* and *Philadelphia*, for example, Friel discusses the difficulties of reconciling the inner life, the saving of one's soul, personal integrity, with the competing claims of the public world, one's family, one's external faith. Columba, the Abbot of Iona, is continually plagued by the irresistible interruptions from his old, familiar, tribal life in Ulster which threaten to destroy his search for spiritual salvation in Iona. Rather than curse his own brothers, whose affective call he must answer, he curses Ireland, as a mother, a *femme fatale*, a place which has taken on all the tragedy of human character: 'Damned, damned, damned Ireland! (*his voice breaks*). Soft green Ireland, beautiful green Ireland, my lovely green Ireland. O my Ireland' (*EW* 70).

In *Philadelphia*, the division of private and public is made explicit by the use of two players to represent the one character of Gareth O'Donnell. [19] The division between hope and disappointment lies in the imagined life that awaits him in Philadelphia, in contrast to the silent war between himself and his father in Ballybeg. This stepping out towards an expectation, or vision, is the religion of ecstasy as opposed to that of control, the placing of one's faith on the edge of the known world.

Somewhat controversially, Friel counterpoints Gar's emabarrassment with two repeated motifs, one the corrupted song 'Philadelphia [California] here I come, Right back where I started from', the other a cryptic reference to Burke's *French Revolution*:

> It is now sixteen or seventeen years since I saw the Queen of France, then the Dauphiness, at Versailles...And surely never lighted on this orb, which she hardly seemed to touch, a more delightful vision. I saw her just above the horizon, decorating and cheering the elevated sphere she just began to move in. [20]
>
> (*Ph.* 23, 26, 80)

Its purpose is to offer gratuitously another vision, of grace, beauty and splendour which has been dashed by a senseless world; against it, Gar and his father can measure their own memories, presided over by the vanished queen of their own lives: 'it was an afternoon in May – oh, fifteen years ago – I don't, remember every detail but some things are as vivid as can be', (*Ph.* 89).

The American vision is familiar to Irish men and women dreaming of emigration in order to escape famine, poverty, rural depression

77

or diseases of the affection, failures of affiliation. To be in America in one's mind and yet in Ireland in one's body, 'chained irrevocably to the earth, to the green wooded earth of Ireland' (*EW* 21), is part of the bifurcation or schizophrenia of the Irish mind, the ability to be in two places at one time, to hold two contradictory thoughts in congruence, to achieve bilocation of the affections. This 'double-vision' gives rise to two ways of perceiving 'reality', subjective and objective, in symbiotic captivity.

In one's roots one thus finds insecurity, 'unhappy and at home'. But one is still compelled to seek those roots, to answer the affective call, in order, one supposes, to confirm uncertainty: we are 'among the ruins' once again. One interpretation of this is Guthrie's view, in 'Theatre as Ritual', that 'we, with our limited vision, by the feeble light of human intelligence, are unable to discern our origin and must proceed blindly towards our darkly incomprehensible destiny', [21] exploring and invoking both 'sight and blindness, light and dark' in order to do so. It is significant that Friel, who knows this essay well, uses so extensively the theory and practice of vision in his stories and plays, as, of course, Beckett does also. (Guthrie continues in that essay to say 'Evil and Good are not, in fact, different ideas, but the same idea viewed from two different stand-points, or considered in two different contexts...Dark and light are not in fact opposites, but different degrees of visibility.' [22])

Between *The Enemy Within* and *Philadelphia* Friel wrote *The Blind Mice*, produced at the Eblana Theatre, Dublin, in February 1963 and subsequently in a radio version by BBC Belfast in November of that year. This is a precocious anticipation of some themes in both *Philadelphia* and *Cass*. Like *The Mundy Scheme*, it is out of the ordinary course of Friel's work because, one feels, he intends as far as possible to refrain from representing the principles of Church and State so explicitly on the stage. *The Blind Mice* is an attempt to exorcise the memory of the years in which he tested the vocation of priesthood and the experience of seminarian Irish Catholicism. It describes the return home to a hero's welcome of an Irish priest who has been imprisoned in China, which turns into calumny and violence when it is revealed that in order to obtain his 'freedom' he has betrayed his 'faith'. The play is so symbolic that the martyred priest is called 'Chris' (an abbreviation of Christopher, the Christ carrying the sins of the world) and the spokesman of the Irish hierarchy is 'Father Green'. Chris is subjected to 'the endless questionings' [23] as Frank Hardy will be later; and he, like Columba, has Christ taken away from him, as he slips out of the emotions into the intellect. But apart from crudely pointing out this dichotomy, the play belongs with the works for radio as a transitional piece.

Perhaps the significance of *The Blind Mice* in Friel's overall development is the fact that, like the story 'The Child', he wishes to suppress it. 'It is far too solemn, too intense, I wanted to hit at too many things. It's a play I'm sorry about.' [24] Quite apart from its crude and hostile characterisation and intemperance, however, *The Blind Mice* reveals more than Friel's admitted reaction to the 'priesthood' and 'the kind of catholicism we have in this country': [25] it also tells us of his preoccupation with the themes of failure and betrayal which he has already sketched in the Columba of *The Enemy Within* and which become the psychological platform for almost all his later work. *The Blind Mice* , in all its rawness, exposes the connection between failure and betrayal, one a condition of weakness which we will find in the Casimir of *Aristocrats* and the Frank of *Living Quarters*, the other a condition of strength which characterises the faith healer and both Hugh and Owen O'Donnell. It is, as Friel put it at the time, about how Columba, and after him Frank Hardy and Hugh O'Neill, 'acquired sanctity. Sanctity in the sense of a man having tremendous integrity and the courage to back it up.' [26]

As a further bridge between the stories and the stage plays Chris Carroll discovers the difference between dignity and respectability: 'I will atone...for all the years when I have been priestly instead of being a priest.' [27] More than simply regretting 'conceit, pride, jealousies', he now craves understanding and sympathy for his act of apostasy. But he is told by his confessor that they are 'luxuries... Never look for them, because once you think you have found them you become righteous again.' [28] Chris committed an act of despair because God had stopped coming to him: 'I was abandoned! He had forgotten me! He had abandoned me; I abandoned Him. We were quits': the beginning of *deus absconditus*. [29] The fears of the mother are projected forcefully onto the child:

> On the day I saw my straight young man step forward to his bishop and take the yoke on his shoulders I knew then that my prayers weren't ending but beginning. And from then on my heart was torn between pride and fear: pride in the greatest thing God could have done to us; and fear that He would be disappointed. It was like – like carrying you again in my womb, a new mothering. [30]

The death of Chris's faith is also the death of respectability. When the angry crowd cries 'Traitor! Traitor!' we discover that the birth of dignity and individuality is fatal to niceties, to localism and to family loyalty. Chris's brother calls him 'that mask of a man' and exclaims 'don't try to justify treason!', [31] little realising that he has explained the whole play: that we all wear masks, especially when we are most sincere, and that treason needs no apology.

At this stage in his career Friel was no doubt unable, as well as unwilling, to face these tensions any more explicitly than he had in *The Enemy Within*. In this sense *The Blind Mice* was a mistake. *Philadelphia*, with its disloyalty and its description of love-in-an-asylum, had yet to be written, and he had still to be liberated by the Minneapolis experience with Guthrie. But he continues to pursue two kinds of love which Yeats expressed as 'love of country' and 'love of the unseen life'. [32] One is logocentric, future-oriented, concerned with the public life, full of rhetoric, fraught with exile, ironic and ultimately tragic. The other is mythopoeic, silent, turned towards the past, concentrating on the inner existence, full of poetry, occupied with the sense of 'home'. In the inner life, love is unspoken – 'emotion recollected in tranquillity' perhaps – it is not challenged by Frank Hardy's 'maddening questions' (*FH* 13). But in the outer life love is reduced to mere 'faith' – the submersion of the individual in authority, the extinction of individual vision in favour of the greater vision of the tribe.

But each love is fragile, because neither can live without the other. Love, like the present, like 'I am', is always consigned to transience, it is already passed as soon as uttered; its hand is at its lips, always 'Bidding adieu'; the only permanence on which one can build a reality is where past *and* future are gathered together in a *nunc stans* [33] – the liminality of Janus who looks into both a past-oriented knowledge and a future-oriented desire. From infinite past and infinite future we can thus achieve an infinite present, so long as that equilibrium can be maintained. In that infinite *nunc stans* all emotion and all intellect can be contained.

Much of the tension between the individual and the tribe is expressed through the conflict between ecstasy and control. Columba is torn away from the spiritual family of his chosen exile, or ecstasis, by the affective memory of tribal affiliation; Gar

O'Donnell doubts the meaning of the journey on which he is about to embark, but the doubts originate in the light of the society he is leaving. In *The Loves of Cass McGuire*, Cass, returning home to 'Ballybeg' after fifty-two years waitressing to 'deadbeats, drags, washouts, living in the past' (*Cass* 19) in the pipe-nightmare of Skid Row, stands outside both memories: those of Skid Row which fixed her mind on the future, and those of the remembered childhood which, until they are proved illusory, provide that future. It is fundamentally important to realise that all her emotions are home-less, because it is in the test-tube of homelessness, when the emotions become restless and start to rampage through the junk-room of memory, that Friel can most effectively explore the nature and – more importantly – the consequences of freedom. Thus in 'Winners' Meg and Joe are leaving their families to commit the tribal offence of exogamy; in 'Losers', Andy Tracey sits downstairs, staring out through binoculars at a blank wall, while upstairs his mother-in-law stares at a plaster saint whose identity is protected by its nameless-ness. In *Crystal and Fox*, Fox Melarkey, with deliberate courage, dismantles the hierarchy and affiliations of his family, his livelihood and his own identity in order to regain his dream of childhood innocence; and the people of 'the gentle island' cannot come to terms with the 'kingdom' where they have chosen to remain while the rest of their tribe abdicates and goes into exile.

The starting point for understanding all these dilemmas is simple: dreamers and visionaries want to make a better life for themselves. By means of their will they have therefore established a future project in which memory and its affects come into conflict with that which it cannot control. This works on the material and emotional levels, which are interrelated by the sense of family and place. Gar O'Donnell sees neither material prospect nor emotional fulfilment in Ballybeg, but he still doubts that he will find them in the unknown Philadelphia; yet he must go in order to escape the asylum of 'home': it is not just a simple question of flying from the emotional centre in order to make a better life, however stifling that centre may be and however attractive that better life might appear.

The real tension in these plays lies in the fact that in stepping outside one set of rules in order to solve a problem of the affections one sets up new demands and new problems one had not 'imagined'. Love knows neither its own strength nor its own consequences. In this sense each play establishes a heroic stance and each hero faces an inevitable tragedy in failing to silence the 'maddening questions'.

There is very little reconciliation or repossession in the early plays which is not contrived and of doubtful validity – the rhapsodies of *Cass*, Columba's 'beginning again' (both Eliotic devices), the deaths of the 'Winners', the nihilism of all the 'Losers' – Andy Tracey, Fox Melarkey, and, in *The Gentle Island*, Manus Sweeney. Possibly *Philadelphia* remains Friel's most outstanding early play simply because he leaves its protagonist in uncertainty:

> PRIVATE: God, Boy, why do you have to leave? Why? Why?
> PUBLIC: I don't know. I – I – I – don't know.
>
> *(Ph.* 110)

an uncertainty which he partially resolves in the later plays. What Gar doesn't know is the way of answering the maddening questions, making the voices silent, which comes from effective communication. Failure of communication is greatest within the family circle. Neither the mother nor the grandfather is there to carry the child away into an alternative vision, and he cannot speak to his father. Friel's own 'project' is to exercise the will in mediating between the inner 'maddening questions' and the ambivalent visions of the public world, and it is only by establishing a liminality in both worlds that he can gain an equilibrium. But, as we will see in the case of *Making History*, the price of the purchase in each world is to lose the right to live or to love within either, because in order to divine, to civilise, within one, he has to be a peregrine, a barbarian, in the other: always other and between.

Cass McGuire solves this by accepting 'election' (in Eliot's sense) to the otherness of 'Eden House', the 'home' to which her dismayed family consigns her. There, the experiences of the past are transformed into dream, in a rhapsody which is inevitably *verbal* in the telling, but predominantly *visual* in the recollection; it is also of a sensual intensity which suggests that the lost children of Eden House would fight savagely to retain their dream, to retain the right to love.

The rhapsodies in *Cass* from two older inmates and, after her 'election', from Cass herself, are of light, and movement, and touch:

> TRILBE: Gordon and I walk hand in hand along the country roads between the poplars...in the shafts of golden sun... still days of sun and children with golden hair, named after princes and princesses; and we travelled and travelled – Russia, India, Persia, Palestine, never stopping, always moving. (*Cass* 30)

INGRAM: She was eighteen with golden hair as ripe wheat...I played the piano and she danced and danced and danced...her hair swinging behind her...I played faster and faster and faster... until her eyes shone with happiness and the room swam with delight and my heart sang with joy. (*Cass* 45)

CASS: One Christmas I saw a man on a green sledge in Central Park and he was being pulled along by two beautiful chestnuts...a man with a kind face...and he looked and he looked at me and he lifted his black hat to me...And I stood at the stern of the ship, and two white and green lines spread out and out and out before me .(*Cass* 63–64)

'Still days', 'always moving'; Friel has captured here the essence of identity: that is, to know oneself and to be known. He has projected it into an imaginary landscape: to sit in the con-trivance of a winged chair in order to deliver oneself of a 'confession' is to take flight into a past which *one can only remember because it never happened.*

The imprecatory leitmotif, to protect 'our truth', is borrowed from Yeats:

But I, being poor have only my dreams,
I have spread my dreams under your feet,
Tread softly, because you tread on my dreams. [34]

But into the fragile carapace of these personal treasures Friel makes savage incisions straight to the heart. The different versions of events in *Cass* are killers: Friel avows that the play is a concerto with Cass as soloist, and Cass fights for her identity by pitting herself against the memories – and therefore identities – of the others, but eventually succumbs to the power of the rhapsody. Meanwhile in 'Losers' Andy Tracey finds himself submitting to the greater truth of the womenfolk – the worship of plaster saints, conducted by his mother-in-law and Cissie Cassidy; Cissie, the spokeswoman for his 'eden' days, says, 'You're coming closer and closer to us' (*Lovers* 112), but Andy shatters that truth by smashing the plaster saint. Dreams can be shattered on a much more mundane level too. In *The Gentle Island* Peter's initial announcement 'My God, it's heavenly' – another pseudo-Eden – has already been negated by the spectacle of mass emigration. The question of heaven and hell depends on one's perspective. In *The Gentle Island*

Friel uses the conventional cherishing of the rural way of life, the psychological and emotional pull of the island, sending up the observance of pieties, as he does later in *The Communication Cord*. And beyond this he uses the island as a device for testing out the characters' ideas and fantasies about themselves.

In *Faith Healer* also we are asked to test memory against time itself. There is very little corroboration of the alternative truths offered by Frank, Grace and Teddy; on only two points of 'fact' do they agree: that they were once in Kinlochbervie, 'in Sutherland, about as far north as you can go in Scotland' (*FH* 15, 21, 34) and that they crossed to Ireland 'from Stranraer to Larne and drove through the night to County Donegal' (*FH* 16, 26, 37). But Teddy recalls that Kinlochbervie was 'bathed in sunshine' (*FH* 34), whereas for Grace it rained. In Kinlochbervie Grace's baby was born and Frank's mother died. No-one is lying. The details are 'immaterial'. Perceptions are disclosed and thus are shown to be imprecise, labile, indeterminate. Different ways of seeing love and affiliation, different ways of experiencing love and affiliation, different ways of loving and touching.

Possibly an even more poignant illustration of the failure of memory is given in *Living Quarters*, in Anna's explanation of her affair with her step-son Ben to her husband (Ben's father):

> ANNA (*quickly*): and I tried to keep you, to maintain you in my mind, I tried Frank, I tried. But you kept slipping away from me. I searched Tina for you and Miriam, but you weren't in them. And then I could remember nothing, only your uniform, the colour of your hair, your footstep in the hall, that is all I could remember, a handsome, courteous, considerate man who had once been kind to me and who wrote me all those simple, passionate letters; too simple, too passionate. And then Ben came and I found you in him Frank.
>
> (*LQ* 84)

To find a father in a son, to allow a trick of memory and perception to reverse time, is to play not the Oedipal, but the Hippolytan, card, and that is to ask us to look not only at horror and guilt, but also at fantasy, the only-so-slight distortion of ourselves in the world. As we discover in the first scene of *Translations*, a distorted vision, if only slightly at odds with the rest of the world, pulls one's perspective of home, name and means of survival seriously out of kilter. And in the operatic soliloquy in which Hugh

O'Donnell rhapsodises on his childhood memory of the great Sir Henry Sidney (*MH* 34–5) the one irresistible spur to the intensity of his affections as a Gaelic prince has been put at nought – the time-bomb has ceased ticking. But in these scenes from shattered childhood Friel is not insisting on the re-integration of those worlds – the hedge-school or the island or the Gaelic kingdom: he is, indeed, showing us that, ancient or modern, they represent the island in the heart of everyone who inevitably sets out imperfectly attuned to the greater world.

The most powerful tensions established by Friel in these love plays, therefore, are not those between father and son (private love) but those between the individual and his tribe and place, the 'public faith' of family and extended family. Ballybeg *represents* the affective images of an affiliatory culture moving through both time and place. Everyday Ballybeg, like love itself, is destroyed by violation of its boundaries, and renewed through the rewriting of the texts, its sacred institutes. Sometimes this disintegration is treated with comic sarcasm: at the evacuation of Inishkeen (the Gentle Island) one footless islander asks, 'D'you think the flight of the Earls was anything like this?' (*GI* 9). At others, realistically:

> MANUS: Fifty years ago there were two hundred people on this island, our own school, our own church, our own doctor. No one ever wanted.
>
> JOE: Scrabbing a mouthful of spuds from the sand, d'you call that a living?
>
> (*GI* 9)

Homecomings and intrusion, more than departures and exile, highlight the sense of fragility, the inherent instability, of homes and families: Cass, Owen O'Donnell, and the family reunions of *Aristocrats* and *Living Quarters*. In *Philadelphia* it is not Gar's impending departure but the homecoming of his aunt Lizzy which triggers recognition: up to the middle of the second episode everyone lives or acts a lie in complicity. Then Lizzie admits the emptiness of her materially successful life in Philadelphia:

> LIZZIE: And it's all so Gawd-awful because we have no one to share it with us.
>
> (*Ph.* 63)

Similarly in *Cass* none of the statements about the McGuire family is 'true' until her brother Harry admits in Act 3 that Cass is 'better off' in Eden House because the family itself has disintegrated: there is no longer a 'family home', merely a nursing home – one kind of asylum has given way to another.

Columba in *The Enemy Within* is in a different category, because he is a displaced person. In his chosen life he is the Abbot of Iona, having forsaken his Ulster homeland, but the calls of that homeland frequently make him an exile from Iona. Both families suffer by his absence, and in a sense he himself is never at home, he is always celebrating or fearing a homecoming. The community of Iona appears to be fraternal, Columba 'looks for no subservience' (*EW* 16) but in practice when faced with a dilemma, he acts in one of two ways: either he exercises his authority as Abbot or he pleads with Grillaan, his prior and confessor, to exercise authority over *him*. His relations with his siblings vacillate equally between the authoritative and the submissive: he is either the manipulator or the victim of the lie.

Friel establishes these tenuous relationships and uncertainties in order to show that 'a man's enemies shall be they of his own household' (*EW* 20), that the external world is not as dangerous or as precious as the inner, because it holds neither the same threats and penalties nor the same hope of reconciliation. Thus a future-oriented love is inevitably at risk, while a retrospective love must live with all the failures of ecstasy.

The pivotal work which capitalises the earlier experiences of *Philadelphia* and *Lovers* and predicts both the later family plays and the plays of language is *Crystal and Fox* (1968). Fox Melarkey (a clever linguistic pun combining the restlessness and wildness of the animal with the insecurity and riddling of the player [37]) is a lost cause, a creature who dreams brief glimpses of perfection, and finds it necessary to destroy the world because he cannot grasp paradise. The play is a parody of a play, in which everyone becomes deranged or confirms the original sin of the derangement within them. '"What's my name?"..."What am I doing here?"' (*CF* 12) is the motif of the characters, each of whom is playing some other part in another play. The central impossibility of both action and plot is voiced when one member of the cast denounces Fox: '"I know that character!" Fox's response is non-verbal: *'he hides behind a mask of bland simplicity and vagueness'* (*CF* 19). The inscrutability hides Fox's desolation because he recognises not only the impossibility of regaining his dream – when he was 'like a king' (*CF* 22) and Crystal was 'a princess' (*CF* 24–5) – but also the futility of any kind of action at all. The audiences for his fit-up show pre-echo the hopeless cases who come to the Faith Healer: 'conning people that know they're being conned' (*CF* 36). It elicits the feral in him: he is 'desperate...restless. And a man with a restlessness is a savage bugger' (*CF* 36). Unlike Manus Sweeney, who is described in similar terms, Fox says this about himself because he has recognised that one cannot measure or balance hope against despair. Crystal says 'We had more courage than sense' (the impetuosity of the lovers) and Fox retorts 'And more hope than courage' (*CF* 25): if despair, in Friel's terms, is the corollary of hope, then fear is the complement of courage. Fox's revenant son tells him 'you're full of hate' (*CF* 48), but the only way we can understand that word 'hate', Fox's principal motivation, is by seeing it as the quotient when hope and courage have given way to despair and fear. Fox is left in the fifth province of hate, at 'a signpost pointing in four directions...in the middle of nowhere' (*CF* 55–6), confident of the proof that, in Wilde's words, each man kills the thing he loves. The homecoming that precipitates the final savagery is external: it is nothing compared to Fox's own homecoming to the private void of his central space.

EMBARRASSMENT

Hannah Arendt and Rimbaud suggest that one can understand oneself as another: Rimbaud says *Je est un autre*, and Arendt says that one can only think of, or judge, oneself through a *retour secret sur moi-même.* [35] This we find transcends the father–son relationship. But it also underlines one of the more equivocal themes of Irish fiction, which, if we can learn to read in the interstices of tragedy, tells us that there is no such thing as silent love, even self-love. Friel has managed two significant developments both in his stories and, much more successfully, in his plays. In *Philadelphia*, particularly, he has, in conceiving Gar as two personae, expressed the otherness of our conscience and thus used what appears to be a technical innovation as an integral part of his intentions. Secondly, he has, out of his own ingenuity, shifted the traditional emotional balance so as to concentrate on the relation of will to time, a way of dealing with continuity and silence which, due to his peculiar vision, involves following a father into the future, dark indefinite rather than a mother into a golden past pluperfect. 'Say something father!' is, as we have already noted, not only the demand for communication, it is also the imperative which calls into existence, which commands the other *to be*. In order to establish some kind of relationship with his father, Private Gar urges Public Gar to keep talking, if only to coax grudging and embarrassed monosyllables from his father:

> S.B.: Which tea chest?
> PUBLIC: The one near the window.
> S.B.: Oh, I see – I see ...
> PRIVATE: You're doing grand. Keep at it. It's the silence that's the enemy.
>
> (*Ph.* 102)

But the initial statement holds good: '*We embarrass one another*' – father and son offend and upset the psychic order of their tribal culture. It is possible, of course, to see *Philadelphia* as 'the tail-end of a bad Irish tradition', [36] rather than opening up new ground. Such a view would see S.B. O'Donnell, and Arthur Carroll in *The Blind Mice*, as successors of the miserable Ulster shop-keeper depicted by George Shiels in *The Passing Day*. (It might also seek to connect Friel's Ballybeg with the 'Bailebeag' which was the setting for 'The Microbe', a rural tragedy which appeared anonymously in *The Leader* in 1940 and contains an explicit but arcadian account of some of the themes explored in *Philadelphia*. [37]) The exile theme is *still* being pursued by Irish writers: Tom Murphy's *A Crucial Week in the Life of a Grocer's Assistant*, first premiered after *Philadelphia* in 1969 but in fact written before it, contains the same elements and pathos as *Philadelphia*; it was eventually followed by *The White House* (1972) and, after revision, *Conversations on a Homecoming* (1985). Murphy's drama, despite the fact that it has taken different paths from Friel's – for example in the violence and anti-intellectualism of what Christopher Murray (after Peter Brook) has called 'rough and holy theatre' [38] – still emanates from the same historical source which makes exile and homecoming also the centre of Friel's drama: dispossession. Spiritual dispossession and emptiness, as a result of physical deprivation in the land clearances in the nineteenth century, [39] fills the cistern of the Irish diaspora and, as I have shown elsewhere, [40] makes Murphy the blatant successor to Eugene O'Neill. But it also makes him a cousin, if not a brother, of Friel. Murphy has said of his *Famine* (1968): '*Famine* to me meant twisted mentalities, poverty of love, tenderness and affection; the natural extravagance of youth wanting

to bloom ... but being stalemated by a nineteenth–century mentality.' [41]

Murphy may write differently about the wounded; certainly he
makes little attempt, except in *The Gigli Concert*, to cure them, and
he shows them little compassion. But he describes the same creatures.
The lost children of *Famine* reappear in Mommo's litany in
Bailegangaire:

> the wretched and neglected, dilapidated an' forlorn, the for-
> gotten an' tormented, the lonely an' despairing, ragged an'
> dirty, impoverished, hungry, emaciated and unhealthy, eyes
> big as saucers ridiculing an' defying of their lot on earth
> below, glintin' their defiance, their defiance an' rejection,
> inviting of what else might come or *care* to come! Driving
> bellows of refusal at the sky through the roof. [42]

Murphy's dispossessed suffer the same embarrassment as Friel's: if
there is no yesterday and no tomorrow, there can be no set of
shared beliefs, no common cause for social or cultural continuity.
There can only be a grinding, self-destructive knowledge of the
here-and-now, which makes both Friel and Murphy apocalyptic
writers. [43]

We live in a constant state of mutual embarrassment because of
our failure to reconcile myth with logic, past with future. We invent
the conceit of indifference in order to circumvent, to circumlocute,
this embarrassment. Yet just as it seems impossible to keep silence,
it also seems impossible to achieve this state of indifference, because
the essential condition of our instability is that of *cultural difference*.
Just as it is impossible to live without hierarchy, without difference
of rank or quality.

Here again, embarrassment is acute in both Friel's and Murphy's
work. A community secure in the knowledge of its inner strengths
defines itself in relation to its heroes and its heroic myths. In Friel's
work the heroes have been deposed: S.B. O'Donnell, because of his
failure to speak ritual words of healing, Columba because of his
inability to lead, Hugh O'Donnell because his authority and therefore his usefulness have fossilised, District Justice O'Donnell
because of the stroke which symbolises the muteness of the tribal
tongue. Here Friel, too, shows himself the son of Eugene O'Neill,
the author of the afflicted O'Donnells in direct descent from him of
'all the four haunted Tyrones'. [44] Murphy, likewise, shows us the
brutal Carneys (*Whistle in the Dark*), an animal family with no

effective, commanding presence; the failure of young men's dreams in the absent father-figure of the publican 'J.J.' (*Conversations on a Homecoming*); and the close parallel of S.B. O'Donnell and Gar in the pathetic father and son in *A Crucial Week*.

When Friel's Gar and Murphy's John Joe (*A Crucial Week*) try to establish a fluency they resort to shouting, trumpeting their failures, their hurt and their unique vision of the non-event: as Murphy says, 'one has to slay one's own town by getting away from it', [45] but one must also return, and Murphy has done this by associating closely with drama in the West of Ireland, as Friel has done in a homecoming to Derry.

But of course Friel and Murphy are both also inheritors of Shaw: Shaw's Larry Doyle dreads his homecoming to Rosscullen, 'that hell of littleness and monotony', because he and his father have nothing in common: 'What am I going to say to him? What is he to say to me?' Below this superficial embarrassment is the shifting ground between two apparently polarised world-views:

> Live in contact with dreams and you will get something of their charm: live in contact with facts and you will get something of their brutality. I wish I could find a country to live in where the facts were not brutal and the dreams were unreal. [46]

In *Translations* Lieutenant Yolland, captivated by that charm, will become a foil to the efficiency of Shaw's Broadbent and to Lancey's 'brutality'; while Murphy sets about much the same business with Betty among the Carneys in *Whistle in the Dark* and J.P.W. King in *The Gigli Concert*. It is as if they endorse Shaw's, and without a doubt O'Neill's, statement, that Ireland 'produces two kinds of men in strange perfection: saints and traitors'. [47]

The comfortable idea that father and son exert some equal-and-opposite symbiotic force on each other is challenged by silence and strength. Private Gar examines a mythic past relationship:

> On that afternoon a great beauty happened, a beauty that has haunted the boy ever since, because he wonders now did it really take place, or did he imagine it. There are only the two of us, he says; each of us is all the other has; and why can we ever not look at each other?...To hell with all strong silent men!

(*Ph.* 98)

'Silence', Private declares, 'is the enemy.' He urges Public to keep talking to his father in order to get an admission of complicity in this 'great beauty' that once happened (*Ph.* 102). One cannot survive in symbiotic captivity with a ghost to whom one is also merely spectral.

But it is not only the public discourse which must be maintained, but also the dialogue with self, which is only possible if it tries to evade embarrassment by means of strange, oblique speech:

> An' you just keep a'talkin' to you'self all the time, Mistah, 'cos once you stop a'talkin' to you'self ah reckon then you jist begin to think kinda crazy things'.
>
> (*Ph.* 26)

The statement represents an acknowledgement of self, but one in which its inevitable vehicle of language con-fuses the distinction between embarrassment and strangeness. Plain speech would have enabled the embarrassment to survive, whereas this patter fails to resolve it, and simply makes it go away by introducing a new form of strangeness: 'with intimacy', says Steiner, 'the external vulgate and the private mass of language grow more and more con-cordant...Inside or between languages, human communication equals translation.' [48] For Friel, this osmosis between his private and public self is spelt out in the persona(e) of Private Gar and Public Gar; elsewhere, for example, in *The Enemy Within*, it is expressed in Columba's self-examination as evident in the title of the play, as well as in his confrontation with himself-when-young in the person of the novice Oswald. Oswald has a preconception of Columba as a saint, 'the man of heroic virtue'. But Columba himself denies this: he says 'young boys need heroes' (*EW* 50-1), an idealised way of projecting themselves onto a public screen. Yet he eventually accepts the need for unity with himself, as revealed through the appearance of Oswald, and a new beginning. But Private Gar bitterly attacks his public self: 'how you stick yourself I'll never know!'(*Ph.* 28).

When Friel was writing *Translations* he recorded in his diary:

> One of the mistakes of the direction in which the play is presently pulling is the almost wholly *public* concern of the theme: how does the eradication of the Irish language and the substitution of English affect this particular society? How long can a *society* live without its tongue? Public questions,

issues for politicians; and that's what is wrong with the play now. The play must concern itself only with the exploration of the dark and private places of individual souls. [49]

This exploration, which began privately with the stories, through, as we have seen, the techniques of the affection, has at its core the intercourse of the public and private selves. This is exemplified in Columba's inability to identify the eponymous hero of the play, the enemy within, and the impossibility of Gar's *seeing* his alter ego (*Ph.* 12) – in other words the haunting of one's familiar. The development from Columba's attempted dialogue with his hidden enemy to Gar's verbalised encounters with his alter ego exemplifies J.S. Mill's view that 'our internal consciousness tells us that we have a power which the whole outward experience of the human race tells us that we never use.' [50] That power, we might crudely say, is the power of love. In the face of this, some of Friel's characters withdraw so far into the inner hermetic life that the only realities are those of another order. Jimmy Jack Cassie in *Translations* encounters reality only in relation to 'the world of the gods and ancient myths [which] is as real and as immediate as everyday life in the townland of Baile Beag' (*Tr.* 11). Jimmy Jack's commerce is with the sole reality, the mythical. For him life is active but meaningless, whereas for others, such as the inmates of Eden House, it is meaningful but merely contemplative. If love is a fiction, as the whole of *Cass* suggests, then Cass and the other rhapsodists learn to love by coming to terms with their fictive powers.

But the long inward journey of self-realisation of one's alter ego becomes for Friel much more than a retreat to the interior, or even a knowledge of one's intricate relationship with 'Ballybeg'. It rests on the idea that one can in fact become the membrane which separates, but only just, one world from another, and by which those two worlds are mediated into each other. Columba, to his spiritual community, is an 'alter Christus' (*EW* 30), mediating between God and souls, whereas to his earthly family he is an *alter frater*, [51] who mediates between men and God – 'the inner man, the soul, chained irrevocably to the earth' (*EW* 21). It might best be described as 'I live in a world, and another world lives in me.' This is the ecstasy of love in which all time is contained in every moment of time.

Beckett says in *The Unnamable*:

I feel an outside and an inside and me in the middle, perhaps neither one side nor the other, I'm in the middle, I'm the partition, I've two surfaces and no thickness, perhaps that's what I feel, myself vibrating, I'm the tympanum, *on the one hand the mind, on the other the world*, I don't belong to either. [52] (*my emphasis*)

Remember Hegel. We come back again to the urge to speak, but now it has a more positive, active role – mediation of the *will* – which is, in the Nietzschean terms employed by Arendt, 'to sing the future', not in a quest for truth so much as in a quest for meaning. [53] As Hugh O'Donnell says, 'confusion is not an ignoble condition' (*Tr.* 67), adding to his son's 'Uncertainty in meaning is incipient poetry' (*Tr.* 32). Thus, in the Irish mind uncertainty and meaning come together in double, or multi-vision, seeing many possibilities rather than one enduring truth. Poetry, rather than rhetoric, is the preferred mode of love.

'I was back there in Tirconaill', says Columba (*EW* 21). *Back* moves him both in time and place, and he imagines, he calls up images from memory. As Steiner says, 'It is not the literal past that rules us...it is images of the past...Images and symbolic constructs of the past are imprinted almost in the manner of genetic information on our sensibility.' [54] Friel 'translates' this into Hugh O'Donnell as: 'it is not the literal past, the "facts" of history, that shape us, but images of the past embodied in language' (*Tr.* 66).

The 'genetic information' is the power of love, while the images translated into poetry become love itself. There is also an echo of Paul Valéry in all this: like Steiner, Valéry emphasised the problems associated with translating from time into experience: 'the past is a thing entirely mental. It is only images and belief.' *But* Valéry says that we must use the 'time of the mind' – 'the idea of the past takes on a meaning and constitutes a value only for the man who finds in himself a passion for the future'. [55] Friel's future volition, or passion for the future, is contained in the realism of extending Steiner's metaphor: 'we must never cease renewing those images, because once we do, we fossilise'.

It therefore emerges from this reading of Friel's psychology that his 'project' is to translate the mind into the world and the world into the mind; intellect into emotion and emotion into intellect; that the writer's function is not only to celebrate 'Ballybeg' but to transcend the mythological present by judging the past and exercising a will over the future. [56] The pilgrimage he makes from the known centre consists of a journey which in itself has no meaning, it is a journey in which the arrival is all, the homecoming to the transfigured place. This is a uniting of private landscape and public world. In terms of Friel's own craft it is a translation from story-writing to play-writing, to hold the private and public voices 'in one receiving sensibility and craft'. Arendt says that conscience and consciousness are interrelated as thinking and judging, and that this is indispensable to survival. 'The ability to tell right from wrong, beautiful from ugly...at the same moment when the stakes are on the table, may indeed prevent catastrophes, at least for the self.' [57] In this process – we come back to that word of healing and humbling – the artist must acquiesce in himself, in anticipation of homecomings which, in Arendt's terms, might otherwise be catastrophic.

4

PLAYS OF FREEDOM

When people have no real life, they live on their illusions
Anton Chekhov [1]

DISPOSSESSION

For Friel, as for Beckett, the compulsion to speak implies the destruction of the world. For his creatures it means the recognition of their vulnerability, the fragility and ambiguity of language itself, the dismemberment of family and the revocation of affiliation. To be is to fracture, never again to make whole. To break silence is automatically to begin an odyssey, the aim of which is to return to silence. Friel marked this odyssey first with a private conversation, as near to silence as possible, a monologue close to soliloquy, and then moved, somewhat reluctantly, into a public domain which the occasion demanded. Now he explores the family and its affects in more clinical intellectual detail in *Living Quarters* (1977) and *Aristocrats* (1979); coming out of the period of the 'love' plays he also writes his one explicit treatment of the northern troubles, *The Freedom of the City* (1973), and two others, although widely differing, on 'political' themes, *The Mundy Scheme* (1970) and *Volunteers* (1975). In *Faith Healer* he returns to the personal, the monologue, the private discourse, in an attempt to re-examine the artist's role in, and affiliation to, society, to find out whether he is a 'civilian' or a 'barbarian'.

Now he discusses *freedom*, the freedom which is known and enjoyed and that which is simply imagined. Through the concept of freedom he is able to approach the culture of poverty itself, and thence the issues of dispossession and repossession. In *The Freedom of the City* Friel sets about celebrating the type of liberation which marks a release from poverty, a repossession of wholeness. It is essential to stress that freedom (*eleutheria*) derives from the concept of movement, free to go as I wish (*eleuthein opos ero*); clearly, therefore, as Descartes realised, [2] it is not simply a matter of exercising some God-given right; the *will* is central to the idea of freedom, as we see both in this play and in its sequel *Volunteers*.

That one may achieve freedom by an act of will is of course countered by the fact that one may acquiesce in one's own dispossession. The fine balance and distinction between will and acquiescence is examined in both *Living Quarters* and *Aristocrats*, in which Friel shows that the will, and therefore freedom, however absolute they may seem, are in fact hedged about, safeguarded by institutes designed both to translate the inexpressible into reality and to reduce the irreducible. These plays constitute a *pathos* in the sense that the exploration of these boundaries, and the freedom permitted within them, is carried out by the 'volunteers', Lily, Michael and Skinner in *The Freedom*, Keeney, Pyne, Knox and Smiler in *Volunteers*, the Butler family in *Living Quarters*, and the O'Donnell family in *Aristocrats*. It is a struggle against fixed and immovable odds. Within the institutes of boundary, text, icon and tribe they find the measure of their own freedom, the degree to which the will can apprehend space, time, being and otherness, and the extent to which they can acquiesce in the consequences of such an act of will. In *Faith Healer* that exploration is taken further in the *sparagmos* in which Frank Hardy continually hurls himself against the barbed wire of apprehension until, after he has torn himself to shreds, he succeeds in making himself whole for the first time. Once Friel has made some vital homecomings in *Translations* and *Fathers and Sons*, he is able once more to confront this *sparagmos* in the Hugh O'Neill of *Making History*, who fails to achieve or maintain his integrity.

The 'love' plays, with the exception of *Philadelphia*, are not *great* plays: not because they fail to answer any 'great' questions, but because they do not set out to address those questions. They don't rise above, or attempt to rise above, the everyday circumstances which give them life. In this sense they are 'naturalistic' plays in the manner of Chekhov. Naturalism of course gives rise to great drama, and, as I have already indicated, Friel goes beyond some of Chekhov's achievements in taking the normal and regular and ordinary, and uniting it to great themes, rather than addressing those themes directly. This is particularly true of *Fathers and Sons*.

But, in looking at the problem of freedom and poverty as a natural issue of the themes discussed in chapter 3, we are looking specifically at the result of drawing boundaries, of inclusion and exclusion, of delineating 'us' and 'them' in the crudest form, as in the polarisation of the two main 'communities' in Ulster, with a mutual suspicion and antipathy which is much stronger than an antagonism, each with its own omphalos, text, icons, culture, affections and ways of naming. We are also looking at the different versions of love, especially the reduction of private *love* to public *faith*, where it concerns the affiliation of individuals to different communities and their relations with those communities.

To the Greeks the *barbaros* was a foreigner, a non-Hellene; later the term was used by any dominant tribe to describe that which was *other* – rude, wild, uncivilised, uncultured. That the divisions of Ulster should be seen as 'battle-lines' is a natural result of this polarisation, but the lines are more recognisable in the mind than on the 'narrow ground', a ground on which each community is dispossessed by the other, in which it is impossible for either culture to know its own place with integrity. The sense of dispossession, although more eloquently and frequently expressed by the 'Catholic Gael', works both ways, as Louis MacNeice says:

I was the rector's son, born to the Anglican order,
Banned for ever from the candles of the Irish poor [3] –

a sense repeated more recently by Longley, Hewitt and Mahon. For example, John Hewitt's poem 'Once Alien Here':

as native in my thought as any here
who now would seek a native mode to tell
our stubborn wisdom individual
yet lacking skill in either scale of song,
the graver English, lyric Irish tongue. [4]

In the 'Gaelic' tradition that dispossession was confirmed in the final disintegration of the Gaelic order in Ulster in the sixteenth and seventeenth centuries, a collapse which parallels, and was only partly caused by, the Elizabethan and Jacobean plantations. The seventeenth- and eighteenth-century poems of 'the dispossessed' express the loss of heroes, and also look forward beyond the politically dead present to redemption in some future age. [5] The achievement of these poets was in establishing a 'mythological present' in which future hope reflected, and was kindled by, the lost

world. Heaney cleverly expresses the retrospective vision of this
culture in his 'An Open Letter':

> The whole imagined country mourns,
> Its lost erotic
> Aisling life. [6]

Irish poetry seems to have kept alive, through various phases, the
concept and the practice of the homeless mind eventually achieving
the cultural (and eventually political) renaissance of modern Ireland;
as Eoghan Rua Ó Súilleabháin's epigram says:

> Loss of our learning brought darkness, weakness and woe
> on me and mine, mid those unrighteous hordes.
> Oafs have entered the place of the poets
> and taken the light of the schools from everyone. [7]

It is worth noting that a century earlier an English poet, with much
the same intent, expressed the idea of loss and redemption:

> Of man's First Disobedience and the Fruit
> Of that Forbidden Tree, whose mortal tast
> Brought Death into the World and all our woe,
> With loss of *Eden* till one greater Man
> Restore us and regain the blissful Seat,
> Sing Heav'nly Muse. [8]

One laments the usurpation of hearth-rights and the flight of the
philosopher-poets while the other sets about dealing with absolutes
– 'to justify the ways of God to men'. Yet although they inevitably
use the same paradigms, light and darkness, good and evil, Eden
and wilderness, one comes from a culture which accepts the double
vision of Janus (*demon est deus inversus*) while the other rationalises
out of existence the Satanic proposition 'Evil be thou my Good.'

The flight of the philosopher–poets created the 'hedge-school'
atmosphere of continuing an education not only in semantics but in
culture and semiology itself. Such schools thus complemented the
natural repugnance of colonial subjects towards external authority.
We have already seen Friel's humorous side-sweep at this mentality
('D'you think the flight of the Earls was anything like this?' *GI* 9)
and we will meet it again in the send-up of his own work, *The
Communication Cord*. Here, however, we should note how in
Philadelphia he uses the image of 'old Ireland' in two perspectives:
that of the retrospective Lizzie Sweeney and that of the

introspective Gar. America, suggests Boyle, the hopeless school-master, is 'A vast restless place that doesn't give a cuss about the past...Impermanence and anonymity, it offers great attractions' (*Ph.* 44). 'Don't keep looking back over your shoulder', he advises Gar. 'Be 100 per cent American...Forget Ballybeg and Ireland' (*Ph.* 46–7). Gar accepts this *aisling* of America, because he believes he is 'Free! Free as the bloody wind! Answerable to nobody! All this bloody yap about father and son and all this sentimental rubbish about "homeland" and "birthplace", yap! Bloody yap!' (*Ph.* 81). But there can be no failure, or abridgement, of memory for Gar (such as his father can achieve) because time intrudes too powerfully. As Private says to Public:

> You know what you're doing, don't you, laddybuck? Collect-ing memories and images and impressions that are going to make you bloody miserable...Just the memory of it – that's all you have now – just the memory; and even now, even so soon, it is being distilled of all its coarseness; and what's left is going to be precious, precious gold.
>
> (*Ph.* 54, 79)

Friel, through the medium of private discourse, is making an inventory of the affections. The question he poses is whether it is possible to stay outside the sacred circle of those affections without feeling the centrifugal force of their gravity. To have gravity within oneself is quite different from obeying the affective pull of the tribal centre. But to be able to ignore that pull is to become a barbarian, a stranger excluded for his uncouth culture, and worse, a sibling exiled, expelled for his lack of piety, his unwillingness to conform; and worse again, one who is *willing* to leave the tribe, and explore unknown territories. The traditional pattern of Irish emigration to America involved two inter-related elements: sending the young to safe places already established by elder siblings (in this case the aunt), and remitting the next passage money. In both ways the 'old Ireland' is maintained at home and recreated in the new world, a colonisation of its own future.

This works very well on the physical and material level, and to a certain extent on the emotional level, but it ultimately breaks down because it is not enough just to foster and protect a culture: that culture must also be *lived*. The successful encounter between cultures, whether they intend to antagonise each other or not, involves, in semantic terms, a decoding of affects and intentions which is beyond most experience; when this is translated into emotional terms it presents a psychological problem on an acutely embarrassing scale, which throws up inconsistencies that a once homogenous culture no longer has the power to rationalise. As Eugene O'Neill says of Irish America in *Long Day's Journey Into Night*:

> none of us can help the things life has done to us. They're done before you realize it, and once they're done they make you do other things until at last everything comes between you and what you'd like to be, and you've lost your true self forever...the things life has done to us we cannot excuse or explain. [9]

This is touched on in *The Gentle Island*: Manus Sweeney regards himself as 'king' of the almost deserted Inishkeen, and his hero-warrior son, plundering the sea, as 'a prince' (*GI* 11). But to possess, in the light of the family disaffection which is taking place, is not enough. As his other son tells him, 'King of Inishkeen, King of nothing' (*GI* 9). We are left with three choices in order to maintain a precarious grip on freedom: going back completely into the hermetic past, *or* exercising some kind of rational, logical rejection of that past and its myth, *or* (the most extreme choice) a jump into the dark. The first choice is implosive, a negative embrace; the second makes the heart brutal, and calls for painful reconstruction of the incised/excised parts; the third obeys the principle that 'he who hesitates is lost', and demands explosive action, where the jump is 'now or never'.

The underlying factor of all this is the fear of dispossession rather than the desire for freedom, and this is instilled by our knowledge and understanding of the past. Security is only as certain as today's seat by the hearth, today's crop, today's reassuring discourse. Irishmen have traditionally survived by distinguishing a sense of 'the past' from a sense of 'history', by recognising that they are liberated by one and oppressed by the other. If 'the past' is regarded as an empty expanse of time, its potential is immense. It becomes possible to equate 'the past' with 'the future'. The only affects which are 'fixed' are the horizons themselves. But if we look at 'history' as a way of filling up that immeasurable past with quantifiable effects – injustices, inadequacies and failures – then the ideas of self-defeat and oppression as affective characteristics of time itself become inescapable. Whether it is military defeat, civil incompetence, lack of juridical or economic prowess, or imponderables such as climate, world wars or the run of the salmon, the notion of time, land and language becomes oppressive, once the events of history are allowed to superimpose themselves on 'the past'. Thus, in the view of history the future, too, becomes impossible. The Irish irony lies in the fact that it is logic, the rational child of history, which offers a course towards freedom, whereas it is the fictive imagination of the past which oppresses by its *embarras de richesses* – a 'precious gold' which denies its own dross.

In order to avoid dispossession and poverty the people of Friel's plays adopt a variety of stances, but there is little idiosyncracy in their basic behaviour. They make one of those three choices. Few of them, like Meg and Joe in 'Winners', jump into the dark; most remain trapped in the paths of their inescapable consciousness. The 'winners' revel in their loss of sense rather than feel themselves disoriented by it. Meg's wild exuberance, powered by her immensely strong intuition, creates a curious ambivalence – a wounded animal who is yet supreme, on a collision course with fate, welcoming the abdication of status, and the rejection of certainty, embracing risk. [10] Most, however – the 'losers' – find their social currency reduced by blindness, deafness, dumbness, their inability to see the world, to hear the texts, to utter their names. (Meg says, 'I'd rather be deaf than dumb, but I'd rather be dumb than blind', *Lovers* 26.) The eventual redemption of Maire Chatach in *Translations* and that of Cass McGuire is achieved by their acquiring a new vision, a new 'method of replying to inevitabilities' (*Tr.* 42).

LOYALTIES

In his early work Friel's characters escape; *time* regained is in a sense synonymous with *place* regained. In 'Among the Ruins' Joe acknowledges that:

> the past is a mirage, a soft illusion into which one steps in order to escape the present...What had he expected to find at Corradinna, a restoration of innocence? A dream confirmed? It had robbed him of a precious thing, his illusions of the past, and in their place now there was nothing, nothing but the truth.
>
> (*Diviner* 133–4)

But most of Friel's retrospection is 'golden'; its success lies in the fact that it recreates and therefore, as with Trilbe, renews the images for the affection. The power of 'that time' to command the present images is escaped only by the kind of inner dialogue, close to silence, which eludes most of his characters, but not Frank Hardy or Beckett's Krapp. Beckett captures it in identical terms in *That Time* (1974–5): 'that time you went back that last time to look was the ruin still there where you hid as a child', [11] and in *Endgame*, a few years before the conception of Cass: 'we once went out rowing on Lake Como. One April afternoon.' [12]

Escape into the future is no different; a homecoming has to be a future project of the will. The point of coming home, whether it is physical or metaphysical, is to complete an odyssey which began with leaving home. Chekhov's three sisters want to regain 'Moscow', more a place of the mind than a place on the map; in Friel's case, this is only imperfectly approached until he writes *The Freedom of the City*, but even here one cannot repossess that which one never possessed. As Eliot says, 'You do not know what hope is, until you have lost it.' [13] For this reason, perhaps, he does not ask us to tread softly on their dreams; the poor of Derry have much more than their dreams, because their dreams are of a state never yet experienced, and beside them they live daily lives of hardship and indignity. They are future-oriented, substituting 'what might be' for 'what might have been'.

These parallel lives of deeply felt indignity, and a dream of an imagined future past, are a form of schizophrenia natural to the 'culture of poverty'. As Oscar Lewis says, 'there is no such "condition" as "schizophrenia", but the label is a social fact and the social fact a *political event*' (*my emphasis*). [14] We must recall Friel's statement that politics is implicit in 'language, attitudes and style'. We thus become aware of two types of despair within the one mind, the despair which energises and the despair which enervates, a struggle to reconcile reality with autism; in the words of the sociologist Dodds, who is adopted from Lewis's *La Vida*, 'the way the poor adapt to their marginal position in society' *and* 'their method of reacting against that society' (*Freedom* 19). It also explains the difference between reality and the perception of reality, which we see in the opening of *Translations*. Lewis calls this the difference 'between what they say and what they do'. [15]

Friel has previously displayed this through Meg in *Lovers* and now particularly in Lily's use of demotic/mandarin vocabulary and syntax. This is Friel's response to the malapropisms of O'Casey's noble citizens, those whose hurt is more than material because through their poverty they have been wounded in their psyche. The ultimate failure is the failure to find any redemptive quality in the death which is inevitable: the failure is as inevitable as death itself, because one cannot stand outside oneself and take the alter id-entity residing in one's schizophrenia: one has renounced that kingdom. R.D. Laing borrows Mallarmé's phrase to explain this, 'l'enfant abdique son extase'. [16] One simply wanders round within the circle of one's inadequate personality, within the ring of one's own enemies, like Columba. There is little hope of the *beau geste*, and one's concentration is limited to the anti-heroic. As Friel has said,

> Since God is dead, and with Him the tragic hero, the only concern of the modern dramatist is man in society, in conflict with community, government, academy, church, family, and essentially in conflict with himself. [17]

He therefore emphasises the dramatist's concern

> with one man's insignificant place in the here-and-now world ...to portray that one man's frustrations and hopes and anguishes and joys and miseries and pleasures with all the precision and accuracy and truth that they know; and by so doing help to make a community of individuals. [18]

This is yet another reminder of Friel's artistic determination to remain a spectator, even though it is required of him to participate (cf. *LQ* 14); and therefore yet another instance of schizophrenia. For as he told Eavan Boland in 1970: 'everyone suspects that when the violence does come it will be very short-lived, quite brutal and very ugly and that it will end, and we're keeping ourselves in reserve for the situation which will never evolve'. [19]

The three victims in *The Freedom* (like the sisters in *Living Quarters* and *Aristocrats* and of course in Chekhov's own play) jointly form that 'community of individuals'; in *Volunteers* it is not so much the 'community' of the internees as the solitary figure of Leif, the excavated skeleton, who draws the others together in a community of alternative story-telling; while in *Faith Healer* the peregrine figure of Frank Hardy embodies both forms of despair and brings them alive: enervation and energy, that which resigns itself to dispossession and that which goes out to embrace its fate.

The specific form of despair which poverty imposed on the Catholic community of Derry reinforced the connection between religion and politics. As one of the participants in the civil rights campaign has recorded, 'nationalist candidates were not selected, they were anointed. Religion and politics were bound up together, were regarded, indeed, as being in many ways the same thing.' [20] This was created by two converging elements: the redemptorist martyrdom of Irish nationalism: 'one learned quite literally at one's mother's knee, that Christ died for the human race, and Patrick Pearse for the Irish section of it', [21] and the effective gerrymandering of local elections by the Unionists which disenfranchised the Catholic majority by denying them houses. The culture of poverty therefore resulted from the fact that people 'were born into misery and raised in squalor. They lived from day to day, fighting to tear some dignity from life.' [22] As O'Neill's James Tyrone would say: 'there was no damned romance in our poverty', [23] because poverty is the worst kind of violence. It was made more acute by the fact that they had lost self-respect through their inability to function as citizens because they did not have the 'freedom' of the city – midnight's bastards.

Friel has commented on the two aspects of Derry which commanded his loyalty and coloured his own sense of loss: 'One was of a gentle and in those days, sleepy town; the other was of a frustrating and frustrated town in which the majority of people were disinherited.' [24] He was a member of the Nationalist Party but resigned circa 1967 'because I felt the party had lost its initiative, I felt it was no longer vibrant and I think this is the reason the conflagration started in Derry'. [25] The Civil Rights movement became a 'conflagration' because confrontation led to police and army brutality, to rioting and then to open aggression on the part of a people determined to win back self-respect by reversing the trend of exclusion and disinheritance – a desperate, autistic people who inevitably became, like Manus Sweeney and Fox Melarkey, 'dangerous', prepared to destroy their own families and affiliates in pursuit of integrity. To destroy love in the pursuit of freedom is the ultimate tragedy and, perhaps, the ultimate necessity.

As Eavan Boland has observed, the reaction of northern writers to political events took the form of a growing awareness 'of a crisis of division in their communities, and therefore, in them as members of those communities, vulnerable to their incoherences as they had been in childhood to their values'. [26] In the 1960s Sam Thompson's *Over the Bridge* and John Boyd's *The Assassin* (1969) were followed by Boyd's *The Flats* in 1971; Wilson John Haire wrote

Within Two Shadows (1972) and *Bloom of the Diamond Stone* (1973); Patrick Galvin's *Nightfall to Belfast* (1973) was the only other significant response at that time to the growing violence in Northern Ireland. It seems that the playwrights have been incoherent themselves in expressing this drama. Perhaps Friel was right when he said that there was no drama in the situation. (Among novelists, Ben Kiely's *Proxopera* and Jennifer Johnston's *Shadows on our Skin* [1977] dedicated to Brian Friel, approached the subject.) More recently, of course, Graham Reid, Frank McGuinness, Anne Devlin and her father Paddy Devlin, Stewart Parker and Martin Lynch have addressed the issue directly.

We have already seen how Friel's attitude to the northern troubles changed from that expressed at the beginning of the decade. The focus of, and reason for, that change was the events of 'Bloody Sunday'. In 1971 Friel said that 'I have no objectivity in this situation; I am too involved emotionally to view it with calm.' [27] He also believed that a 'drama' of the north of Ireland was not possible because it required a 'conflict of equals'. In *The Freedom* we can detect a controlled rage which is utterly characteristic of Friel's personal confluence with those events, and yet it further indicates the control he exercises over that part of him which is more citizen than artist.

Friel has been silently criticised by the Catholic community in Northern Ireland for his supposed 'failure' to represent their predicament through the medium of the theatre of protest and violence. The implication is that Friel is not engaged in the 'realities' of contemporary Northern Ireland since he locates his plays outside it, in Donegal, and concentrates on relatively private issues rather than the unequivocally public domain which younger writers like Martin Lynch and Graham Reid insist are the proper concern of playwrights.

Like the late Stewart Parker, whose play *Northern Star* (1985) deals with the career of the eighteenth-century United Irishman, Henry Joy McCracken, Friel has preferred to think historically about the problems of Ulster. [28] In only one play, *The Mundy Scheme* (1969), has Friel paid explicit attention to modern (and in this case *southern*) Irish politics: the play is 'about' the plan to turn Ireland into an international graveyard, by trading on its pastoral, restful image ('France is the recognized home of good food; America is the acknowledged centre of art; Switzerland is the centre of Europe's banking. Let's make the west of Ireland the acknowledged eternal resting place'(*MS* 204). But the author's *intention* is to ask:

what happens when a small nation that has been manipulated
and abused by a large colonial power for hundreds of years
wrests its freedom by blood and anguish? What happens to an
emerging country after it has emerged? Does the transition
from dependence to independence induce a fatigue, a medioc-
rity, an ennui? Or does the clean spirit of idealism that fired
the people to freedom augment itself, grow bolder, more
revolutionary, more generous?

(*MS* 157)

Friel prefers to look at the wider context in order to learn his
lessons. As the subtitle to *The Mundy Scheme* emphasises ('May we
write your epitaph now Mr Emmet?'), Friel wants to learn whether
a nation has emerged, or can in fact emerge, from the collective
psychologies of its people: the implications for Derry's search for
'freedom' are obvious. The reference is to another United Irishman,
Robert Emmet, who asked that his epitaph be not written until
Ireland could take her place among the nations of the world.

Moreover Friel's position as a 'Catholic playwright', [29] a spokesman for the Catholic 'community', as he is perceived by the
'Protestants' in Northern Ireland, and as a 'Derry (and therefore
Catholic) playwright' as he is perceived from Belfast and the
Republic, makes this doubly difficult. He does not occupy such a
position from choice: he disowns it because, as we have seen, he
disclaims all loyalty to, and succour from, a 'community' in this
sense. But the position has been bestowed on him, however
undesired and unjustified, and either to accept it (to follow certain
implicit tribal dictates) or to reject it (to step outside the tribe) are
both courses in which Friel himself is seen to act, to make choices.

Friel's own position, as an artist, is that he must stand aside from
the actual events of the conflagration in Derry or Northern Ireland
generally, in order to describe the greater freedom of which the
Irish psyche is capable. That position, in terms of the implicit
criticisms just discussed, becomes his defence. Friel as a supporter
of the Civil Rights movement did march against the oppression of the
Catholics; his knowledge of the events of Bloody Sunday was
gained at first hand. But Friel *the artist* feels he must stand on the
sidelines and see himself *as citizen* marching past. It makes him no
less conscious of the fact that a war is being waged not only in the
North but throughout Ireland. As Seamus Deane says, 'the society
he [Friel] had known all his life began to break down, publicly and

bloodily'. [30] But in portraying that breakdown in *The Freedom* Friel also tells us of the society which, like that of Ballybeg in *Translations*, had already broken down internally, privately and psychologically. Therefore, it is easy to see why, in 1972, when he was about to meet the first serious challenge of that conflict, by translating the events of 'Bloody Sunday' into *The Freedom*, he was also considering a 'retreat' from the public drama of playwriting to the private fabula of the short story. [31] In the sense that it is a political and military war he has therefore, with one exception, declined to celebrate it or engage in it, whereas to the extent that the same war is cerebral and semantic and cultural he has made it the basis of everything he has written since 1969.

There is another sense in which Friel could not wish to involve himself in the drama of sectarianism: that is, the danger that by portraying terrorism one might condone or legitimise it. The IRA death-wish, the use of martyrdom to encourage bloodshed, has historical precedents. The combination of mariolatry, dying for the *femme fatale* and Cathleen ni Houlihan, is a recurrent theme in Irish poetry; the hunger-strike is one political weapon, the ecstasy of the mystical experience ('I see his blood upon the rose' [32]) is another. It thus becomes difficult, perhaps, for Friel to conceive a play as explicit and psychological as Graham Reid's *Callers* (1985) in which the concepts and contexts of both the assassins and their victims are explored, together with their respective views of the central event of the play itself.

Outside the area of terrorism, however, there remains the mutual aggression, distrust and often contempt between the Catholic/ Nationalist and Protestant/Unionist communities (if they can be so bluntly polarised) and between predominantly rural Catholic western Ulster and predominantly Protestant eastern Ulster. Both 'sides' of this ideological equation are in a state of mutual siege. To ease the acute psychological embarrassment which this causes, both sides resort not only to terrorism and covert violence but also to hysterical laughter, to romping about with the evidence of their dis-ease.

In these circumstances it is perhaps not surprising that Friel abandoned attempts at explicit approaches to the 'war' in modern Ulster because he could not confirm any sense of community. If he has a constituency in Derry, or in Ulster generally, he does not believe it to be best served by taking a play out onto the streets like a gun or a petrol bomb. His current work is nonetheless political, as we shall see in chapter 6, even though it is oblique: in *Translations* and *Making History* he adopts an archaeological approach, drawing his constituency back to another time – 'that time' – in order to divine something in its present condition. In this way like Tom Murphy in *Famine* or *Bailegangaire*, or Thomas Kilroy in *Double Cross* and his translations of *The Seagull* and *Ghosts*, his oblique approach to the concrete events of modern Ireland does not prevent him from describing their psychic and moral significance head-on.

Seamus Deane, who has been the principal mouthpiece for the activities of the Field Day venture, refers to the 'disfigurement' of the Derry poor, a psychic disfigurement with an external appearance usually described as eccentricity or nervous affliction, which he only recognised as an abnormality when he left Derry and noticed its absence elsewhere. [33] Friel has commented on the appearance of such disfigurement as one expression of the culture of poverty, a 'divine generosity and energy existing in dilapidation and despair', [34] in which we can recognise some of the symptoms displayed by the *staretsi*, the Russian *idiots* whose serene privacy passes across the tragic landscapes of Tolstoy and Dostoyevsky. Deane himself has addressed the problem of being a dramatist of the Troubles in the following terms:

> Northern Ireland has never been either State or nation, nor has it ever had any consciousness of itself that has not been fundamentally beleaguered by the contrary consciousness that each of the different sects there know the other to possess. [35]

To the extent that Northern Ireland is a polarised society, therefore, it enjoys the double vision of the Irish people, the ability to hold the two sides of the equation in the mind without resolution. This is underlined by Deane's remark:

> our main experience of alienation has been sectarianism; and sectarianism is one of the deepest forms of loyalty. To be alienated from that to which you are most loyal is a complicated fate. [36]

In discussing Friel's own 'response' to the situation Deane therefore sees that

> conscience (derived from one's political and class culture) is always wrestling and often clumsily with an author's elusive tact (derived from his own sense of himself and his language) ...Brian Friel's problem has always seemed to me to be the

classic one whereby a man must find in a particular crisis its universal implication and is sorely tried by the problem of timing the moment in which he should, in any given play, move from one to the other. [37]

In the sense that *The Freedom* is a play arising from a 'particular crisis' it undoubtedly fails to do this, because although Friel particularises the crisis in each of the three victims, he points the finger of the universal through quite unworthy figureheads: the sociologist, the priest, the balladeer and the television commentator. Lily, Michael and Skinner themselves remain the children of the Bogside, despite their claim for the solidarity of the Civil Rights campaign. It certainly does not serve the cause of a community at war to recapture its name and identity, however eloquently it expresses their predicament. He would no doubt adopt the broader and more dispassionate vision of Conor Cruise O'Brien: 'we are...forced to think, in our village, whatever its exact boundaries, about the relation of violence to our prevailing myths, to our past history, and to the condition of our society'. [38]

'Violence is terrible, but it is not inhuman', says Thomas Kinsella. 'In political terms it is the final response to unredressed injustice.' [39] Violence is of course done – inflicted and suffered – in *The Freedom*, but Friel is addressing more far-reaching themes. Like an American sheriff he is pursuing the bandits of memory across the border not only of space but also of time, seeking in Donegal the causes and cures of violence done to the Irish psyche much longer ago. For many years he worked on the play about Hugh O'Neill which became *Making History*: 'that was a very significant time for Ulster, that was when the first broad primary colours were splashed on the canvas. And what happened then is still exercising us': [40] it is the fact that those colours are still being splashed – especially the implications of the theme of love versus faith, trust and betrayal – that hindered the fulfilment of that play, at least until *Fathers and Sons* had helped to clear the decks.

The plantation of Ulster turned everything on its head and created, or made explicit, many of the dichotomies in Northern Irish society. It is not therefore surprising that Friel's archaeology, first in *The Freedom* and then *Volunteers*, turns itself upside down, subverts time and place in *Living Quarters* and appearance and perception in *Aristocrats*. The 'victims' of *The Freedom* receive the 'freedom of the city' but they are denied freedom from their poverty; they live and die within its institutes. The whole play demonstrates their servility and therefore the irony of 'freedom'. Friel wrote *The Freedom of the City* and not a play about 'Bloody Sunday'; and he wrote *Volunteers* without telling us for which crime the prisoners had been interned or the nature of their imminent death, because in both cases he was not prepared, either as citizen or artist, to describe such forms of ' "institutionalized violence"...the more antique and atavistic parts of the repertoire of legitimation', as Conor Cruise O'Brien describes it. [41] Nevertheless the play can, according to one observer, 'so easily reinforce hatred and prejudice', [42] a reference to an uncritical reception of a poor production by an embittered and partisan Derry audience.

The Freedom of the City, like Kinsella's 'Butcher's Dozen', was 'not written in response to the shooting of the thirteen dead in Derry' but 'in response to the Report of the Widgery Tribunal'. [43] Kinsella refers to 'Lord Widgery's cold putting aside of truth...with injustice literally wigged out as Justice.' [44] If Friel responded by setting *The Freedom* at a different time (1970), in a different part of the city (the three marchers find their way into the Guildhall, which had been the original objective of the Civil Rights march on Bloody Sunday), it could not have been written without either Bloody Sunday itself or the Widgery Report.

The real life Widgery Report made the following statements:

- that soldiers could only fire at a person carrying a firearm or similar weapon;
- that none of the thirteen men shot dead was shot while carrying a firearm (although one of them was later found to have had nail-bombs in his pocket);
- that although the individual decisions of soldiers as to whether or not to open fire ranged from 'a high degree of responsibility' to action which 'bordered on the reckless' this reflects 'differences in the character and temperament of the soldiers concerned' and did not invalidate the standing order under which they operated. [45]

Friel uses the inherent contradictions in these statements in the fictitious tribunal which dominates the action of *The Freedom*. He thus counterpoints the tribunal's 'objective' approach with the 'subjective' text required in order to make 'sense' out of the whole event and its hinterland of hope and despair. But beyond this he allows us the most valuable spectacle of all, the sight of inconsistencies being hammered into a unity in order to validate our preconceptions. As Elizabeth Hale Winkler has pointed out:

> in both cases soldiers and policemen were allowed to give testimony under pseudonyms. And the grotesque results of the paraffin tests, ambiguous at best, are also taken directly from reality...As in the Report, Friel's Judge discounts the evidence of photographers and eye witnesses, subtly discrediting [the priest] who told the 'truth as he knew it' (*Freedom* 60) (cf. 'truth as he saw it' *Widgery Report* 13). [46]

He makes the judge's opening statement the basis for the different 'versions' or perceptions of 'reality': 'these three people came together, seized possession of a civic building, and openly defied the security forces' (*Freedom* 18). Since in the course of the play we 'know' from the evidence of our own senses that Lily, Michael and Skinner 'came together' only by complete coincidence, that they did not 'seize possession' of the Guildhall but only stumbled into it by the same coincidence that connected them in Guildhall Square, and that they only 'defied' the army's order to leave the building through ignorance and ineptitude at dealing with such situations, it is clear that two separate truths are emerging during the play. The final verdicts represent the two ways of living in Northern Ireland, either for or against authority and its implicit oppression of minorities and the individual.

Friel similarly uses Oscar Lewis's *La Vida* to provide sociological 'evidence' from another figure who appears outside the central drama of the Guildhall. But whereas the Widgery Report enables Friel to subvert an unjust text in order to make a statement about the nature of truth, the subversion of Lewis amounts to an unsuccessful attempt to universalise the condition of poverty: where Lily in her own eloquent way expresses that condition emotionally, the speaker Dodds is expected to do so intellectually.

It is possible, judging by the syntax of the following definition by Lewis, that Friel had already made use of Lewis's central idea in discussing the term 'peasant' as noted earlier:

> Throughout recorded history, in literature, in proverbs, and in popular sayings, we find two opposite evaluations of the nature of the poor. Some characterize the poor as blessed, virtuous, upright, serene, independent, honest, kind and happy. Others characterize them as evil, mean, violent, sordid and criminal...Most frequently the culture of poverty develops

when a stratified social and economic system is breaking down or being replaced by another, as in the case of the transition from feudalism to capitalism or during periods of rapid technological change. Often it results from imperial conquest in which the native social and economic structure is smashed and the natives are maintained in a servile colonial status, sometimes for many generations. It can also occur in the process of detribalization...The most likely candidates for the culture of poverty are the people who come from the lower strata of a rapidly changing society and are already partially alienated from it. [47]

Friel tries to incorporate much of Lewis's thesis into Dodds's three main speeches (*Freedom* 19–21, 48–52, 88–9), but to lift the text verbatim would have been an unwarranted interpolation into the action with no dramatic content. It is significant that Lewis's thesis remains implicit in Friel's thinking rather than fully-fledged in his play. This is especially true of his observation that poverty has its own security, a view made explicit in Lily's conversation. Lewis says:

As an anthropologist I have tried to understand poverty and its associated traits as a culture or, more accurately, as a subculture with its own structure and rationale, as a way of life which is passed down from generation to generation along family lines. This view directs attention to the fact that the culture of poverty in modern nations is not only a matter of economic deprivation, or disorganization or of the absence of something. It is also something positive and provides some rewards without which the poor could hardly carry on. The culture of poverty is both an adaptation and a reaction of the poor to their marginal position in a class-stratified, highly individuated, capitalistic society. It represents an effort to cope with feelings of hopelessness and despair which develop from the realization of the improbability of achieving success in terms of the values and goals of the larger society. Indeed, many of the traits of the culture of poverty can be viewed as attempts at local solutions for problems not met by existing institutions and agencies because the people are not eligible for them, cannot afford them, or are ignorant or suspicious of them ... The culture of poverty, however, is not only an adaptation of a set of objective conditions of the larger society.

Once it comes into existence it tends to perpetuate itself from generation to generation because of its effect on the children. By the time slum children are age six or seven they have usually absorbed the basic values and attitudes of their sub-culture and are not psychologically geared to take full advantage of changing conditions or increased opportunities which may occur in their lifetime. [48]

Even though Dodds's speeches are monologal addresses to the audience, they fit within the mediaeval structure of a play which consists of a number of set tableaux linked by a series of textual catwalks which interpret contemporary events by reference to history lessons.

The Freedom of the City opens with a Kafkaesque setting – a judge high up on the battlements of Europe's last walled city, while various witnesses appear below him. The Judge sets out 'the law', the rules within which 'the play' of the tribunal will be conducted, and against the 'logic' of which the three 'volunteers' argue. In the words of the Widgery Report, the official British Government enquiry into the events of 'Bloody Sunday', 'it was essentially a fact-finding exercise', not a social survey, or concerned with making moral judgements, even though the analysis of poverty provided by the academic foil, Dodds, does indicate the need to consider the events of Bloody Sunday in the light of the moral and material poverty of the Derry minority. The judge sets further limits, not to the facts but to the arguments acceptable to the tribunal: the purpose of being in the Guildhall, and the question of whether or not they were armed, which are he suggests, 'different aspects of the same question'. Conversely Dodds, the sociologist-ex-machina, provides different arguments from a theoretical viewpoint, to explain what has happened: he points out that the culture of poverty is not just an economic condition, but also 'a social and psychological condition', in which one feels inferior, marginal, helpless, dependent, resulting in 'inability to control impulse'. The impoverished man 'is present-time orientated...endures his here and now with resignation and frustration' (*Freedom* 49) which, despite its negative aspects, sharpens 'one's attitude for spontaneity and for excitement, for the appreciation of the sensual, for the indulgence of impulse. To live in the culture of poverty is, in a sense, to live with the reality of the moment'(*Freedom* 51).

The humour with which Lily and sometimes Skinner treat their situation is evidence of the spontaneous, excited, impulsive culture described by Dodds. Despite the by now expected plea for 'dignity' which Friel utters through the third, Michael ('this isn't my idea of a dignified peaceful protest', *Freedom* 55), through the priest ('a peaceful, dignified movement', *Freedom* 79), and the RTE commentator ('I think the word would be dignified', *Freedom* 94), they live their life, and face their death, in the manner of the *morituri*: as Dodds says of the poor: 'they become more and more estranged from the dominant society. Their position becomes more and more insecure. They have in fact no future. They have only today. And if they fail to cope with today, the only certainty they have is death' (*Freedom* 88–9).

The priest underlines this disinterested analysis in his role as 'spokesman' for the dead, a function now traditional at funerals of both persuasions in Northern Ireland:

> they died because they could endure no longer the injuries and injustices and indignities that have been their lot for too many years. They sacrificed their lives so that you and I and thousands like us might be rid of that iniquitous yoke and might inherit a decent way of life. And if that is not heroic virtue, then the word sanctity has no meaning.
>
> (*Freedom* 38)

In other words, the culture of poverty means that poverty kills. But behind this we can hear the words of Grillaan, Columba's confessor: 'You are a priest not a rallying cry!' (*EW* 32).

Dodds warns that the society in which the poor are marginalised is 'highly individuated' (*Freedom* 19). That provides us with an important key to *The Freedom* because, while ostensibly the three occupants of the Guildhall, the 'nerve-centre of Londonderry' (*Freedom* 70), have a common bond and culture of poverty, they have no common *purpose* or *will* (except in so far as they serve that of the author). In fact the deaths of Lily, Michael and Skinner illustrate the distinction drawn earlier between the choices open to us in facing fate – the mythic, the logical and the impulsive – because each particularises the condition of poverty.

Superficially the three characters want to make a better world for themselves, an ambition they share with many of Friel's earlier heroes, but an ambition which we might find difficult to reconcile with the condition of resigned frustration: one *can* will oneself into submission and failure, for example, in that we may acquiesce in loss in order to experience the thrill of search and recovery. Skinner alleges that the Civil Rights movement in Derry was part of a universal awakening: 'It's about us, the poor, the majority, stirring in our sleep' (*Freedom* 77). So the exhortation 'This is your city! This is your city!' (*Freedom* 20) (which we can imagine in the voice of Bernadette Devlin-McAliskey [49]) can be regarded as a universal call. But the Civil Rights position in Derry in many ways overrides the general characteristics of the 1968 revolution, however typical it may have been of that movement.

Lily's humour, which carries the play, is more than a spontaneous wit, because it is also used to mask the preoccupation with the grimmer side of being poor: survival. Her concern is to fill, or make less empty, the stomachs of her eleven children, to avoid the shopkeeper when credit goes too high, to maintain appearances; she puts on her good coat to go marching. She is full of the culture of protest; she knows how to cope with the effects of gas and rubber bullets, where to stand at meetings and how to respond to speeches. But the Civil Rights marches are not a means to an end; they are part of a culture, a Saturday afternoon out. Long after it has been achieved, she still marches for 'wan man, wan vote' (*Freedom* 76) and an end to gerrymandering. Eventually the truth comes tumbling out, as it has for Lizzie Sweeney and Harry and Alice McGuire and the narrator of 'The Illusionists':

> He's not just shy, our Declan. He's a mongol. And it's for him I go on all the civil rights marches. Isn't that stupid? You and him and everybody else marching and protesting about sensible things like politics and stuff and me in the middle of you all, marching for Declan. Isn't that the stupidest thing you ever heard? Sure I could march and protest from here to Dublin and sure what good would it do Declan? Stupid and all that I am I know that much.
>
> (*Freedom* 78)

But she is in fact marching in order to win a kind of freedom for Declan. Lily, like Maire Chatach in *Translations*, is one of Friel's most successful creations, and certainly one of those to whom we feel the greatest sympathy as she assumes the autism of her tribe. In her death, which she tells us she knows 'instinctively, the way an animal knows' (*Freedom* 71) a momentary panic is

> succeeded, overtaken, overwhelmed by a tidal wave of regret, not for myself or my family, but that life had somehow

115

eluded me. And now it was finished; it had all seeped away; and I had never experienced it...because never once in my forty-three years had an experience, an event, even a small unimportant happening been isolated, and assessed and articulated. And to feel that this my last experience, was defined by this perception, this was the culmination of sorrow. In a way I died of grief.

(*Freedom* 71–2)

Life, through poverty, has robbed her of meaning. Because Friel has developed his device, first used in *Lovers*, of splitting time to foreshadow death, so that the dead themselves speak, Lily's last two sentences take their place among the most poignant in literature: *The Freedom* in its unfolding is not so much a study of poverty as a tragic attempt to celebrate grieving bewilderment.

Michael, by comparison, is trying to rise above the subsistence level, both mentally and physically. He has lost the insouciance, the spunk of poverty, his frustration has been channelled into orderly protest ('a good, disciplined, responsible march', *Freedom* 43); he respects the symbols of authority, he is confident of the effective way to retain his rights, and that is silence:

that was really impressive, all those people marching along in silence, rich and poor, high and low, doctors, accountants plumbers, teachers, bricklayers, all shoulder to shoulder, knowing that what they wanted was their rights and knowing that because it was their rights nothing in the world was going to stop them getting them.

(*Freedom* 43–4)

(Skinner's response is 'Shite'.) Michael pities what he considers to be Lily's ignorance of the true aims of civil protest, and he objects to Skinner's manner. He is baffled by Skinner: 'I don't know what you think you are up to. I don't know what sort of game you think this is' (*Freedom* 55), and he never deviates from the belief, the rational belief in the face of the irrational fate which awaits him, that: 'As long as we don't react violently, as long as we don't allow ourselves to be provoked, ultimately, we must win', (*Freedom* 58–9). Michael 'knows' something which he cannot in fact 'know': 'There is no question of their shooting. I knew they weren't going to shoot. Shooting belonged to a totally different order of things (*Freedom* 71). As Simon Winchester, a journalist with *The Guardian* who was covering the Bloody Sunday march, said: 'the killing of thirteen civilians by soldiers seemed to belong both to another age and another country'. [50]

Michael dies in bewilderment, apparently thinking that the 'terrible mistake' was some kind of waste: 'That was how I died, in disbelief, in astonishment, in shock. It was a foolish way for a man to die' (*Freedom* 71). The attempt at reason, at staying within the boundaries, has failed.

Skinner, Lily reckons, 'never had no mother to tan his backside' (*Freedom* 47). He never submits to orthodoxy, respects nothing, fears nothing, mocks all. He is a 'vandal', a 'hooligan', the agent of the 'sacrilege' on this 'holy of holies'. But he is also the agent of repossession. He initiates the others into the 'freedom of the city', he organises the masquerade in the mayoral robes, plays the role of the Lord Mayor, puts on an 'antic disposition', makes the claim 'allow me my gesture' (*Freedom* 89). He, of the three, has nothing to lose, but he recognises, unlike the others, that they cannot win because they are incapable of 'a solemnity as formal as the army's' (*Freedom* 72).

In terms of military strategy the three were always in a no-win position:

BRIGADIER: My lord, they emerged firing from the Guildhall. There was no possibility whatever of effecting an arrest operation. And at that point we understood they were the advance guard of a much larger force.

JUDGE: Had you known...that there were only three terrorists involved, would you have acted differently?

BRIGADIER: My orders would have been the same my lord.

(*Freedom* 51)

Did Friel, or Derry, send them out to be shot? On the surface it would appear that Friel is turning away from the world of naturalism as it has been practised in the 'Irish' theatre by Shaw and O' Casey, avoiding perhaps the inevitable caricature which even in 1973 might have been implied. But in this exchange between judge and brigadier I detect a reading from between the lines of, possibly, *Arms and the Man*, and certainly *Juno and the Paycock*. In fact Friel is not turning away from the genre, but turning it on its head, showing that figures of authority have feet of clay, while those of the gutter have not only dignity but a valuable sense of living. But Friel has discovered that he cannot liberate this world: he cannot, as a

117

dramatist, will it to be free, because finally he cannot involve himself in its laughter.

As a response to inevitability, is Skinner's defensive anarchic flippancy any more effective than Lily's grief or Michael's bewilderment? Probably we will not be able to answer these questions until we have a wider class base in Irish drama generally, and a clearer understanding of the socialist role in the attempts to solve the Northern (and the ubiquitously Irish) crises of identity. We can, however, note the mutual embarrassment of the two communities in Derry, which results from the cultural and economic imbalance in the overall society, and which in itself, because of incomprehension and suspicion, serves to reinforce reciprocal siege mentalities, to which Derry's topography naturally lends itself.

Skinner's masterly caricature of the council meeting (*Freedom* 83–5) is neither mimicry nor travesty: it is more an enactment, symbolic, mimetic, but also *real*. This is not so much 'Skinner' as, to give him his full, 'proper' name, Adrian Casimir Fitzgerald, as he would be called if this were an official occasion, taking over. The only thing 'wrong' is that the wrong people are taking part in the transaction, people who should not be there, but *are* there. There is a certain foundation in history in Skinner's antic gesture. As Eamonn McCann records, the gerrymandered Corporation

> was the living symbol in Derry of the anti-democratic exclusion of Catholics from power...After the mayor abandoned his chair and adjourned one Corporation meeting, Finbar Doherty (Derry Housing Action Committee) vaulted from the public gallery into the chamber, installed himself in the mayoral chair, declared himself First Citizen, and issued a number of decrees. [51]

But there is also a pathetic side to their regard of themselves as 'distinguished visitors' – Lily's tipsiness, caused by their use of the mayor's hospitality cabinet, is an alcoholic answer to the fact that they know their dreams are empty.

It would be easy to read *The Freedom* as a metaphor of Northern Ireland (just as *Translations* looks not only forward to the present situation but back to the plantations of the seventeenth century and the aftermath of *Making History*). *The Freedom of the City* is dangerous enough as a play which we know to be 'inspired', energised by the events of Bloody Sunday. It is, however, necessary to infer that the play's *engagement* in Northern Ireland, the mutual embarrassment of the minority and the administration, questions the neutrality of the Irish mind, and, by extension, the neutrality of the Irish state in relations with its neighbours.

In such circumstances its artists cannot be neutral. Ulick O'Connor has drawn attention to Yeats's membership of the Irish Republican Brotherhood, in a lecture which locates Friel's writing of both *The Freedom* and *Translations* in the tradition of the *écrivain engagé* identifying in his characterisation the various forces lined up in a post-colonial struggle. [52] But we cannot rely entirely on the engagement as specifically and exclusively local and temporal, because the artist can never be intrinsically and totally part of the situation he describes. Against the image of the *écrivain engagé* we must in any case juxtapose that of the gunman *malgré lui*, the dilemma posed by O'Casey in *The Shadow of a Gunman*. 'In this play', says Frank McGuinness, 'O'Casey reminds every Irish writer they are present at such talks [with gunmen] whether they like it or not.' [53] And at such talks gunmen and poets become interchangeable, as each tries to see the other side, to adopt, however briefly, the other's stance. The shadow of a gunman is an inadequate member of his country's infantry. The shadow of a poet is worse, for failing to provide the right marching songs, since, as O'Casey reminds us, all confrontation leads to war. The inadequate poet is 'a poltroon', [54] and, again illustrating the dilemma of the artist of a community, 'a poet's claim to greatness depends upon his power to put passion in the common people'. [55] In the case of Friel, this is an unresolved dilemma.

Metaphysically, too, Ireland is in conflict with its conscience in the discrepancy between its experience and its decoding of history. As V.W. Turner points out:

> in everyday life people in tribal societies have little time to devote to protophilosophical or theological speculation. But in protracted liminal periods, through which everyone must pass, they become a privileged class...with abundant opportunity to learn and speculate about what the tribe considers its 'ultimate things'. Here we have a fruitful alienation of the total individual from the partial persona which must result in the development, at least in principle or potentially, if not always in practice, of a total rather than a partial perspective on the life of society. [56]

LAYING GHOSTS

Friel sends people out to their fate. A few find their way back; most are hostages to fortune. The distinction lies between those whose odyssey is simply a voyage of discovery and those for whom it is a quest of *re*-discovery, a recovery of a holy grail, a golden fleece, a golden-haired mother, freedom, poetry, time. 'Having set forth from that place, it was only natural I should return to it', says Beckett's 'Unnamable'. This journey from silence to silence is of course an impossible one: the exile, whether or not he is the author of his own expulsion, can never penetrate the *same* centre again. 'The man who returns will have to meet the boy who left.' This journey of self-discovery, to pursue Beckett's thought a little further, 'to know what I am, where I am, and what I should do to stop being it, to stop being there', is a destructive process: 'to depart into life, travel the road, find the door, find the axe'. In dramatic terms 'the search for the means to put an end to things, an end to speech, is what enables the discourse to continue'. [57]

Volunteers pursues what may seem a relentless but remorseful discourse by providing a bridge, for the critic at least, between *The Freedom* and *Faith Healer*. Seamus Heaney has rightly criticised a reviewer who greeted *Volunteers* as a response to 'the great dramatic subject of internment'. [58] While *The Freedom* was a deliberate and risky response to the events, or at least the aftermath, of 'Bloody Sunday', *Volunteers* has little to do with internment. Its metaphor is digging, and its purpose is in sifting the layers of meaning which separate reality from the perception of reality. *Volunteers* may seem a 'problem play', because, as Heaney notes, it 'involves an alienation effect but eschews didactic address', [59] a formula Friel interposed in *The Freedom* as a solution to this particular difficulty.

The key to *Volunteers* is Keeney who, like Skinner, acts the Hamlet in his antic disposition ('the public mask of the joker' *Vol.* 18). He asks 'was Hamlet really mad?' (*Vol.* 66) and ironically sums up his carapace as 'the carefully cultivated armour of a shy man' (*Vol.* 64). Like Skinner he might ask 'Allow me my gesture', but he goes far beyond gesture. Keeney initiates the play-acting which reveals the different perceptions of the 'volunteers' towards the symbolic skeleton of their 'pal', the Viking Leif. The explanations of Leif are told through the perennial medium of 'that time':

KEENEY: 'once upon a time', keep up the protection of the myth,
(*Vol.* 51)

and they occupy three main 'versions' of personal truth: Leif is a young adventurer who marries outside the tribe; he is a lost child of a merchant prince; and a slave who served other men until, his usefulness exhausted, he was thrown away. In any case, he died a 'ritual victim' and the unchanging element in his biography, as told by the surrogate archaeologists, is that he was a voyager and that, whether knowingly or unwittingly, he acquiesced in his own death.

Keeney, like Skinner, takes no heed, his comedy is black but alive. His poverty is not an impediment but a key to the door into the dark: 'I'm feeling reckless, no, not reckless, wild...an almost overwhelming sense of power and control and generosity and liberation...anarchic' (*Vol.* 47). Heaney saw *Volunteers* as

> a vehicle for Friel's quarrel with himself, between his heart and his head...more about values and attitudes within the Irish psyche than...about the rights and wrongs of the political situation...he means, one presumes, to shock. He means that an expert, hurt and shocking laughter is the only adequate response to a calloused condition. [60]

Those words apply even more appositely to the third of Friel's 'problem plays', *Faith Healer*, which succeeded the two plays he wrote after *Volunteers*. If I categorise *The Freedom*, *Volunteers* and *Faith Healer* as 'problem plays' it is because he sets up this inner conversation, the call on the most fearful part of our psyche, in order to engage us in the discourse of the informer. The visual metaphor is that of 'Come here till I whisper in your ear', [61] the genre of the short story, the confessional, the informer, the betrayal of the neighbour or of the self, the destructive ego, bred out of servility and fear, which presages abandonment of the text and the death of the heart; and with betrayal, laughter.

Of course Friel offends and shocks: the spectacle of self-destruction is as seductively dangerous today as it was when *Hamlet* was written. To pursue a little further the Hamlet image which Friel himself has set up in Gar, Skinner and Keeney:

> Let the stricken deer go weep,
> The hart ungallèd play,
> For some must watch, while some must sleep,
> Thus runs the world away.

121

Friel is about the business of dismantling realms and exposing peacocks; [62] he is self-consciously 'other', the *destroyer* of love, freedom and language in order to know himself as the *creator* of love, freedom and language. His faith healer, his diviner, is the instrument through whom he examines his role as an artist in the public world; and the poetic language he adopts, even in the persona of Hardy's Cockney manager, Teddy, is a device in that he permits himself the luxury of questioning language itself, the tendency inherent in words to slip, the distinction between being and knowing, between knowing and meaning; am I a healer or a destroyer? He cuts, with his mockery, into the conscience of kings and courtiers and peasants; the wounded surgeon plies the steel in his search for wholeness, and silence, and thereby questions the nature of freedom itself.

Friel's intention is to keep stage directions to a minimum (*FH* 9) but the play, because it is so personal, is so highly structured that in fact he interposes himself more than usual between the director and the play, a situation of which he himself appears to be unaware. [63] The three protagonists here are puppets, more so even than in the contrived times and action of *Living Quarters* and *Aristocrats*. We are ushered into a private realm of induced mystery. Nothing in this play is real; Friel dispenses with the tribune and defies us to find the consistencies in his narrative. We acquiesce in his deceit as we listen to the opening incantation, and for the first time in his work we realise that the sacred nature of place-names can be illusory, 'abandoned rituals', as he will show us in *Translations*, but only because he specifically tells us so. We accept, *a priori*, the utter freedom of the essential artist – 'a craft without an apprenticeship, a ministry without responsibility, a vocation without a ministry' (*FH* 12). Like Skinner and Keeney, Frank Hardy is effectively an orphan, speaking an orphaned language. We know that it not only does not matter whether Frank Hardy heals or not, it does not matter *one way or the other*. For Hardy, as for the Unnamable, the imperative is to 'become whole in myself, and perfect in myself, and in a manner of speaking, an aristocrat'(*FH* 12), which can only be achieved through silencing 'the questions that undermined my life...those nagging, tormenting, maddening questions that rotted my life' (*FH* 12–13). As we have seen, the only way to avoid madness is to select, to exclude, to fracture, to become partial, to individuate. And as we shall see once again in *Fathers and Sons*, the rotten life is something not only specific to the person but endemic in families.

It is not 'the crippled and the blind and the disfigured and the deaf and the barren' (*FH* 14) whom he has to make whole, but himself because, however disfigured, deprived or damaged these cripples are, their disinheritance is of a different order, a lymphatic not a psychic order; they are not destroyed by voices, theirs is not an aural cancer. In exposing his audience to four monologues, Friel is exposing his own 'voices', the kind which sent Jeanne d'Arc and the daughters of Loudun to the pyre, the children of Salem to the gibbet, and Virginia Woolf to her novels.

In this clinical setting, drugged by incantation, poised between divination and Jerome Kern, 'between the absurd and the momentous' (*FH* 14), Friel sets out to expose the weaknesses of his inheritance, the impossibility of coming into one's own, and the fact that to acquiesce in one's own destruction is in itself a form of relief, a therapy:

> They were a despairing people. That they came to me, a mountebank, was a measure of their despair...they knew in their hearts they had come not to be cured but for confirmation that they were incurable; not in hope but for the elimination of hope; for the removal of that final, impossible chance, that's why they came, to seal their anguish, for the content of a finality. And they knew that I knew. And so they defied me to endow them with hopelessness.
>
> (*FH* 15)

Losers. So afraid of the jump into the dark, so apprehensive lest the Redeemer in fact call their bluff, that they are ready, like Lily, to die of grief, to find a freedom in the extinction of hope, and, by extension, as *legati* (*FH* 15), to let their culture die, to relieve the gatekeeper and let the barbarians in.

For every centrifugal force there is an equal and opposite centripetal force. So just as Frank Hardy says 'If we hadn't come to them, they would have sought us out' (*FH* 15), he, in his turn, comes to Ballybeg, to meet McGarvey, an unreal creature conjured out of the Donegal twilight, who Friel/Hardy paints with sensual realism: 'Saw him and recognised our meeting: an open place, a walled yard, trees, orange skies, warm wind. And knew, knew with cold certainty that nothing was going to happen. Nothing at all' (*FH* 17). Hardy's 'homecoming' sees the dominance of ritual: 'A frenzied excessive Irish night when ritual was consciously and relentlessly debauched' (*FH* 17) – but not mocked; ritual which binds one to the tribe and its icons and texts as fiercely when it is debauched and brutalised as when it is piously observed, because debauch is in itself a form of piety.

Grace, the wife/mistress, and Teddy, the manager, provide commentaries on the diviner's artistry. Despite brilliant characterisation in the word-play, they do not feature in the outcome as anything more than ciphers, because they are bound to him as Rosencrantz and Guildenstern are to Hamlet, except that there is another qualitative difference between Frank and Grace on one side and Teddy on the other. But like Frank Hardy himself, Grace and Teddy are *beyond identity*: Teddy has no other name; Grace has many, according to Hardy's whim – Dodsmith, McClure, O'Connell, McPherson, from Yorkshire or Kerry or London or Scarborough, 'I don't remember, they all sound so alike, it doesn't matter' (*FH* 14). It is the same with places, 'Welsh-Scottish, over the years they became indistinguishable' (*FH* 11).

The ritualistic cadence 'in Kinlochbervie, in Sutherland, in the north of Scotland' (*FH* 21) might be a line from 'Mr Sing My Heart's Delight': 'in the sun, in the Punjab, in the Garden of Eden' (*Saucer* 68). Its quality is not in the names themselves but in the effect of the incantation, a 'mesmerism' or 'sedation' (*FH* 11), as Friel uses them to seduce the audience and dig down into the psyche with this litany of place-names. As places, as names, they do not *matter*, they are immaterial in the metaphysical sense. Grace and Teddy are bound to Frank Hardy in the same ritual of observance and debauchery, because they are the supporting cast of his artistry: 'Me, who tended him, humoured him, nursed him, sustained him, who debauched myself for him' (*FH* 21). Without him, Grace is nothing: 'O my God I'm one of his fictions too, but I need him to sustain me in that existence – O my God I don't know if I can go on without his sustenance.' [64] Without art he is nothing: 'I couldn't even begin to comprehend it, this gift, this craft, this talent, this art, this magic, whatever it was he possessed that defined him' (*FH* 25).

Grace sees him as the *performer*, 'crouched, wound up, concentrated, in such mastery that anything is possible' (*FH* 20), who pursues an almost epicurean critic-as-artist role in recreating people:

> it was some compulsion he had to adjust, to refashion, to recreate everything around him. Even the people who came to him, they weren't just sick people who were confused and frightened and wanted to be cured; no, no, to him they were

... yes they were real enough, but not real as persons, real as fictions, his fictions, extensions of himself that came into being only because of him ... he kept remaking people according to some private standard of excellence of his own and as his standards changed, so did the person. But I'm sure it was always an excellence, a perfection, that was the cause of his restlessness and the focus of it.

(*FH* 22)

Teddy, from his position of professional expertise, can analyse 'artists' and their preoccupations:

they know they have something fantastic, sure, they're not that stupid. But what is it they have, how they do it, how it works, what that sensational talent is, what it all means, believe me, they don't know and they don't care and even if they did care they haven't the brains to analyse it.

(*FH* 29)

Hardy is a 'mediocre artist' castrated by his brains, without ambition (*FH* 31). Loss of ambition suggests loss of will, and in that sense Teddy is correct, although otherwise I cannot see how 'brains' explains Hardy's madness, his anarchic disposition.

In the 'performance' his skill is intuitive; his actions outside the healing circle, however, can only be explained by his surgical power. This distinguishes his behaviour from the impulsive nature of Skinner's 'gesture' in *The Freedom* and Keeney's 'protest' in *Volunteers*; his is a calculating embrace of the unknown, because, through his divination, he does 'know'. The critic James Simmons calls him 'a bastard' but cannot see why, nor 'why he welcomes his unlikely death'. [65] 'There was a killer instinct deep down in that man' (*FH* 35) and there is a coldness in his method, even when he is drawing devils out of the poor, but he is compelled to find an order, to fulfil some pattern which will mark a homecoming – 'Some very important appointment he's got to keep...he had to have his own way of facing things' (*FH* 36). He is like Don Giovanni, anxious to keep his appointment with the Commendatore. And like Don Giovanni, Frank Hardy is of course an anarchist who delights in order, whose sacrifice of his own life is the ultimate act of faith: only a psychopath who realises that the playwright has left him no other avenue of escape could conceive so clearly the need for McGarvey. Hardy's (Friel's) obscene caricature of Jerome Kern

125

('lovely ... just the way you look tonight') juxtaposed against 'the crippled and the blind, and the disfigured and the deaf and the barren' (*FH* 24–5), is typical of the savagery of which Friel is rarely capable: as Tyrone Guthrie said of the closing scene of *Philadelphia*, 'infinitely poignant although not one word of sentiment is expressed'. [66] This poignancy is central to Friel's work and typical of him when he is being *least* central, that is, displaying a soul at the end of its tether, both in the intensity of its utterance and in its savage inevitability. It is not so much the tension of son against father, or the confusion of meaning and identity, so much as the fact that in exploring these themes Irish 'classic' drama is more closely definable as *tragic* than anything to be seen, for example, on the British stage.

It is in this respect that Teddy's role is differentiated from that of Frank and Grace. Teddy's function is twofold: to act as our guide, a point of reference, to the statements of Frank and Grace; and to relieve, with his Cockney humour, the tragedy of the narration. The two functions are interrelated: humour is part of Teddy's character rather than an adjunct, part of the culture which keeps him alive and therefore convincing. He places Hardy not in a pantheon of charismatic heroes but in the absurd context of down-market showbiz, equating him (along with Olivier, Houdini, Chaplin and Gracie Fields) with Rob Roy the Piping Dog and Miss Mulatto and Her Pigeons. The essential difference is that Teddy is unimportant and his stories are inconsequential, harmlessly humorous, because they are not his own. He leads his own life simply because *he is alive*. He shows us that *Faith Healer* is *a play about death*, that it is, at its core, stories from the dark angels, telling us of their inevitable death: Frank at the hands of the symbolic McGarvey, the half-brother who has always awaited the moment for which he was created; Grace as Hardy's fiction, at her own hands, a self-strangling puppet. Teddy himself will probably never die, because there is nothing to push him over the edge; he is resigned to the ambition, talent, and brainlessness of his clients in their waiting-room-for-death. It is a play, therefore, which could not succeed without Teddy, because we need the living, those who in the chemical sense retain their humours, in order to decode the unremitting brutality and nihilism of the dead. McGarvey, the cripple whom Hardy knows he cannot cure, is, on the other hand, the unseen but essential other character in this non-play, a 'figure of infinite patience, of profound resignation', not so much because he has come to terms with his disability but because he is waiting for Hardy to come to terms with *him*.

As McGarvey becomes 'real', the 'real' world diminishes:

> and as I walked I became possessed of a strange and trembling intimation; that the whole corporeal world – the cobbles, the trees, the sky, somehow they had shed their physical reality and had become mere imaginings ... even we had ceased to be physical and existed only in spirit, only in the need we had for each other.

> (*FH* 44)

The closing sequence of this monologue is distinctly visual rather than verbal. In destroying himself we *see* that Hardy comes home. He has passed beyond identity, beyond words, beyond madness, beyond chance, beyond fear, beyond the voices: 'the maddening questions were silent' (*FH* 44).

In *Faith Healer* Friel meets and sees his alter ego, and lays the ghosts of self-doubt and the problem of self-knowledge first explored in *The Enemy Within* and *Philadelphia*. In *Translations*, which we might subtitle 'A Family Reunion', he goes to confront the public world and the context of affiliation.

A QUESTION OF FORM

I have already referred to the fact that Friel's plays often succeed on radio, where argument is allowed to dominate form, in monopolising the 'private conversation'. Conversely, many of his plays, *Faith Healer* in particular, leave themselves open to criticism because they appear to lack dramatic impact. Moreover, in the 'family reunion' plays – especially *Living Quarters* and *Aristocrats* – it might seem that Friel is experimenting with form without involving the audience at all, that he has adopted a self-indulgence which Michael Longley, in his own attempt at poetic freedom, has called 'a fuck off to form'. [67] In this respect *Living Quarters* is a play about playwriting, *more text than experience*. It is due particularly to Friel's sense, also evident in *Aristocrats*, of 'the burden of the incommunicable', [68] the problem of finding ways to place, on the narrow back of dramatic conversation and gesture, a family history, a description of social disease, or a political movement, so that his statements might not only address, but also engage, the audience *within* the fiction, a technique he has been pursuing since he wrote

'Fine Day at Glenties' and Cass's exclamations against her author.

However, while Friel uses the possibilities of stagecraft as tools in a clinical analysis of his own trade, he cannot pour out his absolute concepts of freedom and love without employing the nice paradigms and intermediate levels of knowledge which we have noted, or he would drown the stage with the immediacy of what he has to say; the barbarity of his discourse on language itself might be quite incomprehensible if he did not adopt mediating effects such as we find in *Translations*. Of course we cannot know the nature of such unmediated drama because a form has yet to be found to accommodate its content. One can only speculate what might happen if Friel did *not* use drama to put a distance between himself and the rest of the world, and between his conceptions and their ultimate audience.

But there is a further problem associated with this unknown quantity: is Friel using technical experimentation and distancing in order to avoid engaging in that very discourse which his 'community' demands of him? Does he allow his characters too great a freedom, granting them the same dispensation he gives himself, a distance between them and the real world? In the sense that time itself is a device, then the present, in which past play is experienced, is in fact the future of the play itself. Friel the playwright exists in the past of the characters themselves, while audiences exist in the present and future. In *Living Quarters* Friel mediates the concept of absolute being, with its unlimited possibilities, by means of the adjudicator 'Sir', whose ledger or bible represents all possible and apocryphal texts, both those events which actually happen and all those which might happen. Past possibilities (what might have been) become future choices (what might be).

It is also this, rather than the fact that she is an imagined person, which prevents Cass from communicating, establishing shared meaning with the audience. Revenants on the stage are moving through time as well as space. In *Living Quarters* only the fact that the author adopts film technique in switching the flow of action allows him to arrest the time sequence and interpose the audience's 'now' into the otherwise uninterrupted time continuum. The switch means that at one moment the Butler family believes in its own relative present, while the audience regards its individual members as dispersed, dead, past; at the next, the stage becomes an experimental space occupied by the audience as part of the 'mythological present' directed by 'Sir'. The major question is whether, after we have gone home, the Butlers have any existence. Similarly, some-where in the time continuum, Cass, Trilbe, and Ingram continue to rhapsodise; but they only have meaning each time they are summoned by our reproductive imagination. We are Friel's accomplices in this access to privacy.

In this sense drama is a time-capsule or fifth province in which our problems can be depersonalised and thus solved *without* rancour or acrimony or the penetration of the private by the public world (or *vice versa*) but *with* tenderness, compassion and dignity. As already suggested, Friel has, on occasions, abandoned – superficially at least – those characteristic mediating qualities. Is the stiletto of *Faith Healer*, Frank Hardy's 'killer instinct', mitigated or even transformed, partly by the seduction of the poetry and partly by the inherent finesse of the gesture itself? The medium employed is a simple one, whether it is court of law, court of chivalry, cabinet room or the sacred wood of the senses: the time-capsule in each case mediates between the absolutes of space, time and being, by setting a distance between us and the immediate realities of place, past and person.

If we can for a moment regard Friel's drama as 'ritual' we could profitably consider the 'liminality' of his writing as a special form of communal process; that is, we can see not only how he places himself as tympanum between two worlds or matrices, but how he engages the audience in his liminality, as the drama-ritual translates us from one state to another. As V.W. Turner says:

> it is the analysis of culture into factors and their free recombina-tion in any and every possible pattern, however weird, that is most characteristic of liminality, rather than the establishment of implicit syntax...like rules or the development of an internal structure of logic in relations of opposition and mediation. [69]

This is exactly what Friel sets out to achieve in *Living Quarters* and *Faith Healer*, and to a lesser extent in *Aristocrats*. The 'ledger' of each play is an infinite number of pre-determined possibilities, and it would not matter if the actors in those dramas were to abandon all convention and address each other or the audience in un-precedented babel. But of course this is impossible. Frank Butler in *Living Quarters* 'has no fluency in love words' (*LQ* 64) and all the characters in these two plays lack fluency in 'freedom' words.

In *Living Quarters* Friel gets closest to the idea of time suspended, the frozen action of the body (all the meaningless gestures, exits and entrances of the 'play'), while we experience the *communitas* of mind, and it is to this that he returns successfully in *Translations*. In *Living Quarters* the 'ledger' – which is surely a balance-sheet as well as a list of entries? – is verbalised. 'Sir', the servant and interpreter of the ledger, rather than its author, permits shuffling of the pages, but the interpretation which the participants give to their lines is subtle and frustrating for us who cannot look over Sir's shoulder at the document itself. And the reason, of course, is that 'Sir' himself is a stage direction, one of the author's own distancing tricks. [70] As in all good stories, they only reveal its outcome 'in their own good time'. During the rest of the play they interrupt or forestall revelation, analysis and confidences as it suits them. Friel says, through their untimed and unscripted entrances and exits, that the form given to content is ultimately irrelevant, in the same way that much of the 'plot' is unimportant; it does not seem to matter whether the family of *Aristocrats* assembles for a wedding, as they think, or for a funeral, as brought on by Father's unscripted entry; a giving of a name, as in the offstage christening with which *Translations* opens, or a taking away, as in the baby's wake ('it didn't last long, did it?' *Tr.* 60); a wedding as anticipated in 'Winners' or the drowning which 'in fact' results from Meg's panic spring.

Friel here reaffirms a perennial paradox: that man, by the exercise of his free-will, fulfils a pattern of destiny. It does not in fact matter what is said in *Living Quarters* (or even *Aristocrats*) but it is of 'consequence'. The clearest exposition of this principle is Sir's observation (i.e. the statement): 'no sooner do they conceive me with my authority and my knowledge than they begin flirting with the idea of circumventing me, of outwitting me' (*LQ* 10). And yet Sir tells Anna 'You shuffled the pages a bit, that's all. But nothing's changed' (*LQ* 41). The Butler family are following fate within concentric circles of their own constrained freedom. And not only with the subversion of absolute power and knowledge, but also with impassioned, irrational remonstration, somewhere between energised and enervate despair, against absolute reason:

FRANK: Yes you did say we could speak our thoughts, that was established at the outset, wasn't it? Well, I wish to protest against my treatment. I wish to say that I consider I have been treated unfairly...And I am fully aware that protesting at this stage is pointless – pointless ...The ledger's the ledger, isn't it? Nothing can be changed now – not a thing. But an injustice has been done to me, Sir, and a protest must be made.

(LQ 87)

(Cass also appeals, but in her case her derision of the author is directed towards the audience, until she is persuaded that the reality is on the stage, not in the auditorium.) As with the onset of any psychic disorder, it is irrelevant who says what is said, or that it is said at all, because it would have been said, the embarrassments would have been conceived, *in any case*. Ben and Frank re-enact the disorder between Gar and his father; we might expect some resolution of the problem but that possibility is complicated by the fact that the only truth uttered comes *after* Frank's death (as it takes place in *this* version of the play):

> What I was going to say was that ever since I was a child I always loved him, and always hated her – he was always my hero. And even though it wouldn't have been the truth, it wouldn't have been a lie either.

(LQ 93)

This kind of liminality in fact fails in *Living Quarters* because it does not permit final resolution: the creatures of the play are condemned to return to the ledger to search for old possibilities. There is an uncertainty in Friel's writing here which we *must* take into account because he confuses 'dead episodes' (*LQ* 9) with 'those lost possibilities' (*LQ* 95).

This is the most unfortunate, *impossible* type of peregrination, in which we expect to meet wandering Jews and flying Dutchmen: it is not the sort of world where Friel's 'losers' fit in, comfortably or otherwise. Interestingly, it is the same trap which Chekhov falls into, and again with the sons rather than the daughters (Constantin in *The Seagull*, Andrei in *Three Sisters*, for example). And in the 'unfairness' complained of we can recognise a specifically masculine reaction to events, whereas in the feminine roles Friel's creatures create, rather than react to, their own actions, as if they were more in accord or complicity with the original powers which set them in motion. The frightened child is inevitably the boy, whereas women conquer their fear by creating strength; the discourse *(logos)* is between *father* and son, the emotive affinity *(mythos)* is between *mother* and son. In *Living Quarters* Father Tom (another aid to the stage directions who, as a priest, can mediate between the absolute

131

and the real) expresses this liminality: 'The enormous gift that Christ purchased for us – the availability of choice and our freedom to choose' (*LQ* 47).

We might consider this the only fully successful statement of the play, until we realise that it does not express the awfulness of the *necessity* of choosing, the collision of freedom *and* responsibility in which the will continually defeats itself, as we have seen in the 'spectacle' of Andy Tracey, the loser. From the experience of these plays, therefore, we are still looking for a condition in which the liminality of Friel's ritual can be resolved. Ultimately, what 'matters' is the breaking and repairing of silence, and for that Friel requires only a test-tube, and a volunteer audience. But as Thomas Kilroy warns us, the environment of the theatre is more than histrionics and the devices of melodrama or masque. He says that as a language becomes more suspect and brittle there is a word 'compounded of anarchic humour and deadly serious motivation, which cannot describe anything concrete of this theatre; it is merely a signal. The word is Danger.' [71]

The test of Friel's skill is whether or not he succeeds in mediating, by means of the play, between subject and audience, without also interfering in the internal relationship of the *subjects* of the play with the *objects* of the play itself. This again returns us to the question of form: Friel is not, ostensibly, concerned with 'form' – a play is shaped by the events imagined within it, as they, and the characters who enact them, grow in the author's mind and use it in their passage towards the 'play'. [72]

As Friel noted in the early stages of writing *Aristocrats*:

The crux with the new play arises, as usual with me, with its form. Whether to reveal slowly and painstakingly with almost realised tedium the workings of the family; or with some kind of supra-realism, epiphanies, in some way to make real the essences of these men and women by side-stepping or leaping across the boredom of their small talk, their trivial chatterings, etc. etc. But I suppose the answer to this will reveal itself when I know/possess the play. Now I am only laying siege to it. [73]

Dantanus sees this as a preoccupation with *form* whereas in my opinion it is such *only* to the extent that form must serve *content*. [74]

Having finished *Translations*, for example, Friel notes:

The task of writing the play, the actual job of putting the pattern together, itself generates belief in the pattern. The act and the artifact sustain one another. And now that the play is finished the value of the pattern and the belief in the pattern diminish and lethargy sets in: the life process. But only after the play is produced will I be completely cleansed of my subscription to this particular pattern, this ordering of things. Then a vigour will be summoned. Then a new pattern will have to be forged. The process seems trivial and transient because the patterns are so impermanent. But is there another way? It is a kind of vigilance, keeping the bush from encroaching into the yard. All art is a diary of evolution; markings that seemed true of and for their time; adjustments in stance and disposition; openings to what seemed the persistence of the moment. Map-makings. [75]

Map-making itself would be pointless if we did not accept that it is the content which determines the form. In between writing these two passages, as he moved more quickly and surely towards the completion of *Aristocrats*, he wrote:

the dramatist has to recycle his experience through the pressure chamber of his imagination. He has then to present his new reality to a public; 300 diverse imaginations come together with no more serious intent than the casual wish to be 'entertained'. And he has got to forge those 300 imaginations into one perceiving faculty, dominate and condition them so that they become attuned to the tonality of the transmission and consequently to its meaning. Because if a common key-note isn't struck and agreed on, the receiving institutions remain dissipated and unreceptive. But to talk of 'meaning' is inaccurate. We say 'What is the play *about*?' with more accuracy than 'What does the play *mean*?' Because we don't go to art for meaning. We go to it for perceptions of new adjustments and new arrangements. [76] (*my emphasis*)

'What is the play *about*?' orients and approximates the questioner to the 'impermanent' public world, whereas 'What does the play *mean*?' enquires about the playwright and his private intentions. In *Living Quarters* we might think Friel has failed to make the distinctions we ask of him, because we are seduced into receiving impressions which should rightly be regarded as privacies. By seeking to 'interpret between privacies' (*Tr.* 67) Friel coldly exposes, by means of an open text, those affects which keep families or tribes together. He thus destroys form, not with a mechanical flourish, but by using the 'fifth province' – by arguing not from the general to the specific, but from Ballybeg to the world. He solves the political problem by way of language, by posing the perennial question, like Chekhov, in the accents of the province, the zone, and establishing a world of correspondence. The 'tricks' lie in the way he introduces the hallowed effects of melodrama, allegory, naming, into our sub-conscious: thus, by means of ritual seduction, creating an interdependence of words, images and time.

If we ask 'what is the play *about?*' we find that *Living Quarters* is 'about' a *femme fatale* whose intrusion into family life disturbs the memory and affections. It is 'about' the events of a day when, although the public world sees everything going according to plan, the private conscience is caught up in a scheme of subversion. Beyond this the play is not 'about' anything. As Guthrie says: 'meaning is explicit "between the lines" of a text; in silences, in what people are thinking and doing far more than in what they are saying: in the music as much as in the meaning of a phrase'. [77]

In *Aristocrats*, similarly, it would be difficult to say what 'happens', without discussing 'meaning'. *Aristocrats* is 'about' 'incipient decay, an era wilted, people confused and nervous... *family life*, its quality, its cohesion, its stultifying effects, its affording of opportunities for what we designate "love" and "affection" and "loyalty" '. [78] But we cannot pursue that idea very far, because, as Friel noted in the middle of the writing, the *core* of the play is 'the burden of the incommunicable'. But *Aristocrats* (originally thought of as 'The Judas Hole') is no more 'about' the incommunicable than *Hamlet* is 'about' self-doubt, courage, or madness. But whereas Shakespeare provides us with a baroque backcloth of murders, wars, ghosts, Friel allows us no respite from his rigorous examinations; we can comprehend the spectacle of hypocrisy, or of greed, or of buffoonery in *Hamlet* without being drawn into the 'meaning' of the play, but Friel in these later works is cutting away anything which stands between him and his meaning. He is going out to meet his play and he is dragging the audience/reader with him. He is solving the problem identified by Frank Ormsby in relation to *Philadelphia*, that 'the maddening complexities of circumstance and human nature constantly thwart the seemingly straightforward possibilities for solution'. [79] He is making it difficult to be a spectator, more likely that we will want to become participants. If *Waiting for Godot* is a play in which 'nothing happens twice', [80] *Faith Healer* is a play in which nothing happens four times; while in *Translations* everything never happens, and it is debatable whether *Making History* happens or not.

In his most recent play, *Dancing at Lughnasa*, the techniques of stagecraft subject the ostensible, and very spare, 'action' to the scrutiny of memory, and in so doing they set up a novel momentum which, as I shall suggest in my Afterword, puts Friel's drama on a new footing: one where the difficulty of distinguishing between what happens and what our memory tells us has happened, is resolved by immersing the audience in the action of memory – a new method of involving the spectator and at the same time advancing the playwright's dramatic purpose.

A problem with *Faith Healer* seems to be the intensity with which Friel has approached his 'subject', to the exclusion of the subordinate characters. Frank Hardy, in fact, becomes inaccessible to Grace and Teddy, locked into his own privacy, simply because Friel has conceived of private despair as a medium of healing itself:

> And when you speak to him he turns his head and looks beyond you with those damn benign eyes of his, looking past you out of his completion, out of that private power, out of that certainty that was accessible only to him. God, how I resented that privacy!
>
> (*FH* 20) [81]

As a result of concentrating on Hardy's own psyche, Friel comes close to depriving the 'play' of any dramatic content whatsoever; yet he makes us conscious of the dramatic experience by creating a graphic, visual world out of the elements of ambiguity, chicanery and time itself.

As with *Living Quarters* and *Aristocrats*, Friel's technique is akin to Cubism: cutting the subject open and turning it this way and that to expose planes never normally considered by either the spectator or the subject himself. This leads to a form of psychological investigation which is normally approached only by means of the absurd – Ionesco's apparent *non sequiturs* in *The Bald Prima Donna*, for example – in which extra-sensory perceptions take over from the sort of naturalism we expect from a successor to Chekhov. As Stanislavsky said of *The Seagull*, 'he who invents a new ending for a play will usher in a new era! These damned endings are the very limit! The hero has either to marry or to shoot himself; there is no other way.' [82] And of course Frank Hardy 'shoots himself', as clearly as Frank/Theseus in *Living Quarters*. Friel, however, eschews endings in the sense of dramatic closures. Only the contrived postscript to *Living Quarters* rounds off the chaos of the 'anything can happen' syndrome with a conventional 'they lived happily ever after', the sort of conclusion which the drifters in *Aristocrats* might look forward to in their hopeful 'next summer in Hamburg' (*Ar.* 84). But in most cases we are left in the condition of 'anything can happen': in *Translations* where we are still waiting for something to happen, or for proof that something has happened; in *Fathers and Sons* where a new cycle of happenings becomes possible; or in *Faith Healer* where nothing keeps on happening. The place for resolution, we feel, has been created somewhat unfairly by Friel in our own minds, as we carry away from the dramatic experience a new sense of volition in our own lives, a sense of how to answer the question 'to marry or to shoot oneself?', to make sense or nonsense, which he makes explicit in his treatment of *Three Sisters* and *Fathers and Sons*. In *Making History* he makes it no easier for us to decode his intentions, but he does lighten the problem of the play's closure, simply by eliding it.

In his diary Friel noted this passage from Norman Mailer:

> if he did something wrong, they [daughters] being women would grow up around the mistake and somehow convert it to knowledge. But his sons! He had the feeling that because they were men, their egos were more fragile – a serious error might hurt them forever. [83]

One begins to approach a conclusion, perhaps not inescapable but certainly very compelling, that Friel is almost too concerned with pursuing the relationship of father and son, which is the one consistent 'plot' throughout his work. In *Living Quarters* the superiority and authority of a father-figure, whose military bearing echoes the Inspector/teacher status of the father in several short stories, is firmly on the stage; in *Aristocrats* the admonishing figure which so effectively reduces Casimir to weak-kneed fear is mediated through the device of the baby-alarm (the Judas-hole turned around), as if Friel cannot allow physical indisposition to prevent the metaphysical pursuit. This pursuit at times creates an imbalance in the otherwise orderly analysis of affiliation which he approaches elsewhere. The three exceptions to the main theme (affiliation) and its development (filiation), [84] are *The Mundy Scheme, Faith Healer* and *The Communication Cord*, two of which have earned themselves the status of satire (which at times is synonymous with critical condemnation) and the third (in which there is only an apocryphal father) has so stunned audiences and critics alike that they find it difficult to accept the substitution of aural for visual theatre.

Although, therefore, Friel is almost dismayingly conventional in his view of the playwright's function, and therefore in his pursuit of it through stagecraft, as always (with the exception of *Faith Healer* and *Making History* in which he abandons all convention and returns to the condition of radio drama) he is so *ingénu* in his response to the demands of his characters, that the fusion of form and content is of little moment. In this sense, his greatest innovation, and his greatest potential failing, lies in an originality of which he avows he is only the intermediary, 'a ministry without responsibility'. He occasionally fails because he does not sufficiently warn his audience of the dangers inherent in this, although a good grounding in Chekhov would be an excellent preparation for the demands he makes on us.

We have to accept the 'tricks' which Friel plays on both audience and players in *Living Quarters* in order to see how vitally he needs this distance in order to advance his personal project. Because he has not yet retreated from a position where he claims the primacy of language, these 'tricks', such as sociologist-ex-machina, baby-alarm (Judas-hole), the armchair rhapsody and play-within-play, are less important than they would be if he were more intent on experimenting with silence or with entirely new dramatic structures. The experiment with silence has proceeded as far as the *dance* –a dramatic symbol which, even in his most recent original play, *Dancing at Lughnasa*, cannot be dissociated from the stage device of the intermittent radio delivery – and in *Dancing at Lughnasa* Friel has approached, more resolutely than heretofore, the idea (for that is all it is) of the dance as an alternative to speech: dance assuming (as a visual dramatic device) the role of language. It is, as all Friel's work, risky, and the demands he places on directors through text and stage directions are almost self-defeating. However, there is an indication in *Dancing at Lughnasa* that he is in fact approaching the idea of new dramtic structures, in a manner congruent to that of Tom Murphy but divergent from that of Tom

McIntyre, which, by means of its intellectualism rather than its intuition, will offer a novel challenge to contemporary Irish–English playwriting.

Contrivance tends to interpose itself between the audience/reader and the author's meaning. Like all effective stage design, it should enhance and decorate the play, underlining its subtleties and drawing out its inner meaning, rather than creating them and being their *raison d'être*. Friel's use of the private/public technique and of the quotation from Burke in *Philadelphia*, [85] for example, *are not the reason for the play*. The various devices Friel employs, especially the variety of 'truths' and 'realities' which he presents to us in *The Freedom*, *Faith Healer* and *Cass*, the shuffling of the cards in *Living Quarters*, the anachronisms in *Aristocrats*, would be doing him ill service if they left us searching for consistency among the ample debris of inconsistency and doubt which he provides. [86] These are put before us as examples of the various perceptions, the ranges of possibility which can be experienced between whatever extremes he establishes, absurd and momentous, known and unknown, private and public.

Friel also sets out to catch a conscience with his plays. To that extent (and in that sense only) he places great importance on his traps. The complexity and sophistication of the traps will vary according to whether he simply wishes to seduce his public audience into a vision of the world, or to map out a private territory of the characters themselves. It is as if in the 'love' plays he has dredged up emotion in buckets, and in the plays of the 1970s he looks more analytically and formulates some tentative replies to the maddening questions. As we have seen in *Faith Healer*, he begins to come home with less catastrophe, and he completes the journey in *Translations*. But in looking at the strategy he adopts in *Living Quarters* and *Aristocrats* we must maintain the distinction between the public drama which peoples the actual world with imagined characters, and the private play-within-play which confuses the imagined world with the actual.

VERSIONS OF THE TRUTH

The art of coming to terms with Friel's 'versions' of his truth is not to seek for an accommodation between 'reality' and the 'perception of reality', but to accept whatever version is offered at the time. Thus in *Aristocrats* the lawn is simultaneously a lawn, a former tennis court, a former croquet lawn, or an actual game of croquet, depending on which character is investing it with memory, perspective or travesty. There is no point trying to rationalise this; to talk of various perspectives as operating on different 'levels' is pointless. The antiphonal monologues of 'The Illusionists' have been stretched out in *Faith Healer*, shuffled in *Living Quarters* and sublimated in *Aristocrats*. And the latter two are works which we can regard as early attempts at his versions of *Three Sisters* and *Fathers and Sons*. [87]

This facility allows him to give *Living Quarters* the puzzling subtitle 'After Hippolytus'. While Euripides' and Seneca's (and indeed Racine's) versions of *Phaedra* deal with the penalty inflicted on the innocent Hippolytus who refuses his step-mother's love, Friel has Ben (Hippolytus) actually having an affair with his step-mother (Phaedra). The possibility remains in some latent text that Hippolytus was justly punished by his father, the semantic fact being not that he defiled his father's bed, but that his father destroyed him, one way or the other. As explicitly as Friel treats the subject of exogamy in *Translations* we see him here assessing the politics of an internal exogamy, crossing forbidden boundaries within the tribe.

W.J. Cloonan, writing on Racine, notes that, although Hippolytus does not respond to Phèdre's advances:

> they place themselves in positions where they are in apparent violation of generally accepted social taboos...their real fault, which neither grasps until the play's end, and even then imperfectly, lies not in the identity of those they love, but in the very act of loving...*Phèdre* begins with an awareness that cruel and inhuman powers are toying with a desperate woman... The queen's desire to love and be loved is as innocent as Hippolyte's. [88]

In a sense the possibilities are still endless, and the only certainties are the identities of the actors themselves; as for working towards a conclusion, Friel has remarked that, as with Steiner's approach to *Antigone*, [89] 'it depends on which version you use'. [90]

What *is* important is the exploration of those identities of which we can never be sure, so that we can never be free from the exploration: as Crystal says to Fox (as Ben might say to Anna as the archetypes break down): 'What ... are ... you ... I don't know you ... Don't know you at all ... Never knew ... never ...' (*CF* 63). Even in his use of 'comic relief' Friel fuses form and content: in *Aristocrats*, for example, the nomination of pieces of furniture as 'Chesterton', 'Yeats', 'O'Casey', 'Newman', carries its own farce within it, as Willie Diver mockingly adds 'Shakespeare', 'Lenin', 'Mickey Mouse' and 'Ben Jonson' to the list (*Ar.* 32). And in *Translations* he does not simply relieve a situation with comedy, but uses it in a tragicomic sense to emphasise one aspect of his main theme. For example:

> JIMMY: I'm going to get married.
> HUGH: Well!
> JIMMY: At Christmas.
> HUGH: Splendid.
> JIMMY: To Athene.
> HUGH: Who?
> JIMMY: Pallas Athene.
> HUGH: Glaukopis Athene?
> JIMMY: Flashing-eyed, Hugh, flashing-eyed.
> HUGH: The lady has assented?
> JIMMY: She asked me, I assented.
> HUGH: Ah, when was this?
> JIMMY: Last night.
> HUGH: What does her mother say?
> JIMMY: Metis from Hellespont? Decent people, good stock.
> HUGH: And her father?
> JIMMY: I'm meeting Zeus tomorrow. Hugh will you be my best man?
>
> (*Tr.* 65)

Not only is this as farcical and innovatory as anything in Flann O'Brien's *At Swim-Two-Birds*, [91] it also serves to get across (translate) the idea of two worlds, two cultures, meeting in the tympanum represented by Jimmy Jack: 'the world of the gods and the ancient myths is as real and as immediate as everyday life in the townland of Baile Beag' (*Tr.* 11). It is when the two congress in a supposed reality that we find Jimmy Jack (twice) in a posture of 'pained ecstasy' (*Tr.* 14, 65). And that device, too, is pressed into service as, at the close of the play, Jimmy discusses his own wedding and the fatal attraction of Maire and Yolland: 'Do you know the Greek word endogamein? It means to marry within the tribe. And the word exogamein means to marry outside the tribe. And you don't cross those borders casually – both sides get very angry' (*Tr.* 68).

It is little wonder then, that we read in *After Babel*: 'the history of

western drama...often reads like a prolonged echo of the doomed
informalities (literally the failure to define separate forms) before
gods and men in a small number of Greek households.' [92] In this
version of many Ballybegs, Friel turns time on its head by re-
introducing those gods themselves, underpinning them from tradition by calling up the gods of Irish mythology to create in the mind
of at least two characters, Jimmy Jack and George Yolland, a
convincing, imaginable world, and one which is not merely illusory,
but has commerce with the concrete world, a freedom which can
exploit its limitations:

> JIMMY: *'Nigra fere et presso pinguis sub vomere terra'* [Virgil,
> *Georgics*.Bk.II]
> MANUS: 'Land that is black and rich beneath the pressure of
> the plough ...'
> [...]
> JIMMY: 'And with *cui putre*, with crumbly soil, is in the main
> best for corn.' There you are!... 'From no other land will
> you see more wagons wending homeward behind slow
> bullocks.' Virgil! There!... Isn't that what I am always
> telling you? Black soil for corn. That's what you should
> have in that upper field of yours, corn not spuds.
>
> *(Tr.* 19)

In a sense Friel is pointing out the divorce between the rational
and the intuitive, between *logos* and *mythos,* town and country, as
a basic flaw in our psychology. But he is also saying that the setting
of his plays is irrelevant: they could be in 'a small number of Irish
households', or in a mental hospital. In fact the analogy is apt, for a
mental hospital is a place where *nothing happens* but happens
slowly, and where *everything* is rehearsed. [93] One cannot be cured
of madness or psychic disorder, one can only come to terms with it
by understanding it, by establishing a community of meaning with
the disorder itself, and inhibiting the motive and incidence of
embarrassment and despair. Mental hospitals, like prisons, set
boundaries to both freedom and control, but, within those boundaries, allow the condition of ecstasy – that is, standing outside
one's normal, social self – and permit the celebration of failure.
The Ballybeg of *Living Quarters* and of *Aristocrats* (or at least the
houses of the Butler and O'Donnell families) is in this sense an
asylum, but perhaps the most significant is the hedge-school itself
in *Translations*, in which Friel uses the device as a time-capsule to

work out the meaning of meaning itself.

The danger of talking about layers of experience, or of history, which as I have indicated encourages one to think in terms of 'levels' of comprehension, has to be faced because we do need some such metaphor to help explain the creation of distance: the many versions of truth, we might say, are moments when time and the fact-finding exercise are arrested. In fact, as in *Volunteers* with its explicit metaphor of digging, we are safer in the arms of several conflicting versions, inconsistencies or ambiguities than we are with plain, unadorned truth. As long as we continue to have the power of recollection, as long as dialogue goes on, life goes on. So for Ned, a minor character in *Philadelphia*, one night of dalliance recollected in bravado ('Mind the night Jimmy and us went down to the caves with them Dublin skivvies') is as valid as Gar's contra-diction of it ('so we struggled back home, one behind the other and left the girls dangling their feet in the water', *Ph.* 72–3). In *The Freedom* all four versions of the 'truth' (the RTE newsman's 'fifty armed gunmen', the report of the voices 'there's at least a dozen dead', the army's 'a band of terrorists' and the balladeer's 'a hundred Irish heroes') are all incorrect, as is the Judge's summing up (rationalisation) of the events.

In this sense there are always *two* plays going on, not just the whole range of possible worlds which *might* be, of which the spectacle before us is one, but the play offstage, relating to the play in progress, its alter ego. There is another *Philadelphia* in which Private Screwballs is reviewing his relationship with his son, and his dead wife, of which we only get a glimpse in the gesture he makes by touching Gar's jacket and in his brief conversation with Madge (*Ph.* 100). [94] And in *Translations*, when Sarah runs off to announce the only 'action' which the audience is permitted to 'see' (the love scene between Maire and Yolland), she goes to tell it in another theatre, which, like *Rosencrantz and Guildenstern are Dead*, is taking place in the wings.

In *The Gentle Island*, Manus Sweeney, sitting in the aeroplane seat, and Sarah wearing men's boots, are indications of absurdity or incongruity which Friel manipulates in order to suggest the other world beyond the painted stage. That Manus occupies the chair when he is unable to face reality is only part of the story: he absents himself from us, facing upstage as he does so. The recitation of Gray's 'Elegy' in 'Losers' (*Lovers*) is equally 'absurd': the recitation is interrupted by Mrs Wilson's bell, which the 'elegy' is intended to pre-empt, the dramatic irony being Gray's line 'The curfew tolls the knell of parting day.' The ultimate absurdity in Friel's work occurs at the end of Act 1/opening of Act 2 of *The Communication Cord*, which resembles the opening scene of Stoppard's *After Magritte*: a group of apparently rational people posed – caught up – in entirely irrational activities, which they follow through to their conclusions, whether logical or illogical is for us to decide. This is what Friel wants to say about the absurdity of freedom.

There are therefore two senses in which Friel's 'freedom' plays leave the spectator aghast. One is the fact that he has tried to create *total* theatre by involving us in his, and his characters', drama. In this he succeeded with the awfulness of the direct address in *Faith Healer* and again in the judgement of the audience on the various pleas of *Making History*. But he finds it difficult to 'marry two incompatible types of theatre' as Fergus Linehan has remarked, [95] a fact made all the more terrible by the anarchism and total exposure of Frank Hardy's self-knowledge, a way of turning our double vision inside out. The other lies in the fact that, against every freedom identified by Friel, we have to acknowledge an irony. 'Irony tends towards stasis of action' says Northrop Frye (in particular describing the last act of *Three Sisters*). [96] Freedom in the future (what might be) is taken from Michael (in shock), from Skinner (in flippancy), and from Lily (through grief). Freedom in the past (what might have been) is taken from the Butlers through the Greek fates enshrined in the ledger, from the O'Donnells through the disestablishment of time's constructs, their non-existent family history, their aristocracy. Freedom in the present is achieved only by Frank Hardy who becomes an aristocrat, whose freedom seems to be his prison, the personality ringing him round, which he has to meet coming towards him at the speed of fate. Friel has shown us once again that freedom, like love, is only for those prepared to cast away the crown, to tear themselves to pieces in the pursuit of wholeness.

5

PLAYS OF LANGUAGE

To translate is to descend beneath the exterior disparities of
two languages in order to bring into vital play their analogies
and, at the final depths, common principles of being.

George Steiner [1]

HISTORY AND FICTION

With *Faith Healer* Friel has found answers to some of the problems
he first confronted at the onset of playwriting. In that play he
reconciles the artist, the orphan, to his privacy. In others of his
earlier plays he has identified some solutions to the problems of
homecoming: in *Living Quarters*, for example, a son stumbles
through the same experience as Gar O'Donnell –

> you kept stroking my face, my face, my cheeks, my forehead
> ... but what I want to tell you father, and what I want you
> to know is that I
> FRANK (*leaving*) Some other time.

> (*LQ* 72)

and eventually finds a *possibility* (for that is all it is) of reconciliation
with his father:

> *suddenly Frank opens his arms and embraces Ben warmly*
> Ben! Thank you son, Thank you.

> (*LQ* 76)

Also, in the same play, we see one character, the father, almost
achieving the far-off place as surely as Chekhov's sisters achieve
their 'Moscow': 'At last, at long last, and without one regret. To
Dublin' (*LQ* 78).

144

In *Aristocrats*, too, we see some kind of reconciliation with the future, as the decaying symbols of the family's past – the father, the house, and its contents – are discarded in favour of new worlds and individual destinies.

By the time Friel came to write *Translations*, therefore, he had cleared the way for an examination of issues which had been lurking in the background of his previous plays: preoccupations which were to become explicit with the writing of *Making History*. Having reconciled himself to the inner landscape he now had to map the public world, to project his own psychology onto a street-map of Ballybeg, in order to complete the artist's painful function as membrane between the two. In the course of this he also offers a solution to the problem of the father-figure in his earlier work, through the restoration to Hugh O'Donnell of *gravitas* and *dignitas*. But in *Translations* Friel also opens up new territory, especially in trying to meet the challenge he has announced in *Living Quarters* and *Aristocrats*, of discussing the adequacy of language as a tool of communication. And he sets the stage for the full working out of a preoccupation which he examined in *Faith Healer*: the ultimate right and necessity of betrayal. In looking at the language question, Friel unites the *sense* of place with the *function* of place. This encompasses both the affection (or love) which is inherent in affiliation, and the exercise of will (or freedom) which makes a place *live*. Language itself is the factor which unifies these two aspects of the human spirit – its sense of being, and its method of being – *or* it may be the factor which segregates them, displaces and anaesthetises meaning and paralyses purpose. Naming, which is central to the play and to the theme of identity, is the key to language. As Ngugi might tell us, when a community loses its language it loses its culture and its identity. [2] Thus by examining these issues through the medium of bridge-building or translation, Friel unites his main intellectual preoccupations with his emotional concerns in a single powerful metaphor. The success of *Translations* in terms of its attraction for the public is due to this compelling device.

Tom Paulin (one of the members of Field Day) says:

> The history of language is often a story of possession and dispossession, territorial struggle and the establishment or imposition of a culture...spoken Irish English...lives freely and spontaneously as speech but it lacks any institutional exist-ence...a language without a lexicon, a language without form

...A language that lives lithely on the tongue ought to be capable of becoming the flexible written instrument of a complete cultural idea. [3]

This was written with the hindsight experience of *Translations* and it embodies much of Friel's intention; the political dispossession that provided the *mise-en-scène* for *The Freedom* here becomes a text parallel to the narrative of an impoverished culture threatened by the imposition of a strange and more confident culture, an invasion and implantation. This is a 'fact-finding exercise', a map-making which changes the identity of the region. But Friel is anxious that the political implications of his storyline should be brought out expressly by the characters themselves, rather than imposed as a structure of the play. As he wrote at the time:

I don't want to write a play about Irish peasants being suppressed by English sappers. I don't want to write a threnody on the death of the Irish language. I don't want to write a play about naming places...*The play has to do with language and only language.* [4] *(my emphasis)*

A month later he recorded:

One of the mistakes of the direction in which the play is presently pulling is the almost wholly *public* concern of the theme: how does this eradication of the Irish language and the substitution of English affect this particular *society*? How long can a *society* live without its tongue? Public questions; issues for politicians; and that's what is wrong with the play now. The play must concern itself only with the exploration of the dark and private places of individual souls. [5]

It is doubtful if Friel has in fact satisfactorily resolved this difficulty. He comes close in spirit, if not in technique, to the absurdist drama of Pirandello and Pinter in his use of the non-sequitur, the mutual incomprehension of his speakers in *Aristocrats*, where the inconsequentiality of conversation is at its most Chekhovian, [6] or in *Translations* which is inherently political in the sense that, commanded by our aesthetic and social security system, we choose to hear, comprehend and respond to, only those offers or messages which neither offend nor challenge our identity. As Pinter says: 'the speech we hear is an indication of that we don't hear. It is a necessary avoidance, a violent, sly, anguished or mocking smokescreen which keeps the other in its place.' [7]

There are two sets of speech, in fact: that which we receive and return in the public, possible world, and that which we employ as internal discourse, the discrete method of relating to private psychology. The dialogue which transforms that private psychology into public culture can never do better than fail (as it fails in *Living Quarters*), to communicate not only between privacies but also between a specific privacy and its public expression: this is the inevitable failure of metaphor.

In *Translations* as we receive it Friel is, at least ostensibly, addressing public themes. And as he himself says: 'If it is not political what is it? Inaccurate history? Social drama?'[8] Friel's characteristic distaste for open politics reinforces this difficulty, because it makes him more aware of his own need to explore the 'dark and private places'. The final form of *Translations* is due to his eventual realisation that the 'political' issues were inescapable, at least in the broadest sense, because for the first time in his work the 'inevitability' of change is presented in the form of a cultural encounter. While therefore he succeeds in reducing the specific implications of a military eviction, he cannot eradicate from his text the damage caused by the breakdown of communication implicit in the form of the play itself. Even more than in *The Freedom of the City*, Friel is writing for his own 'community' or 'constituency', because by this act of faith he can bring into existence the Ballybeg/ Baile Beag which represents his hearth.

In this regard the figure of Doalty takes on an extra significance. Doalty is the 'antic' of this play, and yet he is commonly perceived in production as a figure of fun, of light relief. But Doalty's immune system rests in his ignorance: he knows nothing and wishes to know nothing. The opposite, as Lady Bracknell might say, is disaster. To know everything is a form of madness (*Tr.* 67). Frank Hardy knows everything, and therefore he is dead. Doalty, like Teddy, survives. Even in tragedy we need our figures of fun. As a political animal he makes an extremely important statement in the closing scene: 'if we'd all stick together. If we knew how to defend ourselves' (*Tr.* 64). Linking this to the aptitude of the Donnelly twins for survival, Doalty thus unites two kinds of refusal, in saying 'yes' to revolt and 'no' to death. He thus redeems his own imcompetence in the opening scene and earns the sobriquet bestowed on him by Hugh – 'Sophocles from Colonus would agree with Doalty Dan Doalty from Tulach Alainn: "To know nothing is the sweetest life" ' (*Tr.* 24).

Friel also succeeds, therefore, in establishing a private and very simple world, in looking at its inner activity and tensions. It would be wrong, for example, to regard Sarah Johnny Sally's muteness merely as a symbol of a people who had lost their tongue, especially in the midst of such loquacity. Her silence is a private question of identity, not a public issue. Similarly Hugh's ambivalent relationship with each of his sons allows Friel the opportunity to look once more at the concept of the dead mother and the role of the revenant, while his camaraderie with Jimmy allows him to bring together the thread of affiliation (which began with Screwballs, Boyle and the Canon) with the appeal to 'that time':

> Everything seemed to find definition that spring, a congruence, a miraculous matching of hope and past and present and possibility. Striding across the fresh, green land. The rhythms of perception heightened. The whole enterprise of consciousness accelerated. We were gods that morning James.
>
> (*Tr.* 67)

Thus while Friel is equivocally private in this marriage of the particular with the absolute, he is also equivocally public in looking beyond the bounds of familiarity: *'Barbarus hic ego sum quia non intelligor ulli'* (*Tr.* 64).

As D.E.S. Maxwell has noted, this poses the by now well-rehearsed problem of 'being in two places at the one time' which we first met in Columba:

> being in reality, and being in the world of art, and establishing a contour between the two. And within that secondary world to authenticate its happening as events which occur only there. They will not persuade us because something exactly the same happened yesterday. These problems are at their most acute with political matter, for ideology, dogma, is most favourably placed to subvert the allegiance to language. [9]

Let us therefore examine this subversive ideology, one which subverts as it seduces.

In 1851, 1½ million people spoke Irish, about one quarter of the total population. In County Londonderry there were 5,400, or less than 3 per cent of the population, while in County Donegal there were 73,000, or about 30 per cent of the total population. In the country as a whole 20 per cent of all Irish speakers were monoglot, a proportion which reduced in the following half-century to less than 3 per cent: in Donegal, monoglots in 1851 numbered, according to the census, 34,882 (almost half the total of Irish speakers), while in 1911 there were 4,733 or 8 per cent of the Irish speakers. [10]

Against this factual background we can artificially polarise two contemporaneous attitudes to the Irish language, one of which – Daniel O'Connell's – finds expression in *Translations* ('the old language is a barrier to modern progress' (*Tr.* 25)). In 1835 O'Connell said:

> Although the Irish language is connected with many recollections that twine round the hearts of Irishmen, yet the superior utility of the English tongue, as the medium of all modern communication, is so great that I can witness without a sigh the gradual disuse of the Irish. [11]

Meanwhile Thomas Davis, the founder of 'Young Ireland', declared:

> A people without a language of its own is only half a nation. A nation should guard a language more than its territories. 'Tis a surer barrier and more important frontier than fortress or river. Nothing can make us believe that it is natural or honourable for the Irish to speak the speech of an alien, the invader, the Sassenach tyrant, and to abandon the language of our kings and heroes. [12]

The Young Ireland definition of nationalism is also at the heart of *Translations*:

> It is the summary name for many things. It seeks a literature made by Irishmen and coloured by our scenery, manners and character. It desires to see art applied to express Irish thought and belief. It would make our music sound in every parish at twilight, our picture sprinkle the wall of every house and our poetry and history sit at every hearth. It would thus create a race of men full of a more intensely Irish character and knowledge and to that race it would give Ireland. [13]

Thus the man who restored to the Irish people their religious freedom and gave them the franchise was also the agent of one form of cultural suicide, while the author of the Young Ireland movement swore fealty to a means of communicating in the 'precious gold' of the past. This ambiguity and tension of modern Irish nationalism becomes the ground on which *Translations* and *Making History* are played out, both publicly and privately.

The significance of this shift, whether or not it was inevitable, from predominantly Gaelic-speaking to predominantly English-speaking, lies in the fact that it encompassed the question of identity. The fact that English is the language Maire needs to know is the central fact of *Translations*, the central reality in which Hugh O'Donnell ultimately acquiesces. One's changing identity (which hangs upon one's ability to speak, on the language in which one chooses, or is compelled, to speak, on one's attitude to one's name, rank and affiliation) thus becomes more important than what one does with the identity by way of social action. One world-view relishes an identity which can no longer be enacted, the other embraces a new meaning which is not yet clear. By 1922 the enunciation of the new State continued in this contradiction as it insisted that the key to the dynamic identity and culture of modern Ireland lay in its language and customs, that is, in an intimate relation of speech to the land, despite the statistical realities already evident from the facts quoted above.

In this sense the seduction of the two world-views, one past, one future, caught in the present which cannot decide whether to follow *mythos* or *logos*, crystallises all the contradictions elaborated in chapter 3. As an *historical* play, therefore, *Translations* explores the dark and *public* places; the individual souls mass up into a community (*communitas*) threatened by the choice between the rush to English or the retreat to silence. The validity of *silence* depends on whether it is employed as a means of escape or of resolution. With Friel, as with Heaney and Beckett, the claims and character of silence – silence as a living force in the life of society – are as real and effective as babel. Monoglot and polyglot have at least one common language, which is liberated from silence by laughter. Silence is *agelast*, a condition without laughter. The ice of silence is broken by the axe of laughter. In translating between privacies, therefore, the *public* issues are made fictive in a way that history cannot touch.

This brings us back to the point made earlier, that Friel enables us to accommodate these parallel texts by a fusion of form and content. The land itself (narrow ground) provides the metaphors – naming, crop failure, invasion and evacuation – for carrying over or translating (*metaphorein, transferre*) the absolute into the particular. As one of the Ordnance Survey officers noted at the time, the inquiry *was* in fact sociological as well as technical:

Habits of the people. Note the general style of the cottages ... food; fuel; dress; longevity; usual number in a family; early marriages...what are their amusements and recreations; Patrons and patrons' days; and traditions respecting them?...Nothing more indicates the state of civilisation and intercourse. [14]

The original survey was therefore concerned with the movement of people through *time* as well as *space*. Friel reduces this to a 'triangulation'; the use of 'section' for 'parish' is not a translation but a diminution of a three-dimensional concept to two dimensions, a denial of a social and cultural function in the interest of a political and scientific one, the elevation of form over content. At the same time Friel reduces the community to the definition of the hedge-school within which the off stage action is discussed: a definition which likewise has a temporal dimension as its function shifts in the light of the community's subjective drift into decay and desuetude and of its role as *object* of incursion.

In *Translations* Friel provides a congruence of semantics and history within the framework of fiction: Steiner's *After Babel*, the first chapter of which deals with the art of translation, and John Andrews's *A Paper Landscape*, an account of the first Ordnance Survey in Ireland, which began in Derry and Donegal in 1828–35. Additional background material was supplied by John O'Donovan's *Letters*, Dowling's *The Hedge Schools of Ireland*, and Colby's *Memoir* of the survey. [15]

It is instructive to note how both Friel and Andrews were drawn into a subsequent debate on the subject of map-making. Andrews has said that in experiencing the play of *Translations* he realised 'that there can be more than one kind of historical fiction' [16] (just as Baudelaire commented at the Salon of 1846, 'there are two ways of understanding portraiture, either as history or as fiction'). Within such realisations there lurk two kinds of playing with time and language: one which says, as we shall see in the case of *Making History*, that it is possible to have different kinds of simultaneous truth; and another which allows that for whatever truth is being portrayed, there is one (or more) equal and opposite fiction(s).

This has not, however, absolved Friel from severe criticism both in regard to the 'poetic licence' which he has exercised with the 'facts' of history and in the interpretation he has put on them – the 'uses of history'. In this there is an inevitable, and perhaps un-resolvable, collision of playwright and historian, poet and critic, about the nature of truth and portraiture. To take one example: Sean Connolly argues that *Translations* 'is written in a tone that seems to make clear that Friel believes he is depicting a real experience' and that the programme notes 'vouch for the authenticity of the version of the past which it sets out'. [17] How can we here divorce the integrity of the act of playwriting from the need to be faithful to history? How to allow the writer sufficient liberty to construct a credible fiction while maintaining the 'version' of the past which has been handed down to us in the long tradition of veracity? How to measure one kind of truth, one way of perceiving (aesthetic), against another?

In order to find even tentative answers to such questions, which Friel himself baulks at in *Making History*, we must look at his intentions in writing *Translations* in the first place. In bearing in mind texts like Dowling, O'Donovan and Colby, he was working over the idea of

a play about the nineteenth century, somewhere between the Act of Union and the Great Famine, a play about Daniel O'Connell and Catholic emancipation; a play about colonialism; and the one constant – a play about the death of the Irish language and the acquisition of English and the profound effect that that change-over would have on a people. [18]

These 'fugitive notions of a play about language' gradually developed into an interest in hedge-schools and the Ordnance Survey until, with the appearance of *A Paper Landscape* in 1975, 'suddenly here was the confluence, the aggregate, of all those notions...here was the perfect metaphor to accommodate and realise all those shadowy notions – map-making'. [19] He set out to dramatise Andrews's book, but, failing to capture the essence of its main characters, and obviously subconsciously putting the idea of O'Donovan as a quisling to the back of his mind, he 'embarked on a play about a drunken hedge-schoolmaster', since he had discovered that his own great-great-grandfather had been a hedge-schoolmaster from Mayo who settled in Donegal. In doing so he provides, in one sense, a dramatisation of *After Babel*. As we have seen, Friel insisted – to himself, it should be noted – that 'the play is about language, and only about language'. And the essential point about *After Babel* (as indeed it is about all Steiner's work) is that it underlines the difficulty of translation between privacies, between the deep core of meaning in two cultures, and that it emphasises the difficulty of apprehending the nature of individual truth.

Sean Connolly asserts that *Translations* 'represents a distortion of the real nature and causes of cultural change in nineteenth-century Ireland so extreme as to go beyond mere factual error', which includes 'a picture of traditional Hibernophone culture, prior to the coming of the English, so unrealistic and idealised as to cast doubt, not only on his history, but also on his art'. [20] Let us turn again to Friel, who makes two assertions: first, that 'the imperatives of fiction are as exacting as the imperatives of cartography and historiography', and, second, that equal to the advantages of using established facts or ideas is the responsibility 'to acknowledge those facts or ideas but not to defer to them. Drama is first a fiction, with the authority of fiction.' [21] The issue seems to turn on a *political view of culture* as opposed to *a cultural view of politics*. The political view argues that the writing of history, and the acting out of its events in dramas, poetry and novels, maintains the dominance of the recorded fact at the expense of poetic licence; that the dramatic function is to enhance and illuminate, but not to subvert and distort. The cultural view argues that history has still to be written, that distortion, the provision of other versions and subversions, of received 'fact', are equally valid. The distinction rests on the location of the act of judgement: are actors, playwrights and audience to receive and transmit the immutable experiences of known and documented historical figures, or are they able to participate in the act of history itself? Maps can be false, whether conceptual, moral or cartographical. Therefore, the 'imperatives' are related to the right to falsity as well as to truth. 'History', says Paul Ricoeur, 'begins and ends with the reciting of a tale.' He insists that 'narrative is a redefining of what is already defined, a reinterpretation of what is already interpreted', and that 'our future is guaranteed...by our ability to possess a narrative identity, to recollect the past in historical or fictive form'. [22]

The proximity of history to fiction, the narrative properties of both, are only beginning to be explored by writers like Barthes and Ricoeur. [23] Another aspect of the problem is the conceptual difference between *logos* and *mythos*, which we shall see in discussing *Making History*. Ricoeur puts the emphasis on *mythos*, which 'is the bearer of something which exceeds its own frontiers; it is the bearer of other *possible* worlds'. [24] In putting forward a cultural view of politics Friel falls inevitably into the problem of nicety:

language can not bear the weight of both interpretation and reinterpretation. As if he wished to demonstrate even further Steiner's thesis, Friel shows us that there can be no satisfactory translation between the rational and non-rational: in his approach to the criticism his plays have provoked, he is prepared to go only so far as 'to acknowledge...but not to defer'.

Possibly the most serious of Friel's subversions is to deny the English sappers in *Translations* a capacity to discourse in Latin, presumably in order to suggest that the otherwise inferior society of Ballybeg might have some cultural values unavailable to the colonists. It has caused an English drama critic to call the play 'a vigorous example of corrective propaganda: immensely enjoyable as theatre if, like much else in Ireland, gleamingly tendentious'. [25] That there can be two opposing and apparently exclusive ways of seeing underlines that there are two ways of observing, and commenting on, the events which occupy the course of time in Ireland: law as order or tyranny, popular movement or revolt, dissent as denial. As Andrew Carpenter observes, 'certain terms have double interpretations: loyalist, big house, patriot, perhaps even the word "border"'. [26] One can become tendentious about both the effects and the affects of time, the ways in which we experience the past and the ways in which we react to it. 'Versions' of *Phèdre* (as in *Living Quarters*) can be regarded as tendentious or simply bemusing. Friel has taken liberties with the 'facts' of Bloody Sunday, of the Ordnance Survey and, in *Making History*, of the Battle of Kinsale and the Flight of the Earls.

But, to paraphrase Steiner, it is not so much the literal facts that become subverted, but (and this is what lies behind Connolly's criticism) the cultural environment, the psychic hinterland. The *effect* of time is that the Battle of Kinsale, like that of the Boyne, decided the course of Irish history; the *affect* of time is that the Irish cannot accept this. The act of betrayal becomes the central metaphor for escaping from collective responsibility for, and interpretation of, the past. It is generally considered, for example, that at Kinsale the Irish/Spanish strategy was sold to the English commander by Brian McHugh Og MacMahon for a bottle of whiskey, [27] and Friel incorporates this into his play. But in adding the rider (expressed by Hugh O'Donnell) that 'we never had a chance', [28] Friel puts forward the inevitability of that betrayal. Furthermore, by emphasising the effect on Hugh O'Neill's character of his nine formative years in English society, and utilising the facts of his continual vacillation, inactivity and diplomatic exploitation of his dual loyalties, Friel suggests that it could as easily have been Hugh O'Neill himself who sold out the Irish future and the Counter-Reformation. It is often overlooked by Friel's critics that he identifies himself in *Translations* not only with the revenant Owen but also with Hugh, not as a precious retrospective but as a man resigned to the future. Friel puts his own words – 'we must make English identifiably our own language'[29] – into the text of *Translations*, thus lining himself up with these agents of erosion and eviction. But the real turning points of history are achieved more subtly than winning or losing either military or cultural wars. Hugh O'Neill's strength, as we shall see, lies in inaction, and in subtlety, but of a kind which inevitably traduces both cultures. In this sense he was/is truly the great *sacerdos liminalis* of Irish history. Thus, for example, he makes 'a gesture of loyalty' to the English crown, and appears to aid the erosion by 'bringing in' his peers and vassals: 'and I assure you, it means nothing, nothing. And in return for that symbolic courtesy London offers you formal acknowledgement and recognition of what you already are, leader of your own people! Politically quaint, isn't it?'(*MH* 26)[30] The comparison with Eamon de Valera's approach to the 'oath of allegiance', and his access to power, by declaring it 'an empty political formula',[31] will be obvious. So the true critical argument, which has yet to be engaged, is more truly located within the question of the relation of time to language than it is in the area of faithfulness to fact.

In the words of Dan H. Laurence, therefore, Friel is illustrating that the playwright's task (he is speaking of Shaw) is 'not to reproduce history but to shape it into credible drama, thus changing us from bewildered spectators of a monstrous confusion into men intelligently conscious of the world and its destinies'.[32] Shaw himself, when asked whether an historical play should be substantially accurate as to the facts – the play in question was *Arms and the Man* – replied:

> not more so than any other sort of play – historical facts are not a bit more sacred than any other class of facts. In making a play out of them you *must* adapt them to the stage and that alters them at once, more or less. Why, you cannot even write a history without adapting the facts to the conditions of representation on the stage. Things do not happen in the form of stories and dramas, and since they must all be told in some

form, all reports, even by eye witnesses, all histories, all stories, all dramatic representations, are only attempts to arrange the facts in a faithful, intelligent, interesting form. That is, when they are not intentional efforts to hide the truth, as they very often are. [33]

Obviously the victims of *The Freedom of the City* and of *Living Quarters* are cast by their author into such narrative roles but, more than this, they take on an importance in excess of their own personalities. As Dan H. Laurence noted, speaking of *Saint Joan* and *Antony and Cleopatra*, 'Shaw endowed his characters with sufficient self-consciousness to explain themselves to an audience that was, for the most part, historically misinformed.' Nowhere in Friel's work will we find a more blatant case of this self-consciousness than in the fabrication called *Faith Healer*, which, as far as the audience or reader can tell, is an almost total tissue of lies and incomprehensions, told and experienced across the barrier of death. (In this sense we must once again note the possible importance of Teddy, simply because he is alive and therefore available to verify or discount the stories of the dead.) The adaptation of historical 'facts' in *Translations* scarcely amounts to such a fabrication, in the sense of amounting to 'intentional efforts to hide the truth'. Friel has in fact utilised the already artificial histories of others (O'Donovan's letters for example) in order to create, out of all the available versions, a *possible* world in which the exercise in understanding and expression can take place.

TRANSLATING

In 'Word against Object' Steiner says:

Our languages simultaneously structure and are structured by time, by the syntax of past, present and future...Language is in part physical, in part mental. Its grammar is temporal and also seems to invite and inform our sense of time. A third polarity is that of private and public. It is worth looking at closely because it poses the question of translation in its present form. In what ways can language, which is by operative definition a shared code of exchange, be regarded as private? To what degree is the verbal expression, the semiotic field in which an individual functions, a unique idiom or idiolect? How does this personal 'privacy' relate to the larger 'privacy of context' in the speech of a given community or national language? [34]

Thus to particularise, to individuate a common culture, is to stress the difficulties of adapting absolute feelings such as 'love', 'fear', 'meaning', to real situations where one might need to express some concrete instance of such feelings.

Heidegger, who parenthetically influenced the conception of *Translations*, says 'man acts as though he were the master of language, while it is language which remains mistress of men. When this relation of domination is inverted, man succumbs to strange contrivances'. [35] This 'ontological' view of language as the mediator between man and the world requires some attention.

In *Faith Healer*, as Richard Kearney points out, Hardy's attempt at self-analysis, at an understanding of his 'power' or 'gift', is a series of equivocations which 'amount to the fundamental question: Am I the manipulative master or the obedient servant of the healing word?' [36] In the ontological sense this parodox can never be resolved. It is therefore a rational gesture, if a solution can be both rational (i.e. logocentric) and gestic (i.e. impulsive), can embrace irresolution and turn it into 'meaning'.

But here again we run into problems, because, as Lévi-Strauss points out,

> it is absolutely impossible to conceive of meaning without order. There is something very curious in semantics, that the word 'meaning' is probably in the whole language, the word the meaning of which is the most difficult to find. What does 'to mean' mean? It seems to me that the only answer we can give is that 'to mean' means the ability of any kind of data to be translated into a different language. [37]

In translation, therefore, we are looking for meaning, the ability to carry over, to translate, to metaphorise, the integrity of sense, the wholeness of the signal by which perception is expressed and community is established. And this in itself 'means' that there are two subjective meanings to every crossing, one on each bank of the objective river of apprehension. The idea of a language as an entity over which we have temporary logical mastery, but which exercises continuing affective mastery over *us*, suggests that in order to establish and extend control we must define and distinguish on one hand the irresponsible use of language, which allows it to predetermine its use and to run away from us, and, on another, the calculated use, within prescribed limitations, of language, fully realising the risks that its imprecision and fickleness impose: the civilised institute of the text and the barbaric chaos of babel.

In the theatre this requires that we make a difficult adjustment to distinguish between the direct communication of the verbal dramas with our inner aural senses, and the formal communication with our sensual perceptions. For Friel this means that language can become an instrument of either servility or liberation, and that one can exist in a limbo of meaning in which one is deliciously uncertain about significance. Steiner: 'languages are wholly arbitrary sets of signals and conventionalized counters' (*After Babel* 21). Friel: 'words are signals, counters. They are not immortal' (*Tr.* 43). But they *are* promiscuous, and a translation is not only a release or liberation of a word/concept from one language to another, it is also an act of betrayal, a carrying across from the camp of the true to that of the false, from dexter to sinister, adroit to gauche. Such a tradition, or 'handing *over*' (*tradere*), is a subversion or perversion of tradition conceived as continuity, or 'handing *down*'. [38]

This, as we have seen, is what Maxwell calls a subversion of 'the allegiance of language'. It also, of course, by extension deals a blow to our allegiance to history. If truth is the daughter of time, chaos and betrayal are the bastards of history. Under the sliding weight of babel, our sense of meaning is abolished, because we lose the power of 'faith' or the 'willing suspension of disbelief'; our behaviour becomes as depraved as the polyglot himself: the retreat into silence may be more a resolution than an escape. This, as the Anglo-Irish writer Lawrence Durrell points out, is a dialectical problem: 'how to convey a state for which words are inadequate? How to name a reality which is no longer itself once you qualify it with a name? How to state something which is beyond opposites in a language which is based on opposites?' [39]

Kearney argues that in modern Irish theatre 'words tend to predetermine character, action and plot', [40] as a deliberate response to this condition. History as trader, it appears, is trustworthy while it is on your side, but anathema, traducer, when it crosses over. 'We like to think we endure around truths immemorially posited', says Hugh O'Donnell (*Tr.* 42) whereas we discover that we endure beneath the offensive pressure of the dolmens which ring us round.

In *Translations* Friel attempts to re-establish this situation in order to re-establish the primacy of language as *content* over language as *form*. As Seamus Deane comments on *The*

Communication Cord, 'A colony always wants to escape from history. It longs for its own authenticity, the element it had before history came to disfigure it.' [41] If there is any symbolism in *Translations* it lies in the fact that, apart from an irrelevant phrase which amounts only to doggerel ('in Norfolk we besport ourselves around the maypole'), Maire's only original knowledge of English consists of the elemental words 'water', 'fire', 'earth'; and in the process in which she becomes bewildered and debauched by the traitorous word 'always'. Here again is our 'embarrassment', brought about by the confluence of two incompatible matrices, which leads either to tragedy or comedy.

Friel's whole endeavour here is kept in the balance by the fact that he found it difficult in the writing to propel his characters either forward or back. It would be too easy to regard *Translations* simply as a 'powerful metaphor' of modern Ireland, 'bulled' by multinational and multicultural influences, a senescent, hopeless, incapacity; the failure of the new race to rise against the *urbs antiqua* (*Tr.* 68); a parable of Derry's poor. *Translations* does far more than that; it is not just the transparent 'satire' of *The Mundy Scheme*. But we can see how easy it is for both author and critics to take such a view.

Robert Hogan's general view of *Translations* is that 'the language device also underlines the broad theme of the play, about the gulf between cultures...So Friel may also more broadly be saying that the failure of language is a symptom of the failure of sympathy.' [42] This analysis confuses what the play is 'about' with what the playwright intends or 'means', and it also allows the devices in the plays to come between the critic and the meaning. Hogan regards it as a flaw that:

> the most arresting character, the hedge-schoolmaster, is not the main character, and has little to do with the plot. The three young men who impel the plot are not really memorable. Also, some critical developments of the plot occur between scenes, and the conclusion of the plot is really only implied. [43]

I fundamentally disagree with this interpretation of *Translations* because I read, and see, and hear, a different play. This is not a way of politely differing from Robert Hogan: it means that I take an alternative course towards the author's intentions. I do not see the failure of language as a symptom of the failure of sympathy. It is not symptomatic: it is central, it is chemical, it is the disease itself;

there is a fusion of form and content here, not a confusion. The fact that the characterisation of three actors, Manus, Owen and Yolland, is not 'memorable' (i.e. that we cannot carry away in our reproductive imagination an image of their achievements) or that the play follows the Greek and Chekhovian pattern of keeping its action firmly off stage, or that the 'plot' seems to have no conclusion, is irrelevant. It is a quibble with the *story*, when that story is only a device to set a distance, to mediate, between ourselves and the images of the absolute. One could argue endlessly but fruitlessly whether the plot demands conclusion, when it hardly has a beginning or a middle.

The original Field Day production in 1980 established a considerable *gravitas* not alone for Hugh O'Donnell but also for Jimmy Jack, whereas the production at the Abbey Theatre in 1983 explored more extensively the play's capacity for humour, which at times bordered on buffoonery in the character of Doalty and greatly detracted from his contribution in the final scene (discussed above). I have seen Hugh and Jimmy Jack played with an almost total lack of *gravitas* which made nonsense of the first scene and especially of Owen's line 'back here with you all again, *civilised* people' (*Tr.* 28).

But this is to worry about the crisis of form when the real issue is to look at the failure not alone of language and sympathy but also of the mediating effects of tenderness, as the dominant characteristic of the diviner. As Friel says:

> the cultural climate is a dying climate, no longer quickened by its past, about to be plunged almost overnight into an alien future. The victims in this situation are the transitional generation. The old can retreat into and find immunity in the past. The young require some facility with the new cultural implements. The in-between ages become lost, wandering around in a strange land. Strays. [44]

It would be easier in fact to think of modern Ireland as a cultural metaphor for some of the problems of history – what Beckett also expressed through the character of Malone:

> Then he was sorry he had not learnt the art of thinking...sorry he could make no meaning of the babel raging in his head, the doubts, the desires, imaginings and dreads. And a little less well endowed with strength and courage he too would have

160

abandoned and despaired of even learning what manner of being he was, and how he was going to live, and lived vanquished, blindly in a mad world, in the midst of strangers. [45]

It is therefore about all the problems of *Faith Healer*, projected onto the screen of *communitas*. And it is about the non-historical problem of indignity. The strays are those for whom the poet, the playwright, the shaman or diviner, essays an alternative map-making, a new clutching towards a dimly perceived identity. It is *the coincidence of madness with indignity*, in the sense expressed by Beckett, which has characterised much of Friel's concern with alienation of one's own culture and despair at one's 'political' condition. Madness leads to dream, a dream of continuity and wholeness which may turn to grief or nervous distress when contrasted with reality, when a society realises that it has enjoyed no living past or wholeness in its history. As the psychiatrist R.D. Laing says:

> If we can begin to understand madness and sanity in existential terms, we shall be more able to see clearly the extent to which we all confront common problems and share common dilemmas ... When a person goes mad, a profound transposition of his position in relation to all domains of being occurs. His centre of experience moves from ego to Self. Mundane time becomes merely anecdotal, only the eternal matters. The madman is however confused. He muddles ego with self, inner with outer, natural with supernatural. Nevertheless, he often can be to us, even through his profound wretchedness and disintegration, the hierophant of the sacred. [46]

It needs no quotation to underline the application of such a view to *Translations*, where 'mundane time becomes merely anecdotal'. It is also easy to see how well *The Communication Cord* suits Friel's purposes. The same set which in *Translations* was the centre not only of the house but of the entire known world, becomes, in *The Communication Cord*, a travesty of a 'cathedral' but one with a host of side-chapels ('room down', settle bed, loft) in which a Feydeau-type of bedroom farce, including distorted morals, is enacted. By showing us how very nearly serious our misdemeanours can be, Friel persuades us of the proximity of tragedy to comedy, and the ease with which one can be translated from one 'diocese' to the other.

There are figures on the British stage who would find look-alikes on Friel's: as C.W.E. Bigsby says:

> Beckett's clowns, Osborne's music hall entertainer, and Pinter's caretakers...are not simply images of a society which has lost all purpose and direction, of people dislodged from history. They are images of a world in which the idea of identity and individuality are themselves ironic.

Bigsby also elucidates the fact that 'for Orton and Stoppard the viscosity of language, its ambiguities, its availability as an instrument of social control and moral evasion, is a clue to more fundamental changes of morale and morality'. Bigsby goes on to make a point in relation to Stoppard which we can apply also to Friel: Stoppard, he says, is 'trying to re-establish...the necessity to acknowledge language as in some ways both rationally and morally linked to a world whose reality must be assumed even if it cannot ultimately be proved', and in doing so 'he knows and acknowledges...the contradiction and even the moral evasion...implied by challenging other people's fictions, other people's coercive language, with one's own' [47] – manipulating the relationship between the imaginative and the real, defining truth. This, for example, in *Travesties* and *Rosencrantz and Guildenstern Are Dead*, in many ways poses the same questions Friel asked himself in writing *Faith Healer*.

At first it might appear, as some critics have maintained, [48] that the facility of *The Communication Cord* betrays an absence of serious intent; that we now expect of Friel not only first-class stagecraft, but also drama of an explicitly intellectual type. (The lack of intellectuality, and the re-introduction of some of the animal energy of his earliest work, will no doubt contribute to a problem in critical analysis of his latest play *Dancing at Lughnasa*.) Apart from the high quality of the writing, the weakness of the farce lies in the obvious falsity of the sexual relationships, which, unlike the 'high art' of French farce, lack the serious frivolity of *haut bourgeois* misdemeanour. The liaisons of Tim with Susan, and Jack with Evette, are not convincing, nor is the simultaneous affair of Evette with Jack and Senator Donovan, nor the obvious eventual pairing of Jack with Susan and Tim with Claire. However, the keynote to this quite transparent failure is contained in Jack's solemn avowal to both Susan and Claire (a piety as empty as his 'first cathedral'): 'You and I were fortunate enough to experience and share an affection that is still one of my most sustaining memories, and when we broke up...a part of me died' (*CC* 67).

As Richard Kearney says, 'words have become both the form *and* the content of his drama'. [49] In this sense, also, *Translations* and *The Communication Cord* are twins. In *Translations* the form or 'aboutness' of his intentions, despite its conventional appearance, in fact goes further than his previous plays in promoting its own obsolescence. In *The Communication Cord* the 'meaning' or content is conversely smothered in a riot of action, all of which in itself is inherently pointless. It thus becomes possible to realise how *Translations* does have a tendency towards farce, so that Jimmy Jack's, Maire's and Doalty's lines in particular can be played for more laughs beyond the stage than they rightly excite upon it. It is almost as if the problem were entirely semantic: discussing the naming of 'Tobair Vree' Owen asks 'do we keep piety with a man long dead, long forgotten, his name 'eroded' beyond recognition?'(*Tr.* 44). It is the same difficulty encountered by the pseudo-archaeologists in *Volunteers* when confronted with the skeletal Leif. If therefore identity *is* inseparably bound up with the ability to utter one's name, or to hear another utter it when one has passed into muteness, the semantic problems become central to the 'meaning of life' as evidenced by the chaotic catalogue of mistakes poured out by the frenetic 'Tim the Thesis': 'You're a German they call Barney Munich and you're married to Claire Harkin whose real name is Evette Giroux' (*CC* 49).

LANGUAGE AND IDENTITY

One of the identities which the 'volunteers' bestow on Leif is 'the only child of a merchant prince'; 'all young Leif could say was "I own a well-trained falcon" in seven languages' (*Vol.* 57), like a polyglot version of Mervyn Peake's Titus – a baroque conception who belies the fact that time has made him a skeleton while history has robbed him of all identity. Underlying this imagery is the fact that one can change one's identity with one's language – the carapace which both protects and inhibits.

But further beneath this superficial statement we find that language is dependent on sense, since it is the expression of composite sense. Comprehension depends on vision ('Can't you *see*!') and it also depends, perhaps to a lesser extent, on the other ways of perceiving: 'Are you deaf? Are you stupid? Don't you understand simple words?' (*LQ* 83). And it depends very definitely on an aggregated sense of *being*: in Mozart's *Le Nozze di Figaro* Count Almaviva begins to make love to his wife *because* she resembles someone else. People are not who they seem, our reasons for doing things are not what they seem, and our interpretation of what we do can also be dangerously ambiguous. The possession of two languages by which to decode a single text or icon is a common psychological feature even among monoglots: we think in one language and we speak in another. We are called 'Skinner' in one and Adrian Casimir Fitzgerald in the other. We think demotic but we speak mandarin – like Lily 'phoning from the Mayor's parlour (*Freedom* 64–5), or the subtle changes in Hugh O'Donnell's syntax and the blatant changes in the actual tongue he uses, when he is at home or abroad ('outside the parish'). He puts his house in order when Englishmen arrive (*Tr.* 29) just as Manus Sweeney, paradoxically, begins to speak English when Shane and Peter come to the gentle island. We can be deprived of an essential part of our identity by having our name, or one of our names, removed from us – like Leif, or like 'Smiler', the imbecilic victim of police brutality: 'he hardly knows his own name' (*Vol.* 43).

Changing identity with language, or losing identity through lack of language, is made explicitly tragical in *Making History*, where, depending on the context of circumstance and affiliation, Hugh O'Neill employs either an 'Upper-class English' or a 'Tyrone' accent to express his meaning. I have seen Owen O'Donnell, in *Translations*, played in the same way, very effectively using an 'English' accent to address Yolland and Lancey, and a Donegal accent for his 'constituency'. *Making History* (like the short story 'My Father and the Sergeant') shows us the inflections possible with the use of different names: O'Neill's circumstances differ according to whether he is 'Hugh', 'The O'Neill', 'Earl of Tyrone', or 'Tyrone', or even 'Fox O'Neill' – and so of course do our reactions to, and perceptions of, him.

Under such conditions, communication, meaning and identity begin to disintegrate, and it becomes increasingly difficult to maintain an equilibrium between the inner and the outer voice. Ways of doing things – responses to the perceptible world – become caricatures: the actual difference between English and Irish miles provides a basis for a distinction between efficient and inefficient ways of measuring, and therefore expressing, the world. The English language becomes subverted by its Irish users. Irish

nomenclature is 'bulled' by the Englishman because the ambiguity
of sense and meaning is resolved by anglicisation.

MANUS: What's 'incorrect' about the place names we have
here?
OWEN: Nothing at all. They're just going to be standardised.
MANUS: You mean changed into English?
OWEN: *Where there's ambiguity*, they'll be Anglicized
(*Tr.*32, *my emphasis*)

With the collapse of orientation, community falters:

OWEN: Do you know where the priest lives?
HUGH: At Lis na Muc, over near...
OWEN: No he doesn't. Lis na Muc, the Fort of the Pigs, has
become Swinefort...And to get to Swinefort you pass through
Greencastle and Fair Head and Strandhill and Gort and
Whiteplains. And the new school isn't at Poll na gCaorach
– it's at Sheepsrock. Will you be able to find your way?
(*Tr.* 42)

The 'sense' which this condition appeals to, and indeed engenders,
lies between 'consternation' and 'melancholy', the key elements of
despair which Friel identified in writing *Aristocrats*.[50] The Irish
mind is left in Janus-like desolation between the shock of the future
and the emptiness of the past. When one does not know whether
one's life is a tragedy or a comedy, the only *frisson* possible is that
of despair – as Hugh, the enervate, hands over the baton of hope to
Maire, the energised. At first we don't realise how serious the
position is. There is no experience. The mind cannot will us towards
either pole. It is exhilarating to find oneself in 'uncertainties,
mysteries, doubts', a condition we often dignify with the name of
'love'. We live within the perimeter of a world which offers security,
but one which we would like to escape, if only from curiosity. Then
we know the thrill of discovery; the commanding texts are wrong,
they therefore lose their authority; the maps are incorrectly drawn,
the territory ceases to be closed and becomes open; we turn the
icons to the wall. 'The chart's wrong...The museum's wrong' (*Vol.*
36). Then we discover that, however wrong the text may be (the
Widgery Report, Sir's Ledger, Lombard's 'History'), the discovery
coincides with the hour of our death. The result is grief, bewilderment, 'a casualty of language' (*Vol.* 26).

We adopt language as a means of communication in order to

avoid, or prevent, tragedy and violence, in order to ensure some kind of survival. In the hour of our death, as Heaney says, 'whispering morse', [51] we abandon language as a false god. That is the public world. The inner state is even more consternated and melancholic, because *it* experiences a breakdown in the process of rationalisation:

> MAIRE: Never! There never was blight here. Never. Never. But we're always sniffing about for it, aren't we ...Honest to God, some of you people aren't happy unless you're miserable and you'll not be right content until you're dead!
> DOALTY: Bloody right, Maire. And sure St Columcille prophesied there'd never be blight here. He said
> The spuds will bloom in Baile Beag
> Till rabbits grow an extra lug.
> And sure that'll never be. So we're alright.
>
> (*Tr.* 21–2)

Maire uses 'never' as she later uses 'always'; we know that both are impossible, seductive concepts of *absolute* time which break down in the face of *relative* time. To wish the conjugation of the temporal and the eternal without being able to live it, is to act the fool without cause; to abandon reason is the step immediately before the flight from language: first irrationality, then silence. Perhaps only Jimmy Jack, because of his removal from the rational, quotidian plane, is closest to reality: events as such do not concern him; he has become 'immemorial', part of the fabric of time itself.

The most obvious example of the flight from language in modern Irish literature is of course Joyce. His strategy, in the face of the affective breakdown of Ireland, was 'silence, exile and cunning'. The result, in literary terms, was the renewal of myth and metaphor in the creation of a new language in *Finnegans Wake*. Friel does not attempt to approach Joyce's drastic remedy, but he is acutely conscious of the need for a linguistic revolt: 'we have not yet discovered a language appropriate to the theatre in this country – as singularly appropriate as Synge's invention', [52] and one, we might therefore think, as radical in its own way as Joyce's. What Friel envisages, but cannot feel his way towards, is a 'language' that will encompass the social-political *and* the emotional–familial modes, a dual-purpose method of expressing both opportunities/possibilities and inevitabilities, without double-crossing either. In one sense he needs to move towards a balletic, non-verbal theatre such as that developed by Tom MacIntyre in plays such as *The Great Hunger* and *Rise Up Lovely Sweeney*; in another he requires words more than ever before. The idea is compellingly explored in *Dancing at Lughnasa* which, because it is a 'memory play', counterpoints the way we use words with the way they have been used; and because words are re-interpreted through the central metaphor of the play, the spectacle of the dance.

We will look now at the way Friel actually constructs *Translations* on the foundation of his intention to write a play about the drunken hedge-schoolmaster whom he had discovered in his own ancestry. Then I will suggest how he fills this form with the emotional lessons which he has distilled from his previous work. The hedge-school story in Ireland is sentimentally linked to the notion that 'every Kerry ploughboy has a copy of Homer in his breeches pocket', a notion which is substantiated, though not certified, by Dowling's *The Hedge-Schools of Ireland*. Friel studied this history to assimilate the background to his chosen theme, and thereby reduced Dowling's subject to suit his particular needs. Friel creates a composite school, Ballybeg, from the many instances cited by Dowling: the strength of the classical tradition is transported from Kerry; the 'poor scholar' is transformed into Jimmy Jack Cassie, 'the Infant Prodigy'; and the level of excellence, usually in mathematics and classics, is reduced to a poor and precarious proficiency. The archetypal master, according to one of Dowling's sources, was a

> pure Milesian, short of stature, fiery in temper, with features exhibiting a strange combination of cunning, thought and humour. He swore at his pupils roundly, and taught them to swear. But he was a good scholar and a successful teacher. Like many of his countrymen his love of classical literature amounted almost to a passion and he had the rare talent of inspiring favourite pupils with his own enthusiasm. Among Latin authors he delighted in Horace [53]

– whose odes he rendered quaintly, one supposes in the same way that Hugh refashions Ovid (*Tr.* 41). The children of the hedge-schools become young adults, but the lessons are the same: copying headlines, arithmetic, geography. Hugh becomes the author of 'the Pentaglot Preceptor or Elementary Institute' (*Tr.* 42), a version of a standard textbook of the time, 'the Hibernian Preceptor' , by George Wall of Birr, County Offaly. The schoolmaster was often in an ambivalent position regarding the two languages, English which was 'used in business affairs' and Irish, 'the language of home and the fields'. Hugh O'Donnell calls English 'particularly suited to the purposes of commerce' (*Tr.* 25). [54] Nevertheless:

> the hedge schoolmaster was often proud of his English. In the home parents were particularly careless of imparting a knowledge of Irish to their children; in fact, they sometimes looked upon the ignorance of the younger generation in this respect as an advantage when they wished to discuss private affairs in their hearing. Yet the schoolmaster must have deplored what was happening, for every now and then we find him either defiantly singing the praises of the language or regretting its decay. He has been instrumental, however, in the preservation of thousands of legends, songs and poems, and in helping to perpetuate his native tongue. [55]

And although the master was poorly paid – Friel alters the amounts payable to Hugh from those suggested by Dowling but maintains the same general level of income [56] – his social status was high:

> his knowledge and his very status constituted him the leading authority on all matters of moment to the community. His advice and help were sought and generally paid for in money or kind, and where neither of these were forthcoming he invariably managed to gain in prestige. His social standing in the parish was of considerable importance to him, for the higher it was, the more the people looked to him as guide and counsellor. 'A hedge schoolmaster' writes Carleton 'was the general scribe of the parish, to whom all who wanted letters or petitions written, uniformly applied – and these were glorious opportunities for the pompous display of pedantry.' [57]

We can see in Hugh Mor O'Donnell the relics of 'a leading authority' among the relics of his parish.

Friel also presses into service the fact that while this was a literate culture it was predominantly verbal rather than written. Gaelic society had texts which provided it with the pillars and adjuncts of learning, safeguarded by the *fili*, those native men of learning with the 'responsibility and corporate interest...to maintain the traditional integrity of social organisation and the traditional concepts on which it depended'. [58] But these 'texts' were of course oral: the strengths of a patriarchal and traditional society lie in its verbal culture, not enshrined in books which can be stolen but preserved in the secret runes which have all 'the magic associated with solemn oral pronouncement' [59] – a power which invests the *seannchai* with social importance to this day: why else would the secret-ary of a government department be titled 'An Runai'? With the advent of written texts, the same authority suggests, scholars continued to conform to oral tradition, and we are led to suppose that in Ireland (where content has always been regarded as more important than form, the superiority of the spoken to the written, the aural to the visual, the obedience to inner, heard voices rather than the evidence of our own eyes) the appeal to a text that is more easily uttered than it is read will be a superior appeal.

We turn now to another 'department' in Friel's play-construction, the place-name methods of the Ordnance Survey. (In the same way, of course, Friel 'collects' his place-names such as Termon and Burnfoot and Swinefort, from Derry, Donegal and Mayo. Similarly he brings together the relatively distant Norfolk villages of Winfarthing, Little Walsingham, Saxingham Nethergate and Barton Bendish to make up Yolland's own world.) As Andrews notes, although the policy in anglicising the place-names was to adopt whatever version was recommended by the majority of sources, 'Irish place-names had been too variously mangled by generations of English-speaking settlers for any such assumption to be valid.' [60]

Larcom, one of the directors of the survey, decided

> to adopt not necessarily the commonest version but the version which came nearest to the original Irish form of the name. This was an attractive compromise between the empirical and the antiquarian. It was rational, scholarly and practical. It also showed a well-intentioned deference to the Irishness of Irish place-names. [61]

In *Translations* this difficulty is evidenced in the versions given to, for example, Bun na hAbhann: in the church registry 'Banowen'; in the list of freeholders, 'Owenmore'; in the grand jury lists, 'Binhone'. Owen says, 'I suppose we could Anglicise it to "Bunowen".' Similarly Druim Dubh: Dramduff, Drimdoo, Dramduffy, Drom-duff. But, like Larcom, Owen and Yolland set about finding the original meaning:

Bun is the Irish word for bottom. And Abha means river. So it's literally the mouth of the river...We are trying to denominate and at the same time describe that tiny area of soggy, rocky, sandy ground where that little stream enters the sea, an area known locally as Bun na hAbhann...Burnfoot!

(*Tr.* 35)

We are therefore provided with a framework within which a psychological drama can be worked out: the physical shape, personnel and accoutrements of the hedge-school, and the occupation which disturbs both the daily life and the orientation of the village. Into this framework Friel inserts the 'ontological project' discussed by Richard Kearney.

I referred to the 'distilled emotional lessons' of Friel's earlier work: by this I mean those explorations of individual and collective consciousness as we have seen them expressed in the stories, the 'love' plays and the plays of freedom. In *Faith Healer* we have been offered some form of resolution to the artist's inner problems, a homecoming to the self. We have also seen a steady erosion of the concept of *communitas* in the face of inevitable social change, and a growing awareness of the paucity of dramatic invention where it is needed to meet a 'crisis of form'. In *Translations* most of these lessons are repeated in a way which suggests that the author is using some form of emotional shorthand as an *aide-mémoire*, in pursuit of a further project – that of language itself – and a further resolution. First, therefore, we look at his psychological approach. We realise immediately that the hedge-school pupils, anticipating the entry of the Master, represent a community of doubt and anxiety. A lame man is coaxing an apparently mute girl into the confidence of self-expression, opening the play with the catechetic 'what is your name?' The 'Infant Prodigy' recites Homer's account of the transfiguration of Ulysses by 'flashing-eyed' Athene. The intimacy of the modern and ancient worlds is reinforced by Jimmy's familiarity, and the idea of naming is reinforced by the question of the paternity of Nellie Ruadh's baby: 'she was threatening she was going to call it after its father' (*Tr.*18).

Perception is faulty: they fear the 'sweet smell' even though they are not sure whether or not the smell is the cause or the effect of crop failure. The failure of perception can be fatal: if memory is the link with the past, then the failure of memory (a breakdown in the recollection of past perceptions) cuts us off from history; Beckett, in particular, explores this through the principle 'esse est percipi': since 'to be' is 'to be perceived', then to remember also depends on being perceived. Memory cannot have an independent existence, since it requires a person to operate it and a perceiver to create that person. If imperception or imperfect perception can be futuristically fatal, Beckett suggests that the imperfect perception of the past, or non-perception, can be equally damaging to one's past:

> Instead of resuming me at the point where I was left off, they pick me up at a much later stage, perhaps thereby hoping to induce in me the illusion that I had got through the interval all on my own, lived without help of any kind for quite some time. [62]

The message for the broken traditions of Irish history is clear.

Sarah's slow progress towards utterance begins with the most basic and personal announcement: 'my name is Sarah'; she accomplishes four further holds on the public world: 'Flowers' (compare this with Maire's three words of English), 'Sarah Johnny Sally' (her full patronymic, marking her place in the world), and, as she witnesses the embrace of Maire and Yolland, the name of her fellow-cripple, 'Manus!' – a 'response cry blurted out as an involuntary reaction to what you've just heard' (*CC* 19); her final statement is of place, 'I live in Bun na hAbhann'.

Hugh's appearance is intricately connected with his role in the Tarot of the community, a catalogue which Friel has concentrated into this one personage, the *dominus*, surrounded by Yeats's noble peasants, the *ignari, stulti, rustici*. Hugh has 'residual dignity' (*Tr.* 23); he interprets the events of the parish – the baptism or *caerimonia nominationis* of the baby, the arrival of the sappers, the opening of the new national school; and he draws his pupils closer again to the classical world and its people: 'Sophocles from Colonus would agree with Doalty Dan Doalty from Tulach Alainn: "To know nothing is the sweetest life" ' (*Tr.* 24). As Kearney observes: 'he is an inquisitor of origins and etymologies who speaks in the past tense. He is backward looking for the simple reason that the future holds no hope for his language.' [63] He therefore ignores Daniel O'Connell's challenge thrown out by Maire, who insists 'I don't want Greek, I don't want Latin. I want English. I want to be able to speak English because I'm going to America' (*Tr.* 25–6). The ultimate irony is of course that the *dead* languages, which should be meaningless, paradoxically *live* in Baile Beag. [64]

171

The text maintained by this community and protected by its *dominus* is unwritten. It is the essence of an orally transmitted culture; folklore would hardly describe it, since it is not entirely a matter of custom nor even a simple conjugation of custom and knowledge. It is, as the passage from Larcom quoted above suggests, both the temporal dimension of habitude and the daily way of going about things, and the interaction and interdependence of the two.

Within this text, however, there are secrets, inner truths. In Baile Beag these are at stake. As Sarah succeeds in saying her name Manus declares 'this is our secret...soon you'll be telling me all the secrets that have been in that head of yours all these years' (*Tr.* 12): her private imaginings which are now to be broadcast to a wise and sceptical community. Simultaneously Manus encourages Sarah: 'Nothing'll stop us now! Nothing in the wide world!', but we know that experience stops us, we cannot embrace the wide world because we are enclosed by the limits of the known world, the narrow ground. Manus betrays Sarah, by making public the mute secrets of her privacy. In the public world she is destroyed.

To look to America is to look at a colony, a diaspora – 'the passage money came last Friday' (*Tr.* 20) – and, although Friel uses Jimmy's impending marriage to Athene as a foil to Maire's love for Yolland, even Jimmy's union is across a border vitiated by customary commerce between Baile Beag and 'the parish of Athens'. But to look beyond that world is to contemplate exogamy, and, as Jimmy Jack says:

> Do you know the Greek word *endogamein*? It means to marry within the tribe. And the word *exogamein* means to marry outside the tribe. And you don't cross those borders casually – both sides get very angry. Now, the problem is this: is Athene sufficiently mortal or am I sufficiently godlike for the marriage to be acceptable to her people and to my people? You think about that.
>
> (*Tr.* 68)

There is an obvious analogy between this dilemma and that in *The Enemy Within* where Columba's nephew Aedh has married a Pict – a pagan – with resulting suspicion on both sides: the connection between *faith* and *place* is explicit: 'Let it grow up a heathen, a stranger to the soft lands of Gartan' (*EW*65). And as *Translations* ends, it is the turn of Hugh to intone, invoking the protection of a text he has by now admitted has no authority: [65]

'*urbs antiqua fuit...*'(*Tr.* 69). Friel continues his examination of the role of the revenant by combining elements which we have previously seen in Gar O'Donnell, Cass McGuire and Ben Butler: a disruption, an evaluation of the old ways, and a failure of communication. But he also conducts this visitation in two ways: through Owen O'Donnell, the ambivalent son of the house who doubles as 'Roland', the cartographer's scout; and George Yolland, *his* doppelganger, who is rediscovering or inventing himself, and coming home for the first time (they congress as 'Rowen' or 'Oland', *Tr.* 45). For Owen, 'everything's just as it was! Nothing's changed! Not a thing!' (*Tr.* 27), he is back within the tribe, '*civilised* people' (*Tr.* 28), but he realises, in an echo of *The Gentle Island*, that permanence is false and civilisation dead:

YOLLAND: It's really heavenly.
OWEN: For God's sake! the first hot summer in fifty years and you think it's Eden.

(*Tr.* 38)

He taunts his father with the new topography (*Tr.* 42) and asks 'Is it astute not to be able to adjust for survival?'(*Tr.* 43). Owen is the go-between, the traducer of cultures who inserts himself between the worlds of past and future. For Yolland the 'homecoming' is perhaps even more acute, because, like Private Gar, he is aware of the *inner* tensions which his 'crude intrusion' (*Tr.* 32) sets up. He realises the problem of translation: that one must live *within* a culture, the dark and private places of pre-verbal life, rather than seek a transference: 'Let's leave it alone. There's no English equivalent for a sound like that' (*Tr.* 35). But he also realises the impossibility of living within the culture of Baile Beag, even though he has experienced 'a momentary sense of discovery – not quite a sense of discovery – a sense of recognition, of confirmation of something I half knew instinctively' (*Tr.* 40). He acknowledges that 'I may learn the password but the language of the tribe will always elude me...The private core will always be hermetic' (*Tr.* 40).

For Yolland there can be no going back, however: 'I couldn't face father' (*Tr.* 39): he is exiled from both worlds and he cannot live up to his father's aspirations for a new world. For his father (again echoing Steiner [66]) 'ancient time was at an end...There were no longer any frontiers to man's potential. Possibilities were endless and exciting' (*Tr.* 40). Once again, a world without boundaries is, as we already know, an explosive culture without immunity, a prey to

173

the bacteria of the unknown. And Yolland knows that to live in the world one needs 'energy – coherence – belief' and believes that he has found it in the calm possession with which Baile Beag conducts its daily life, whether it be the pastoral, hallowed by consuetude, or the appeals to the classical world which it has made familiar – 'a totally different order, a consciousness that wasn't striving nor agitated, but at ease with its own conviction and assurance' (*Tr.* 40).

The *dominus,* the *paterfamilias,* extends symbolic welcome to this adopted son: 'I understand your sense of exclusion, of being cut off from life here; and I trust you will find access to us with my son's help' (*Tr.* 43). Hugh has coherence and belief and knows that 'to remember everything is a form of madness'. This is one key to Hugh's character, to the fact that the play revolves around him, as its central persona. He and Rowen/Oland/George are accomplices in the fate of Baile Beag, this 'erosion' or 'eviction' (*Tr.* 43) of one culture by another. O' Faolain calls it an 'infiltration' and comments: 'today we have sometimes disguised our outposts as tourists; then, they disguised them as traders; in either case they ended up as soldiers'. [67] The inference being that, however civilised the infiltration may be, it ends in armed confrontation: the map-making evolves inevitably into what it always contained, a military exercise.

There is also a fierce reaction to this process, not from Hugh but from the lame son, Manus, from the unseen villains whom he protects and excuses, the Donnelly twins, and an ineffective response from Doalty. For Hugh and his cohort, Jimmy Jack, the real eviction excites only a verbal, nostalgic response in a dead tongue ('ignari, stulti, rustici') and an appeal to an heroic engagement in which they did not fight – the 'Thermopylae' of 1798, when they returned to their undefended omphalos before the battle was joined (*Tr.* 58, 67). Manus O'Donnell wants to maintain *communitas* when it is obvious that a larger society is in the wings. Like Manus Sweeney in *The Gentle Island* he is 'the lame scholar turned violent' (*Tr.* 55) when the secrets are penetrated and laid bare and the language is 'bulled'. But he is only capable of 'the wrong gesture in the wrong language'.

Therefore, Friel addresses the problem of possibilities, not only inconsistencies between different versions of the same event or perception (as we have seen in *Philadelphia, Cass, Living Quarters, Aristocrats, The Freedom*) but also the meanings which lurk within the words themselves, the range of ambiguities which stretch from blatant falsehood and traduction to misplaced or uncomprehended tenderness.

There is a blissful state in which one can be in 'uncertainties' without reaching for meaning; this immaterialism comes out at several points in *Translations*: 'I don't know a word they're saying, nor they me, but sure that doesn't matter does it?' (*Tr.* 17); 'Owen/ Roland – what the hell. It's only a name. It's the same me, isn't it? Well, isn't it?' (*Tr.* 33). But communication depends on shared meaning, and between languages there must be a common code. In *Translations* we see that in language, as a gesture of discourse, this commonalty cannot be found, because the symbolic points of contact represent different cultures, different ways of looking at the world. Owen calls Irish 'archaic' and English 'good' (*Tr.* 29); Hugh sums up the difference between Irish and English as that between the aristocratic and the plebeian (*Tr.* 41).

In the scene of *Translations* where this incapacity for communion is expressed most poignantly, Friel creates a tragi-comic situation which he manipulates into a post-verbal exchange based on the nonsense-talk of lovers – the place-names of Baile Beag and Norfolk. This scene is difficult to encompass because it has many elements: the comedy (Maire: The grass must be wet. My feet are soaking. Yolland: Your feet must be wet. The grass is soaking. *Tr.* 49); the pathetic attempts at communication, grasping at wisps of meaning ('if you could understand me....I would tell you how beautiful you are', *Tr.* 52); the induction of Maire into English speech, like Manus coaxing Sarah ('Water. Water. Oh yes – water – water – very good – water – good – good ... fire – indeed – wonderful – fire, fire,' *Tr.* 50) and the use of the traitorous 'always'. [68]

As the Englishman and the Irishwoman come together in a tenderly orchestrated movement towards union in exogamy, they adopt signals, meaningless but not inappropriate, in order to avoid the failure of meaning, but which convey ideas of which they themselves are not capable. They are limited by the same difficulties as Frank Butler ('he wants to smother her, wash her in words of love, but he can't, because he has no fluency in love words', *LQ* 64). And in recompense for the appropriation of the place-names George offers Maire the topography of his own world – a mental map of an imaginary world, an otherness ('Aren't they odd names? Sure they make no sense to me at all', *Tr.* 60) which replaces the invaded ground in her secret memory ('strange sounds...nice sounds, like Jimmy Jack reciting his Homer', *Tr.* 60).

So we see a further turn in the language-play, as meaning is twisted for the purpose of betrayal. In his role as Roland, Owen

deliberately mis-translates the explanation of the map-making exercise (*Tr.* 31–2); it is significant that Manus, *but not Hugh*, draws
attention to this. Owen's version is a sub-version of the militaristic
intention. He is, in fact, the instrument of his own tribe's destruction,
working through the medium of linguistic distortion.

The disposal of Yolland is not merely the dramatist's inevitable
response to the situation he creates in the love scene. In the symbolic
metaphorical embrace of Owen and Yolland in Act 2 Friel replicates
the welcome dreamed of by all those who fear and yet desire their
own destruction – a gnostic death-wish to embrace my-brother-
my-executioner. Moreover, Yolland rushes to meet this fate: his exit
with Maire from the dance is a 'sudden and impetuous escape' (*Tr.*
49) and their leap into the dark makes him, like Meg in *Lovers*, a
winner, whereas Maire is repossessed by the tribe, a relict of
ecstasy. So, in addition to Hugh's masterly surrender to fate, power
in quiescence, a tragedy without heroism, we have Yolland's paradoxical renunciation of life and love.

In the figure of Hugh O'Donnell, however, Friel has drawn his
most convincing and impressive character to date. Although, following Dowling's caricature of the typical hedge-schoolmaster, he
espouses the dead and dying tongues, he possesses, and can use, the
inner strength to resolve their crises. He admits the situation, and
while for himself he prefers to favour a detumescent culture, he is
willing to aid – he bestows his will upon – those frightened children
like Maire who need to learn a new song, in order to recapture faith.

It is Yolland, the usurper of this Eden, who notices this. While
Owen taunts his father – 'will you be able to find your way?' –
Yolland quietly states: 'He knows what's happening' (*Tr.* 43). And
Hugh confirms it by accepting the need for new place-names, for a
new way of seeing the familiar. Here once again Friel has borrowed
from his O'Neill project, by giving the schoolmaster some of the
stature of the Earl. As O'Faolain tells us, 'it is because he did
understand what was at stake that he was of such size in his own
day and of such interest in ours'. Later, describing O'Neill's
recognition of impending catastrophe, O' Faolain says 'the decisions
of such a man are real decisions where every hesitation is to be
honoured for its courage and humanity in that it springs from a
profound knowledge of the consequences of the final choice'. [69]
To give, as O'Faolain's O'Neill and Friel's O'Donnell, 'a speech
that it could understand and which made it realize itself
intelligently', [70] is both a form of salvation and an act of trreachery.

Hugh, from a position of historic but wavering strength, that of crepuscular myth, also rewrites the local past, by admitting that he and Jimmy Jack never went to Sligo in 1798, but, fortified by drink, retreated to repossess those familiars whom in their heroism they had deserted. He realises that he is one of a dying race, because 'ancient time is at an end', and yet when he says '*we* must learn where we live, we must make there our new home' he speaks for his people but not for himself: he intends to fossilise. In his line 'Yes, I will teach you English, Maire Chatach' there is an operatic quality because, as he moves towards the stairs and ascends from the room he has been regarding 'as if he were about to leave it forever' (*Tr.* 62), he begins to sing the threnody of his own life. Hugh is the complete realist, because he *knows* what is happening. He makes the final statement: 'I will provide you with the available words and the available grammar. But will that help you to interpret between privacies? I have no idea. But it's all we have...As for "always" – it's a silly word, girl' (*Tr.* 67).

In Hugh the drunken schoolmaster father is repatriated, restored to dignity. The way Manus nurses him is indicative of this restoration. Friel, having come to terms with the artist's responsibilities, perfidies, inherent anarchy, finds a way of rehabilitating the figure who has been most defiled and assaulted, the patrician, the father of the aristocrats. Through the necessary conceit of the Latin tongue he salutes him as 'Dominus'. In the conjunction of Owen and Hugh, Friel finds himself. From the silent S.B. O'Donnell, to the eloquent Hugh Mor O'Donnell, via the stricken Judge O'Donnell of *Aristocrats* is a strange odyssey, but a homecoming nonetheless.

Translations closes with a triologue which repays close attention: Maire says 'When he comes back, this is where he'll come to. He told me this is where he was happiest' (*Tr.* 68). George in a new epiphany will revisit his new home, he will redeem the waiting girl, who represents that which made him most happy, but least fortunate. Jimmy pronounces on the difficulties of becoming a god. And Hugh's threnody, uttered in confusion and forgetfulness, looks back at an uprising, a search for civil rights, for freedom against the ancient city. As he speaks, the lights come down, and, in his own version of Ovid, 'evening comes with its sacred song'. [71]

TRAVESTIES

Even in its baroque appeal to language, *Faith Healer* is a play against language.The language of *Translations* by comparison is lean and spare. Friel uses every word to advantage. He does the same in *The Communication Cord*, the play in which he stands the world on its head to examine it through the spectacles of farce. He took this step for two reasons: to allow himself the freedom of speaking openly and in the vulgate which he had been denying himself in his earlier work; and, with a flood of words, to free his work from the tightness of *Translations* and from the trap of sentimentality; from the danger of being treated as consecrated testament. [72]

In 1980 Friel had written a short parody of the language difficulties in *Translations*, in a playlet entitled *American Welcome*, requested by the Actors' Theater in Louisville, Kentucky. A European play-wright arrives in America for the production of one of his plays. He is told by the American director that a revision of the play has been commissioned from an American writer due to language difficulties: 'there is a lot of it we don't understand...simply a question of our ignorance of your usage'. The American adaptor 'took all those little confusing words – 5 or 6 thousand approximately – and with wonderful delicacy and skill and *with the utmost respect for the rhythm and tones of your speech* he did this most beautiful job of *translating the play into the language and speech we understand.*' [73] Furthermore the monologal form of the original (which in fact caused *Faith Healer* to flop in New York) is recast because Americans 'talk, we exchange, we communicate'. The irony in Friel's wry humour is that it is impossible to 'translate' from one 'language' to another in the same tongue without completely changing the 'rhythm and tones', the cadences and inflections, of the original, and the meaning which lies between the words them-selves – as anyone knows who compares English common speech with Hiberno-English or English short stories with Irish short stories.

Kearney points out that, like Synge's Christy Mahon, Friel persuades 'by the power of a lie' – asking his audience to make his fiction true. [74] That skill, a word-play that conjures with aural images like an illusionist, is pushed even further in *The Communica-tion Cord*, since Friel uses the farce to highlight the absurdities of the action while continuing to show us a catalogue of mistaken identities, misunderstandings and opposing value systems, all based on a clearly presented semantic theory ('Discourse Analysis', *CC* 18) which summarises and underlines, in a light-hearted way, many of the subtleties and implicit notions of its forerunner. Friel wishes the two plays to be read/seen in tandem.[75] *The Communication Cord* is the mirror image of *Translations*, the key to the author's serious intentions, and thereby qualifying itself as one of the most purposeful and effective applications of farce.

Furthermore, lifting some of the conventional limitations of his accustomed genre, Friel is able to allow his characters more anarchy and more space even though the situations he contrives for them are more tightly constructed. So much so that the characters spill over into one another, their identities merge because, due to their lack of common code, they fail to discriminate adequately between what each of them says and does not say and between who says what. Where, in *Translations*, words control the experience of life, in *The Communication Cord* 'life' controls words. But does language have a life of its own? Things fall apart (they literally do at the end of the play); disused agrarian utensils suddenly spring to life; and the fine balance of interpretation on which we depend for the connection between language and meaning is continually upset. In its mockery of the furniture of the cottage, and in the way its inhabitants are trying to erect a tradition upon them, it is also a parody of *Aristocrats*. The time direction also changes in both these plays: whereas previously those who looked into the future were uncertain but articulate about their doubts, the futurists are now in love and unable to communicate; the retrospectives are those with a coherent but incorrect view of where they have come from.

In *The Communication Cord* there is no attempt to summarise past work or to introduce new concepts. Friel indulges in a phenomenal send-up of the ideas which make *Translations* such a valuable play. This involves him in a great deal of simplification; whereas for example the traducer or agent of death has been in a position of trust, ritualised by the community (the revenant son, the faith healer, the pastoral father or *dominus*) here no one trusts him, except the prissy Susan (*CC* 67–8):

JACK: Just trust me Timothy, will you?
TIM: When someone says that to you, you know you're being betrayed (*CC* 20)

CLAIRE: Trust you? I never trusted you!

(*CC* 28)

The parody of *Translations* begins with the opening stage directions, indicating that the barn of the hedge-school has been refurbished as a country cottage ('three wooden posts complete with chains where cows were chained during milking', CC 11); a travesty of history, a mythological present, a syntax opulent with *yesterdays*, within which it is quite natural that absurd things should happen. It turns on its head the relation between thinking and experience. In Steiner's words 'analogies, metaphors and emblems are the threads by which the mind holds on to the world even when, absentmindedly, it has lost direct contact with it, and they guarantee the unity of human experience'. [76] But, as in *Aristocrats*, this simply does not happen. All the metaphors seized on by the players in *The Communication Cord* fail to unite experience with thought, and in fact plunge them into deeper communicational difficulties. It is indicative that the only refugees from Friel's earlier work are Senator Donovan and his prissy daughter Susan, who re-enact Senator Doogan and Katie from *Philadelphia*.

Jack invariably refers to this travesty as 'our first cathedral': 'this shaped our souls. This determined our first pieties. Yes. Have reverence for this place' (*CC* 15). Immediately 'piety', 'soul', 'reverence' become signals not of the deep structures of culture but of doggerel: the fucate travesty, 'an artefact of today making obeisance to a home of yesterday' (*CC* 11). We see the museum of pastoral as a product of an imagination 'imprisoned in a contour which no longer matches the landscape of fact' (*Tr.* 43). Nora Dan is 'the quintessential noble peasant obsessed with curiosity and greed and envy' (*CC* 21): Tim salutes her as 'Mrs Dan', the same error which Lancey makes about 'Mr Doalty' (*Tr.* 63) and thus the series of mistaken identities begins: 'the queer way we have of naming people about here' (*CC* 22); Barney the Banks: 'but sure, that wouldn't be his real name at all' (*CC* 23); Nora Dan becomes 'Nora the Scrambler' – but of eggs or motor cycles?; Barney the Banks, because he lives on the edge of the river or because he is very rich? Jack the Cod – a fisherman: 'call a man Jack the Cod and you tell me his name and his profession, and that he's not very good at his profession. Concise, accurate and nicely malicious' (*CC* 42). Claire becomes Evette:

SUSAN: She has hardly any English.
JACK: She was born and bred in Omagh.
SUSAN: Her name is Evette.

JACK: Her name is Claire Harkin.
SUSAN: She's married to a German.
JACK: She's single

(CC 66)

Translations run amok: 'My name is Willie. In English that is Barney...just a little bit gallagher'(CC 76, 51). Nicknames are demolished: 'His name isn't Teddy, it's Patrick Mary Pious' (CC 74), or created: Tim becomes 'Tim the Thesis' (CC 84). With the arrival of Senator Donovan the already devalued culture of Ballybeg receives a rude shove in the direction of sacrilege:

This silence, this peace, the restorative power of that landscape ...Despite the market place...a small voice within me still knows the responses...This transcends all those... hucksterings. This is the touchstone...this is the apotheosis...the absolute verity.

(CC 31)

Later he debases the idea still further, assisted by the half-witted schemer Nora Dan:

DONOVAN: Renewal Nora, Restoration. Fulfilment, back to the true centre.
NORA: The true centre surely.

(CC 43)

Tim falls into Nora's Synge-song:

DONOVAN: That is where we kneel to pray. That's where we gather at night to tell our folk tales and our ancient sagas. Correct Tim?
TIM: Our ancient sagas surely, Doctor.

(CC 55)

Eventually the pretence and the myth are abandoned, exploded in Donovan's outburst, 'This is our native simplicity! Don't give me that shit!' (CC 70). Friel has already indulged in one send-up of this attitude in *The Gentle Island*: 'I envy you, Manus, the sea, the land, fishing, turf-cutting, milking, a house built by your great-grandfather, two strong sons to succeed you – everything's so damned constant. You're part of a permanence. You're a fortunate man' (GI 53).

Tim's 'Discourse Analysis' contains the kernel of the

communication theory on which Friel builds a sense of community. Here, however, it can be played for laughs:

> Words, language. An agreed code. I encode my message, I transmit it to you; you receive the message and decode it. If the message sent is clear and distinct, if the code is fully shared and subscribed to, if the message is comprehensively received, then there is a reasonable chance – one, that you will understand what I am trying to tell you – and two, that we will have established the beginnings of a dialogue. All social behaviour, the entire social order, depends on our communicational structures, on words mutually agreed on, and mutually understood. Without that agreement, without that shared code, you have chaos... An extreme example: I speak only English; you speak only German; no common communicational structure. The result? Chaos.
>
> (CC 18–19)

There is, however, a serious side to this also: it is only the circumstance of farce that dictates that it should be delivered in a humorous tone. As a commentary spoken by an extraneous 'expert' it would fall nicely into place in *Translations* itself. As Laing says in *The Politics of Experience*:

> Two people sit talking. The one (Peter) is making a point to the other (Paul). He puts his point of view in different ways to Paul for some time, but Paul does not understand. ...The dissociation of each from his phantasy, and the phantasy of the other, betokens the lack of relationship of each to himself and to each other. They are both more or less related to each other 'in phantasy' than each pretends to be to himself and the other. [77]

The process by which private 'phantasy' becomes public reality is an arduous political and cultural struggle; that language is at its centre is the single fact that places on us, as differentiated from the other animals, the twin burdens of tragedy and comedy. The seriousness of Friel's apparent farce is further underlined by the fact that he has employed the example of Erving Goffman's *Forms of Talk* which engages in 'dialogic analysis', [78] but which also explores the idea of 'footing', which Goffman calls 'the dance in talk', [79] something which Friel makes anatomical in the staging of *The Communication Cord*. [80] In the light of this intellectual involvement with the use of words, and the way words use us, which is one of the chief considerations of *Making History*, it is easy to see why Friel wants us to regard *Translations* and *The Communication Cord* as twins, each feeding off the other's dramatic form to impress on us the atrocious dangers of communication of any kind.

So the latter is not simply a farce on the serious theme of 'discourse failure' but an underlining of the lesson of the former, that a whole culture can lose its command over the encoding and decoding of its messages, its commerce with the civilised and barbaric worlds. And within this there is the artist's dilemma, an attempt to find both sense and justice in the situation. The chaos which Friel creates, or allows his characters to indulge in, proceeds directly from the lack of 'communicational structure' – although this is a farce, although it is quite clearly a 'language play' in the same sense as *Translations*, we are nevertheless encouraged to be healthily sceptical of our previous concern for etymologies, our 'means of finding our bearings' (compare the opening of Act Two of *The Communication Cord* with Owen's 'Will you be able to find your way?') and our particular 'condition of madness', travestied in Claire/Evette's 'I understand perfectly' (*CC* 33). And we see some things more clearly than they are shown in *Translations*: for example the idea of the *omphalos,* the centre of cultural gravity. Donovan says 'You're right Tim, absolutely right. This is the true centre' (*CC*. 46), of which Tim observes:

> An interesting discourse phenomenon that. Called statement transference. I never used the phrase 'This is the true centre' but by imputing the phrase to me, as the Doctor has just done, he both seeks confirmation of his own sentiments and suggests to listeners outside the duologue that he and I are unanimous in that sentiment.
>
> (*CC* 46)

We might call 'statement transference' a form of wishful thinking. It creates currency for an idea which was originally worthless or spurious and implicates members of the community in a common bond of cultural affiliation to that idea which in itself validates it; one *can* thus repossess that which in fact one never possessed, whether it be called 'dignity', 'freedom' or 'control of the means of production'. Friel thus safely exposes us to the dangers of subverting not only culture but the means of culture – perception, thinking and willing.

The successful formula for this type of exercise is the same as that employed in tragedy: pretence. Pretence as a fictional process runs parallel to history. This cottage is in fact no one's home. The falsity of the spectacle reinforces the inherent falsity of the thing portrayed. No one's culture is being debased because this is no one's 'true centre' – no one actually claims it. I have already used the metaphor of the stage-as-mental-hospital. Here we see the cottage farcically employed as the stage-as-French-hotel; the bedroom capers of that genre help to persuade us, by encapsulating the extra-marital misdemeanours of the bourgeoisie, that mutual deception by husbands and wives is justified because it bestows its own rewards and penalties and thus polices its own morality. In the case of *The Communication Cord* the capers are, as in Alan Ayckbourn's *Taking Steps*, purely directional, rather than occupational, hazards. At the climax of *The Communication Cord* Claire and Tim, like Maire and Yolland, move towards one another talking lovers' nonsense, and realising that the words they are actually uttering have nothing to do with their intentions. Absurdity reinforces the truth of that which is absurd. But they serve the same purpose – to show us how easy it is to mistake our invented culture for a re-invented one. Manus Sweeney tries to do this in *The Gentle Island*; the inmates of 'Eden House' achieve it in some measure in *Cass*; the family in *Living Quarters* rejects it; and in *Aristocrats* they signally fail to find it. In *Translations* we have seen how, through a combination of human and temporal betrayal and obsolescence, a culture may make the journey into the 'dark places of the soul' and begin again to flourish. In this farce, Friel also shows us that chaos can be resolved not by language but by silence.

Part III
POLITICS

6

A FIELD DAY

Words – they're all we've got to go on.

Tom Stoppard [1]

I'm sick and tired of words, words, words...this madness.

Brian Friel [2]

A FICTION IN SEARCH OF BELIEF

The transactions between oneself and the rest of the world, particularly when they are fraught with the burdens of 'community', 'loyalty', faith', are, on the tragi-comic stage which writers like Beckett, Friel and Murphy have been making in the past thirty years, potentially lethal. The problem of artist-as-gunman is as evident in Friel's *Faith Healer* as it is in anything by O'Casey. And at the same time the faith healer, like Hugh O'Neill, is also a Prince – as O'Faolain calls the latter, 'a man of terrific arrogance and terrific ambition'. [3] Divided loyalties explain only part of the dichotomy: we must also look at tragedy as simply the business of living, as a search for ways of tolerating the waiting-room-for-death.

In Friel's *Three Sisters* a man touches his mirror-reflection with his finger-tip: 'Maybe you're the reality. Why not? Maybe this [body] is the image...I wish you [reflection] were the reality, my friend. I wish — oh God, how I wish this [body] didn't exist.' He breaks down and exclaims 'What the hell do I care?...Oh, you are magnificent' (*Sisters* 73). 'This' is Chebutykin, a doctor whose patients die, who assumes social graces which he neither merits nor possesses, who kills his self-esteem. Such failure is 'magnificent'. As another character, Vershinin, says, 'We Russians are a people whose aspirations are magnificent; it is just living we can't handle' (*Sisters* 43).

187

43). The similarities between Irish and Russian society in the nineteenth century have fascinated both Friel and Thomas Kilroy, whose complete translation of *The Seagull* into Irish was produced in the same year (1981).

Kilroy's introduction to the programme for Friel's *Three Sisters* discusses Chekhov's generosity as a writer: 'there are no heroes in Chekhov because he understood how the process of history diminishes even the most Napoleonic ego'; instead, we see a playwright concerned with 'inconsequentiality...ordinary helplessness...who accepted completely that he was himself subject to the same life as that of his creations'. In suggesting that 'at this stage of our century this single fact may appear revolutionary', Kilroy is expressing much of the difficulty encountered by contemporary critics in assessing Friel.

In the course of the preceding chapter Friel the diviner has been usurped by Friel the deceiver. This is (at least in part) due to the weight of critical opinion. Synge, for example, also divined the condition of the Irish psyche and altered conventional form and content to express that condition, and the invention of Synge as a manipulator of truth/untruth has tended to obscure his original divination.

The Irish mind which has been present throughout this book is ambivalent because its sources and its means of expression are bifurcated. This ambivalence is present both in its vision and its use of a tongue which is not its natural form and which it adulterates with its strange inflections and intonations. Friel has explored this psychology with subtlety and compassion. But at times he runs the risk not so much of confusing form and content, or of failing to expose its disorder, as he does of falling a victim to the ambivalence itself, of opening himself to too many possibilities and insufficiently disciplining the squads of perception. This in turn may result in an indefinite approach to truth/untruth. D.E.S. Maxwell suggests that 'what might be or might have been, is being asked...to relieve, to displace, facts which have become intolerable' [4], that is, that Friel is sometimes in danger of creating his own *aisling* as a substitute for the fact which he regards as tyrranous or impossible. But even in 'uncertainties...' we need to be presented with a disciplined schedule of options, a certainty *about* uncertainty.

In the case of Friel we have to decide whether or not resolution matters: for example, whether the conclusion to *Translations* successfully resolves the central dilemma of cultural decline. Since Friel has resolved the problems of affiliation, those of dramatic form become less significant. He is now moving towards a new kind of resolution, that of a philosophic *regard sur le monde politique* (the judas-hole again) [5] in which he can also send his audiences home with their sensibilities nicely restored to equanimity. This would be a theatre in which the Irish mind would be engaged, as it has been at certain anatonic moments [6] in his previous plays, in issues of volition; where it has up to now been the psychiatric patient, it may be required to ply its own steel. In doing this Friel would be abandoning the characteristic generosity which he shares with Chekhov.

If there is any actual validity in the idea of the 'both/and' of the homeless mind, it is in its activity, its willed life, in its function as the membrane between the two worlds which exclude it but which depend on it for their mutual translations. And gradually this mind takes on its own temporal dimension, the life of the mind, an intellectual tradition, able to hold in the balance the opposing tensions which would otherwise demand a choice of either/or.

It seems as if Friel wants to use this mind, that he feels there *is* now drama in the situation, that the artist has a duty to take over from the politician in certain aspects of governing (*gubernator*, the helmsman) social directions. Friel has consistently argued for the role of the artist in shaping not only cultural but political perceptions and in this sense helping to 'govern' society. In 1972 he said 'we are obsessed with ourselves and cannot see ourselves in a global context. One of our great misconceptions is that Ireland can be ruled only by its government and that the best government is composed of businessmen. This is a fallacy. I see no reason why Ireland should not be ruled by its poets and dramatists' [7] – an opportunity which he had the opportunity of exercising during his membership of the Senate of the Republic from his appointment in April 1987 until July 1989.

Friel is, of course, involved in political theatre in the sense that that he has been signalling the collapse of the public world, whether through corruption (*The Mundy Scheme*), indignity and dispossession (*The Freedom*) or entropy (*Translations*). Effectively he is still asking the question posed in *The Mundy Scheme* in 1969: 'What happens to an emerging country after it has emerged?', but the issues have now become much broader and more pervasive because in the meantime Friel has begun to divine those levels of the Irish psyche which are much deeper than the questions about 'love' which he had previously been able to ask. And this is pre-eminently political theatre in the sense that Heaney says 'the imagined place is what politics is all about. Politicians deal in images' [8]. In the Irish context the inference is obvious: republican nationalism outside Northern Ireland 'imagines' the repossession of its fourth, lost field; inside the Six Counties the implications are far more complex. But for the writer himself the paradox lies not so much in the tantalus of the inaccessible as in the power lessness of the word as an idea: the easy propagation (and manipulation) of freedom *as a concept* which cannot be reconciled with freedom *as exercised*. This too is a political impasse.

Friel thinks that he can offer an alternative to this. The 'public address' is the 'technique of the preacher and the politician...through the collective mind' [9] and the purpose of looking at man 'in the here-and-now-world' is to 'help make a community of individuals'. But since 1968, when he said this, the events in his own community have intensified that view and given it a specific focus. In theatre it resulted in *The Freedom of the City*, a play which, two years earlier, had been inconceivable to Friel. In 1972 he wrote:

> The future of Irish drama...must depend on the slow develop-
> ment of the Irish mind, and it will shape and be shaped by
> political events...The revolt in Northern Ireland is going to
> spread to the Republic; and if you believe that art is an
> instrument of the revolutionary process, then you can look
> forward to a spate of committed plays. I do not believe that
> art is a servant to any movement. But during the period of
> unrest I can foresee that allegiances that have bound the Irish
> imagination – loyalty to the most authoritarian church in the
> world and devotion to a romantic ideal we call Kathleen – will
> be radically altered. Faith and Fatherland, new definitions will
> be forged, and then new loyalties and then new social
> groupings. It will be a bloody process. And when it has
> subsided, the Irish imagination – that vivid, slovenly, anarchic,
> petulant alert to the eternal, impatient with the here and now
> instrument – will have to set about shaping and interpreting
> the new structures in art forms. [10]

In doing so Friel wished to re-establish the position occupied by Synge and O'Casey from which, he asserts, they *were* able to shape society. He has not retreated from his earnest position; he in fact believes more strongly today that the artist can help, if he cannot achieve it entirely himself, to build communities. In 1980 he said that perhaps it was *only* in the artistic province that the new voice could be found: 'perhaps this is an artist's arrogance, but I feel that once the voice is found in literature then it can move out and become part of the common currency' [11]. We might have assumed that Friel would contribute to the common currency by speaking in Seanad Eireann on artistic affairs, although he disavowed any intention of participating (other than voting) in political matters [12] – yet in the outcome he almost ostentatiously allowed the opportunities to pass.

The political role of theatre in Ireland has been intimately connected with cultural renaissance. Thus, the political implications of the founding of the Irish Literary Theatre (1899), National Theatre (1904) and Ulster Literary Theatre (1904) are clear, as was the advent of Synge in the first decade of the century. The coincidence in 1929 of two expressionist dramas, O'Casey's *The Silver Tassie* and Denis Johnston's *The Old Lady Says 'No!'*, underlines this. But until the 1970s there were no similar milestones.

It was the 'conflagration' in Northern Ireland which disturbed an otherwise complacent Irish theatre, and then, as we have seen, only fitfully. The attempt, as expressed in the manifesto of the fledgling National Theatre, to portray 'the deeper thoughts and emotions of Ireland' was not sustained, and even in Friel's own divination we can see that there is an added ferocity and sense of urgency after 1972 which, with the exception of *Philadelphia*, was almost entirely implicit and subliminal in the earlier 'love' plays.

In order to promote more explicitly some of his 'political' ideas, Friel participated in the formation, in 1980, of the Derry-based theatre company and publishing house, Field Day. Up to the end of 1988 it had produced, in addition to *Translations*, *The Communication Cord*, *Three Sisters* and *Making History*, adaptations of *Antigone* (Tom Paulin's *The Riot Act*) [13] and *The School for Husbands* (Derek Mahon's *High Time* [14]) Fugard's *Boesman and Lena*, and three new commissions, *Double Cross* by Thomas Kilroy [15], *Pentecost* by Stewart Parker, [16] and *Saint Oscar* by Terry Eagleton. [17] It has published Heaney's version of the Sweeney epic *Sweeney Astray*, [18] twelve pamphlets on aspects of nationalism, language and the relationship of Ireland, England and the various cultures co-existing within Irish society [19] and an anthology of Irish literature. [20]

This venture is in part a response to the need for an Ulster theatre, which Friel (and before him Tyrone Guthrie) has strenuously advocated, and in part a method of ensuring the closest possible collaboration between the 'writer's theatre' and the 'director's theatre' – an elimination of the divergence evident in Ireland since the inception of the drama renaissance. (Molière, Ibsen, Chekhov and Pirandello similarly collaborated in the formation of such companies.) Friel, much earlier than 1980, acknowledged that 'I have never seen myself writing for any particular theatre group, or any particular actor or director,' [21] but he would undoubtedly disown this now, since it is an underlying assumption that Field Day Theatre Company will give the premieres of his plays and that he will be involved in their production. It is therefore pertinent to consider Field Day as an extension of Friel's interests. It is a 'coterie' in the sense that its members – Friel, Heaney, Deane, with the actor Stephen Rea, the poet and academic Tom Paulin, and the musicologist and folklorist David Hammond, joined in 1988 by Tom Kilroy – are well-known and loyal to each other, and committed to altering the political perceptions current in Northern Ireland by working through the dramatic dimension.

It is highly significant that, while all the directors with the exception of Kilroy are northerners, three are Catholics from Derry and three are Protestants from other parts of Northern Ireland. This fact may often be overlooked by those critics who tend to see Field Day's activities as predominantly Catholic and partisan propaganda. Field Day's self-definition is: 'A day on which troops are drawn up for exercise in field evolution; a military review; a day occupied with brilliant or exciting events; a day spent in the field e.g. by the hunt, or by field naturalists.' [22] *Translations* was therefore a fitting first production.

In explicating this definition Seamus Deane says that 'Field Day is a sense of risk', that it pursues the people 'not for their sake but for its own'. [23] More recently he has said that Field Day's 'theme' or 'obsession' was 'the analysis of, a lament for, the fact that the failure of various forms of authority has long-term social effects'. [24] In this sense, once again, we can see how plays like *The Freedom* and *Volunteers* are much more than a straightforward representation of specific acts of political or social violence: they are 'a method of replying to...inevitabilities' and, to invoke Kinsella once more, a way of locating 'the poetry...in the response'.

In this we can also detect Friel's further purpose in highlighting the inherent right of the artist to selfishness, or to put it in Deane's political terms 'a double secession – from the North and from the Republic'. Field Day is, Deane asserts, 'like the Abbey in origin in that it has within it the idea of a culture which has not yet come to be in political terms. It is unlike the Abbey in that it can no longer subscribe to a single nationalism as the basis for its existence.' [25] The concept of a 'fifth province' (discussed earlier), a zone removed, or seceded, from time and place, is particularly apt here (although, while it has been used in its self-description by Field Day, it was first announced as a metaphysical device by the editors of *The Crane Bag* in 1976). It is worth comparing this with the intentions of the founders of the Moscow Art Theatre which set out, overtly, to achieve a certain social and artistic objective, largely through the work of a single playwright, Chekhov. As Nemirovich-Danchenko noted, its objectives were

> to free the theatre from the fossilised layers of stage conventions and literary clichés. To bring back to the stage living psychology and colloquial speech.To look at life not only from the top of its towering peaks or from the bottom of its sheer precipices, but also from the flat places of every day life that surround it. To look for the dramatic quality of plays not in the stage effects which have delivered the theatre for many years into the hands of a special kind of stage expert and driven all vital literary forces away from it, but in the hidden, inner psychological movement. [26]

It is therefore possible that a new political culture is in the making – we have seen the materials brought on site and in these terms Field Day is already creating a climax for the discussion of 'complex nationalism': its pamphlets especially address this question. In *Translations* (as also with *Making History*), as Deane asserts, Field Day also becomes 'a force involved with history', and its audience becomes involved with the theatre it witnesses. Another of the directors, Stephen Rea, has said 'people accuse us of being too intellectual. And perhaps we are making some kind of pretentious attempt to justify what we do', [27] i.e., to move away from the worst aspects of populism and elitism in contemporary theatre, to set free 'a congealed idea of theatre'. The company has been accused of 'semi-mystical formulations of their own meaning' [28] which may do more harm than good for the concept of intellectual theatre, and James Simmons's critique of 'Brian Friel: A Catholic Playwright' is more an attack on Deane as spokesman for Field Day than a balanced assessment of Friel's playwriting career. I don't want to play with words unduly but the word *pretentious* expresses the essence of the company's purpose. Just as Synge conceived the need for a new form as well as new content in Irish theatre – and found an answer which embraced naturalism with intellect – so Field Day has, in its self-conscious way, found an answer to the identity problem in Irish society. 'The power of a lie' is, in Friel's terms, a *pretence*, a fiction of theatre, which persuades his audience of a certain truth which they themselves can act out in their lives. There is, however, another side to Field Day's collective problems – that of the solitary artist. Friel himself must also continue to be regarded not only as the leading director of this company, but, principally, as a sole playwright. It could be catastrophic (to invoke Hannah Arendt again) for Friel to attempt a homecoming which identifies the author of *Translations* as the ship's captain of Field Day and it is perhaps typical that one of the most significant developments in his recent drama, *Fathers and Sons*, has taken place altogether outside Ireland, as a result of a commission from the National Theatre in Britain.

For every excursion from the psyche (*ekstasis*) there must be a return to, and occupation of, the psyche (*entasis*). The 'sense of risk' for Friel himself is that, while on an ideological manoeuvre for Field Day, Friel the private dramatist might be stranded by developments on the political plane. As Deane says:

> if Field Day can breed a new fiction of theatre...which is sufficiently successful to be believed in as though it were natural and an outgrowth of the past, then it will have succeeded. At the moment [1982] it is six characters in search of a story that can be believed. [29]

In these terms the 'pretence' is like the *aisling* of the dispossessed, a belief in search of tradition, and in that lies the 'danger'. This quest for public credibility of an already established inner meaning is of course extremely dangerous, in the sense established by Kilroy's use of the term. Cultural nationalism will always be tendentious simply because, unlike Eden, words and things do not naturally coincide; belief and meaning are forced apart and their respective loyalties create sectarianism. In an interesting discussion of cultural nationalism as 'Homecomings and Diversions' Colm Kelly combines the imperative of naming with that of homecoming in the cases of both *Translations* and *Faith Healer* (*Bailegangaire* would be another obvious example). Kelly argues that 'the cultural nationalism represented by Friel and others is involved in a contradiction'.

While national integration is acknowledged to be a dream, the idea of harmonious discourse perpetuates that dream by denying the likelihood of that discourse ever resulting in a homecoming: 'the new cultural nationalists retain a teleological conception of understanding as agreement and union towards which dialogue must lead'. [30]

In so far as Friel can be said to 'represent' anything at all – and here his own choice of the term 'constituency' must stick – it is an intellectual and didactic tradition, that of the schoolteacher and 'spoiled priest' who has to find other, different satisfactions in pursuit of private and public visions. It is a 'constituency' in which Field Day's activities and those of the *Crane Bag* journal (1976–85) to a considerable extent coalesce and overlap. [31] But there is also Friel's point, quoted by Kelly, that home is a destination to be pursued but never finally reached. Just as in *Bailegangaire* Mommo eventually completes the tale of homecoming and reaches base truth, so Hugh O'Donnell and his son Owen achieve some success in their liminality. But it is always time for a new departure. Hugh's other son, Manus, is simultaneously leaving home; in *Fathers and Sons* another revenant comes home to die; in *Making History* Friel begins a new cycle by starting up once again the themes of exile, frustration, remorse and misunderstanding.

In a sense Field Day's 'mission' is to produce problem plays, of which there are three types: those that present problems to the audience, those that present problems to their author, and those that are problems in themselves as plays (I am of course using the term as discussed earlier in chapter 3). The play which falls into all these categories is quite clearly *Faith Healer*, precisely because it is the most *dangerous* in its atrocity. Because Friel always puts himself at risk in the relationship of form and content, his inventiveness itself becomes problematic. Like Chekhov, Friel has contented himself with locating his treasures in the everyday; the problems he encounters there, particularly when his public expects him to address 'great' themes, are no less elemental because they are 'ordinary'. *Philadelphia*'s success is due to a considerable extent to the device by which Friel solved the problem of portraying the 'invisible' alter ego, but because of that device it remains a problem play in itself. The Eliotic device in *The Loves of Cass McGuire* likewise constitutes an artificiality with which the audience may have little faith. Those plays which have been most problematic for the author, and which seem in theory to present the greatest difficulties in production, are in fact those which are most successful and effective in performance – *Living Quarters, Aristocrats* and *Translations* – particularly the last, where the 'device' of simultaneous language proves, despite its ostensible dangers, to carry the play to acclaim.

In this sense Friel's (and Field Day's) work represents a *bildungs-drama*, a celebration of the achievement of certain types of freedom, as there is a tradition of a sense of development, of growing towards wholeness, of the exercise of will, of increasing strength and maturity, which necessarily contains an awareness of struggle. In Ireland, both north and south, drama, as we have already noted, has yet to move, in Friel's terms, towards a possession of the English language, and, with it, to a knowledge of its own powers. Ironically English drama, built upon certainties, is today meeting the same challenges of the failure of language, of a search for words to satisfy a condition of wordlessness. The two experiences, however, are separated by differences in perception and realities: one working from the starting point of poverty which ironically provides it with a certain security or rootedness of its own, the other from a position of wealth which has found its security shattered by the implosion of its own strength, the collapse of empire. Much of this irony is written into the bond tentatively established between Owen and Yolland in *Translations*.

The versions of *Three Sisters* and *Fathers and Sons*, however, seem to present none of these problems. As I have suggested, Friel has been able – no doubt with a certain degree of self-indulgence – to step back from the problem of contemporary society to examine the way in which a previous master of the craft treated the 'great' themes of life through the idiosyncratic. His translation into modern speech 'adequate to our predicament' (which has been skilfully analysed by Ulf Dantanus [32]) is, however, unlike Kilroy's translation of *The Seagull*. Where Friel translates the words, Kilroy translates the setting and context of the characters (and of course their 'proper names') into Ireland. But where Kilroy is largely transposing ambience and manners, Friel is attempting an equation of mind and roots: 'I never considered setting *Three Sisters* in Ireland. My first purpose in translating the text was to make the full experience of the play more available to Irish audiences – to offer them the text in Irish-English, a text they have known only in English-English or American-English'. [33]

The everyday parable of childhood has already been introduced in *Living Quarters*: 'God bless Mammy and make her healthy again. God bless Daddy and have him transferred to Dublin' (*LQ* 20). The Chekhovian 'Moscow' is overwhelmed, however, in *Living Quarters* because the characters are set an impossible puzzle by their creator: to find 'some tiny forgotten detail buried here' in the Ledger; the 'if only' of achieving a future is inverted into a retrospective hopelessness – 'if only it would be found and recalled' (*LQ* 9). So that 'what might have been' can be translated into 'what might be'. The problem posed by *Living Quarters* typifies Friel's dilemma as a playwright: is a play 'a feast laid out for consumption or a trap waiting to spring' (*LQ* 9)?

Because Friel is not particularly concerned with form, allowing it to find its own way from the content of his plays, he is not especially aware of any 'crisis of form' – nor is he concerned with a 'crisis of language' *as form* , however much he is aware of dealing in a slippery commodity *as content*. But he is aware obliquely of the call for a theatre of language, one which sets more emphasis on the non-verbal *appearance* of things, perhaps alluding more strenuously to the visual qualities implicit in the Irish words for theatre, *amharclann* and *taibhdhearc*, than to the eloquence with which its authors have addressed their themes. 'Words', says a member of the 'Operatic Theatre' group, 'may even distract from the inner life of the show...they are such a limited way of communicating. They reach an audience only through the intellect. The body and the voice without any words have much more potency on stage.' [34] To follow the non-verbal as a way of expressing the pre-verbal is also of course part of the natural tendency of Beckett's motion towards silence, particularly in his last 'plays for dancers', *Quad 1 & 2*, designed for German television. [35] The contrast between Friel and Tom MacIntyre is also striking: for MacIntyre 'it's past the time for talking' and 'goodbye to the literary discursive as a satisfying mode', preferring 'the language of dance and the best in contemporary film as offering a high voltage idiom that has an instantly recognisable connection with contemporary living, the crisis we are in'. [36]

It can be argued that Friel and Beckett represent very different theatres: in form, yes, but not so much in content, since they are both involved in a search for meaning through language itself and through naming. (Friel particularly admires, and acknowledges a debt to,

Krapp's Last Tape, *Not I* and *Molloy*.) I have already discussed Beckett's Berkeleyan interest in the metaphysical and its importance as a basis for the concept of identity: in *naming* Friel and Beckett both exercise a catechetic influence and control over their characters. [37] There are also significant similarities between *Play* and *Faith Healer*: where one indicates the *esse est percipi* principle by permitting speech only when the face is lit, the other separates the discrete discourses in time. [38] Both rehearse versions of the ego's intricate confessions, and both owe something to the concept of Evreinov's *The Theatre of the Soul* (1915). These two plays underline the fact that their respective authors create languages of the mind, whether it is the perceptional landscape translated into intellectual tradition in the case of Friel's Ballybeg, or a purely conceptual landscape of Beckett's 'Molloy country' centred on a town called 'Bally'. [39] But the most important area in which these two writers operate is one where they cannot – yet – be compared, and in which Beckett made significantly greater advances: that is the relation of form to content and the placing within that area of the language/silence issue.

One is led to the conclusion that silence may be the most effective way of expressing the 'dark and private places' – for just as, in Pater's terms, all art aspires to the condition of music, so may all drama, even voiced drama, tend towards the state of wordlessness, thus marking the 'continuous claim of silence upon the spoken word', a feature noted by Guthrie in Friel's early work. There are indeed points in *Making History* where one feels that Hugh O'Neill's dilemma could be expressed more effectively through either MacIntyre's balletic genre or otherwise a full-blown operatic treatment, so painfully and pitifully does he stumble through the vocabulary of tenderness, rage and morbidity. It is as if we see a man alternately weeping and laughing in silence while offstage his twin brother screams his madness into the night. But Friel is only tactically or psychologically concerned with silence: as in the conclusion to *The Communication Cord* ('saying anything, anything at all, that keeps the occasion going...Maybe even saying nothing. Maybe silence is the perfect discourse' *CC* 86); or in the more pathetic attempt to 'keep the occasion going' against the father's silence in *Philadelphia*. In *Dancing at Lughnasa* he employs the metaphorical dance as a means of bringing onto the stage emotions that cannot be expressed in words – elemental, chthonic madness and gaiety, a hovering, like that of Burke's Dauphiness, above the mundane and its vocabulary – as a potential resolution of the problem of translation. He is still caught in the mould of Irish writing which insists, because English is not its native tongue, in re-writing its adopted, imposed and grafted tongue.

AT HOME AND ABROAD

Where does Friel stand in relation to his contemporaries at home? To place him in the context of contemporary Irish playwriting is in fact to create the context itself. Fintan O'Toole has drawn a severe and incisive picture of theatre in Ireland today which explains this problem: 'contemporary Irish dramatists are the orphans of the Irish Literary Renaissance'; he says that Ireland 'has no genuine theatrical tradition' and that 'to go beyond the dominant nationalism' is 'to construct individual solutions in an often unyielding environment'. [40] There is no common thrust among today's Irish writers but some – Friel, Murphy and Kilroy in particular – seem to have some affinity, both on a personal basis and in their work. Murphy's *The Gigli Concert* (1983) is in the mainstream of the psychological drama I have been discussing, if mainstream there be. It is concerned with *naming* (the man who wants to sing like Gigli will not reveal his identity); with a *dream* ('I want to sing'); with *survival* ('there are too many facts'): and with *condition* ('You do not like what you are' – 'Better than not knowing who or what I am!'). In *The Morning After Optimism* (1971) Murphy also pursues the question of *time* ('What is the Past?...A broken promise'), and *identity* ('I am not me'). [41] Murphy's *The Sanctuary Lamp* (1975) also provides a curious parallel with Friel's work, in the similarity between its affected, disabled trio and that of *Faith Healer*. Meanwhile, Hugh Leonard's *Da* (1973) owes much to *Philadelphia* in its treatment of dialogue between father and son. A younger playwright, Bernard Farrell, also discusses the affects of dignity, appearances and meaning, and the nuances between these and everyday behaviour, in plays such as *I Do Not Like Thee, Doctor Fell* (1979) and *Canaries* (1980). Even more important than this apparent obsession with identity, meaning and ambiguity is the fact that the artist himself seems to be isolated by intelligence: the intellectual, rather than the poet, is marginalised in Irish society because of the political implications of much of his work. Friel himself has, in many ways, been the leader of a generation of playwrights who affiliate to intellectual exercises in other disci-plines, moving away from a violent, bitter and alienated description of their cultural identity towards a more suitable, humane and positive pursuit of identity and purpose. It is as if Friel would say with Gandhi [42] – of the unionists, of the southern nationalists, of the British government, of the terrorists – 'I want to change their minds – I don't want to kill them for weaknesses that are in us all.'

As Friel said in 1972:

> The persistent cry in Ireland at the moment for a more relevant drama...is interesting because it is not a genuine demand for the revelation of a new 'truth' about the country, but for a confirmation of a false assumption. The assumption is that Dublin is a miniature New York, London, Paris, Tokyo, and that it shares with those capitals identical social, economic, moral and cultural problems...But what the critics are not shouting for, and what may well be worth the dramatist's probe, is the deep schizophrenia of that city, because it is there, and only there, that the urban man and the rural man meet and attempt to mingle. [43]

At the same time he was also writing more explicitly:

> How difficult it is for an Irish writer to find his faith. He is born into a certainty that is cast-iron and absolute. The generation of Irish writers immediately before mine never allowed this burden to weigh them down. They learned to speak Irish, they took their genetic purity for granted, and soldiered on. For us today the situation is more complex. We are more concerned with defining our Irishness than with pursuing it. We want to know what the word native means, what the word foreign means, we want to know have the words any meaning at all. And persistent considerations like these erode old certainties and help clear the building site. [44]

If that clearance had not taken place, it is doubtful if Friel could have written *Translations, Fathers and Sons* or *Making History*. In that case Friel's public project would therefore have continued to concentrate on the erosion of old certainties in order to come to terms with schizophrenia not only in Dublin but in the northern communities, and to deconstruct the false assumptions on which those communities have so often based their 'truths'. At the same time the issues have become much more obvious and immediate. 'What we in Field Day are asking is this: "What is it that constitutes an Irish reality?" ' And here Friel quotes Seamus Deane: 'Everything, including our politics and our literature, has to be re-written, i.e. re-

read. This will enable new writing, new politics, unblemished by Irishness, but securely Irish.'[45] It is this strength which underpins *Fathers and Sons*.

Fathers and Sons is a study in nihilism, and as such it is inevitably about homecomings, the same kind of *retour sur soi-même*, that has been made by Frank Hardy and Owen O'Donnell. Yevgeny Vassilyich Bazarov possesses, as Colm Toibin says in his review of the play,[46] 'an extraordinary brutality', and in his pursuit of this quality Friel, as Toibin noted, abandons many of his theatrical methods in favour of a straightforward narrative approach, a two-dimensional portrait of terror. It is, once again, as if the dramatisation of Turgenev's novel had been carried out by Chekhov – a Chekhov pursuing a private vision of despair which ultimately makes the play a private triumph but, especially in the light of the naive production it received at its premiere, not an obviously public occasion.

It was as necessary for Friel to write *Fathers and Sons* as it was to address the homecomings of *Faith Healer* and *Translations*. Without it, the challenges he makes in *Making History* would not have been possible. In this sense *Fathers and Sons* is the vital bridge between the homecoming of *Translations* and the new departures of *Making History*. In a sense it is almost as if he had returned to the short story as a form of conversation in which the family saga can be conducted away from overtly political and social issues. To locate nihilism in such manifestly rustic surroundings is a risky venture at uniting the local and private with the public and distant. Friel approaches this by providing us with echoes, clues, from his previous work. In many ways we can in fact read *Fathers and Sons* as a 'translation' into Russia of the characters and psychologies of Ballybeg. Thus the father and uncle of the revenant Arkady Nikolayevich Kirsanov respond to the exposition of nihilism as if they were Hugh and Jimmy Jack expressing their despair at the English lack of civilisation: to Arkady's assertion 'the most useful thing we can do is repudiate, renounce, reject' Pavel Petrovich replies 'Civilization has just been disposed of' (*FS* 11). Nikolai Petrovich remonstrates: 'surely rejection means destruction; and surely we must construct too?' Arkady retorts, in the accents of Captain Lancey, 'Our first priority is to make a complete clearance. At this point in our evolution we have no right to indulge in the gratification of our own personal whims.' And in the original version of *Fathers and Sons* (which was substantially cut to bring it within a more satisfactory playing time) Pavel Petrovich responds:

> Well I'm sure the Russian people will be pleased to know that they are about to be relieved of all those things they foolishly hold so sacred – their traditions, their familial pieties, their sense of faith. Oh yes, that will be welcome news to them' [47]

The impact of Bazarov in Friel's play, whether in his own words or through his acolyte Arkady is as Turgenev intended: blunt, crude and brutal. But Friel has added a new aspect to his sweeping nihilism: the awareness that we cannot 'gratify our personal whims' because we, as personae, do not yet exist: *ex nihilo* we must create both a public and a private world. Sweeping everything away is the work of a disillusioned faith healer, a repudiation, renunciation and rejection of past *and* future, a dramatic act based on the realisation that civilisation, if it is to exist at all, must be created out of a void. The possibilities are simultaneously endless and absolutely finite, our assets invaluable and yet worthless. For Yolland's father, we recall, 'ancient time was at an end' and, out of this negation, new time, 'the Apocalypse', began; for his alter ego, Senator Donovan in *The Communication Cord*, ancient time is only just beginning. For Yevgeny and Arkady, the predictors of revolution, their nihilism has already produced the apocalypse. Of all Friel's tortured personalities, only Frank Hardy has found the liminal way to tread between them: apocalypse *now*.

In *Fathers and Sons* Friel thus tells us much that was implicit, but not easily approachable, in his earlier work. He did so particularly in the original script by corrupting Turgenev's text to introduce an explicit statement of the theme of betrayal, its antecedents and its consequences. Friel intended to introduce into the final scene of *Fathers and Sons* the name of Leonard McNally, composer of the song 'Sweet Lass of Richmond Hill':

> PAVEL: McNally's story is interesting. He was a key member of a revolutionary group called the United Irishmen. I'm talking about 60 years ago, in Ireland, obviously. Anyhow, years after McNally was dead and buried, his revolutionary friends made a remarkable discovery: that right from the very beginning and all through the revolution [sic] McNally had betrayed them – he had been a spy for the English all along. Interesting, isn't it?
> ARKADY: What is?

PAVEL: That a man who composed some good songs and wrote a few good plays [48] was also capable of betraying his friends. Maybe the two instincts – for creativity and for betrayal – maybe they're complementary. Maybe they're identical.

. . .　　　. . .　　　. . .

KATYA: I think I know what he's suggesting. Perhaps that creativity and betrayal are of a piece. Perhaps that loyalty and betrayal are of a piece. Perhaps that love and betrayal are of a piece...that freedom, real freedom, cannot co-exist with loyalty or with love...And I think he is also asking what happens when revolutionary friends fall out. Which is the more important – loyalty to the friendship or loyalty to the revolution?...And that's what's fascinating about Mr McNally. He was faced with neither of those dilemmas – betrayal endowed him with real freedom from all attachments. [49]

Thus while this 'version' has not received public expression, there exists unequivocal evidence of Friel's intentions during the silent years after *Three Sisters*. For several years he had approached McNally's 'freedom' as a dramatic subject equivalent, in the public arena, to that of Frank Hardy in the private. *Fathers and Sons* marked a new departure in Friel's work because it demonstrated his capacity for having his own field day. It is indeed significant, as already noted, that it took place in another society and that he was thus free of the constraints and demands of his own problematic constituency, its subject matter and its preoccupations. There is, in fact, the obvious suggestion that 'a man...who wrote a few good plays was also capable of betraying his friends'. And yet, by a parabolic method and route, he arrives at a point where we can learn more directly from his Russian Ballybeg than from his Irish Chekhovian dramas. The 'Russian Friel' can look, as he did through the eyes of Columba and Frank Hardy, at the Ireland that robbed him of Christ, silence, freedom. Only by approaching Ireland the terrible, beautiful, damning and damned with an equivalent brutality and *from the outside*, can he come home without catastrophe.

The fellow who comes home is the same who went away, but changed. [50] In *Fathers and Sons* Friel gives us graphic evidence which helps us to understand more fully the homecomings of Owen, Casimir, and indeed Gareth O'Donnell. Not only do Arkady and Yevgeny, in relation to their own fathers, return from Moscow changed by the political tenets of nihilism but they also experience another form of change in the *transitus*, the crossing of the domestic threshold. Stepping back into the familial past with its pieties and niceties also involves stepping into a new future. Macro-civilisation may be at an end, but the Kirsanov and Bazarov households begin a new relationship with barbarism: who, here, are the '*civilised* people'?

With characteristic sympathy Friel extends the treatment of Bazarov's death in describing the determination with which he throws himself against the typhus epidemic to which he himself succumbs. Yevgeny is thus not only brought round to a positive, forward-looking attitude by the selfish device of love (which in Turgenev's novel is somewhat overdone) but by a social, humanitarian altruism which Turgenev had seriously underplayed. Nevertheless Bazarov remains brutal, or at least dangerously cynical, to the end: 'Everything for the bloody peasants, damn them!' (*FS* 76). But it is a brutality or cynicism tinged and mediated by love between father and son: when Yevgeny is dying he tells his father (at least in the uncut version of the play): 'I'm glad you and mother have your religion. I hope it is a comfort to you' [51], a sarcastic but affectionate recognition that not all ancient time can come to an end at once, that some time dies more slowly than others.

Bazarov's exemplary death is used as a means of inspiring Arkady's positive motivation for the revolution. He has moved from his original nihilistic stance to embrace his own father's viewpoint that after destruction there must come regeneration, an assertion in fact that without *a project of the will* our attitude to life remains unmotivated, that we are incapable of response. The project of will, however, must be based on freedom, whether it be the freedom of Bazarov to throw himself into death or that of Kirsanov to go on living, with all the rage against order and disorder that that demands. Once again the cutting-room floor provides us with strong evidence of Friel's own determination to effect the revolution in the relations between father and son that he has only hinted at in *Translations*:

> ARKADY: Why must you always be stupidly flippant about things that are vitally important, Father? What are you afraid of? You are all casually tossing about large words like loyalty and betrayal and love –
> KATYA: And revolution.

ARKADY: And revolution – yes, and revolution – as if they existed only [in] the abstract. Good. Great. Splendid. Be as cavalier, as flippant, as you wish. Plan the ideal world to your heart's content...but sooner or later you have got to acknowledge that the splendid new world you're concocting is inhabited by ordinary people, real people, your friends, your neighbours, your servants, and that they may not share that magnificent vision. And then you have to face up to your real responsibility: because if those people can't share your vision and if you cannot persuade them, are you going to coerce them into acceptance?...Yes, I want a new and better order. Yes, I demand the rejection of all that's mean and ugly and corrupt. But rejection alone is merely destruction. And surely we must construct too? [52]

This is the apocalypse for 'the bloody peasants, damn them' of Ballybeg; it is the acceptance by Hugh O'Donnell of Maire's need for English; and it is the recognition that it is not enough for the oppressed masses to stir in their sleep: they must have a reason for waking. No clearer blueprint is needed for the re-reading and re-writing of the nationalist, republican project. That alternative project, to which Field Day directs its energies, is the imperative which Arkady calls 'the primary and enormous task of remaking an entire society...not only a social obligation but perhaps even a moral obligation and indeed it is not improbable that the execution of that task may even have elements of *artistic pursuit*' (FS 24–5, *my emphasis*). We begin to see how a modern Irish playwright, following the example of Yeats, could accept appointment to the Irish Senate, having asserted the right and ability of artists to participate in government. We see that the antic gesture of a Skinner or a Keeney or of a Doalty, has been abandoned in favour of a reasoned and easily accessible exposition which is also free of diatribe.

In *The Mundy Scheme* Friel, the potentially political artist, had spoken out against the fact that 'the enormous task of remaking an entire society' had been funked by a neo-colonialist native administration which still carried within it its old subservience to the larger world, its deviousness in the face of oppression now turned in upon itself, its desperation for a name and an identity leading it into supermarket politics. In *Fathers and Sons* he pushes those crudities aside in the interests of greater issues: 'we know there is starvation and poverty; we know our politicians take bribes; we know the legal system is corrupt' (*FS* 11). But the world does not revolve on political slogans:

> Liberalism, progress, principles, civilization – they have no meaning in Russia. They are imported words. Russia doesn't need them...What Russia does need is bread in the mouth. But before you can have bread in the mouth, you have got to plough the land – deep.
>
> (*FS* 13)

We have gone beyond *The Freedom of the City*, where individuated dignity was the focus of revolt, to a scenario where the persona, like civilisation itself, is a *res nullius*. Bazarov, as he is dying, asserts: 'I am no loss to Russia. A cobbler would be a loss to Russia. A butcher would be a loss. A tailor would be a loss. I am no loss' (*FS* 79). But at the same time we are left with the absolutely personal claim of the nihilist, as recognised by his father: 'an extraordinary man cannot be judged by ordinary standards. An extraordinary man creates his own standards' (*FS* 42). It is the rock on which the revolutionary friendship founders, because, as Arkady wryly and jealously observes, 'only Bazarov has the courage and the clarity of purpose to live outside ordinary society, without attachments, beyond the consolation of the emotions' (*FS* 45). His exit raises issues in the quiet rhythm of his own home. In his father's exclamation 'Damn you, Almighty Father! I will not stand for it! I certainly will not stand for it!' (*FS* 78) Russia (and Ireland) creates another *deus absconditus*.

In recreating Frank Hardy Friel is doing more than simply showing us once again the prototype bastard: he is also demonstrating the symbiotic chemical relationship of two half-brothers. As Bazarov says of Arkady:

> He thinks he loves those damned peasants. I know I hate them. But I know, too, that when the time comes I will risk everything, everything for them, and I'm not at all sure that Brother Arkady is prepared to risk anything.
>
> (*FS* 44)

One half of the brother remains in civilisation, the other is an out-and-out barbarian. Bazarov tells Arkady:

> We are now into the area of hostilities – of scratching, hurling, biting, mauling, cutting, bruising, spitting. You're not

equipped for those indecencies. When it would come to the bit you would retreat into well-bred indignation and well-bred resignation. Your upbringing has provided you with that let-out. Mine didn't. I am committed to the last, mean, savage, glorious shaming extreme!

(*FS* 67)

Arkady's resolve to continue the nihilist revolution is fired by the fact – shameful to him – that Bazarov's final act of freedom has carried him off, whereas his own gentility has kept him the prisoner of ambiguous loyalty. Only a similar unequivocal choice of freedom can bring him out of the losers' enclosure.

It is in the changed relations of father and son – in the Kirsanov household – that Friel's Russian field day brings us fully back to the Ballybeg of *Translations*. Bazarov *père* has said:

There's something not right about a father burying his son, isn't there? Some disorder in the proper ordering of things, isn't it? It's not the way things should be, is it?

(*FS* 78)

And after Arkady's resolution, Kirsanov *père* announces in the closing passage of the play:

Some people might think that there is something inappropriate about a father and a son getting married on the same day, some disorder in the proper ordering of things. But I know that for both of us it will be an occasion of great joy and great fulfilment. And who is to determine what is the proper ordering of things?

(*FS* 94)

The son has recognised the wisdom residing in old age, as well as the right of old age to behave youthfully (for example in begetting children and marrying) while the father acknowledges that it is not *necessarily* either the old *or* the young who have the management of society. Maddening questions can rot the life of the hopeful as well as the hopeless, especially when their attempts at communication bring them into conflict; as Kirsanov *père* tells us early in the play, 'You never really know what people are like, do you? We all have our codes. We all have our masks' (*FS* 16).

Back in Ireland Friel continues to acknowledge the danger of sentimentalising an attachment to anything one might describe as 'roots': 'the ideal would be to retain the attachment but transcend its pressures as – for example – Beckett has done...The hope is that Field Day – working through particulars [the local thing, the interest in language, the political situation] may help to forge an analysis, fashion a new model that isn't inhibited or bogged down by the stereotypes of the past.' [53] This is a first step towards admitting, and embracing, the qualities of tribalism. But the fact that it is not yet possible, that the situation remains 'absurd...crass', was one reason for writing *The Communication Cord*. The situation is of course changing and Friel clearly believes that Ireland may be finding some advantage in its move towards the 'European lodestone': firstly, that its imagination is 'escaping from the German romantics, encouraging propensities that are fatal for us' and, secondly, that it is 'not so neurotic about England'. [54] There is, moreover, no need now to follow Joyce and Beckett into exile and separation; in fact it is important to live in Ireland – 'a sense of home...a sense of duty'. [55] Friel's continual concern in the 'theatre of language' is obviously to reconcile, to whatever possible extent, two apparently irreconcilable elements, the Irish imagination and the English language. It might seem more sensible for the Irish to speak Irish to the English, and that both sides could avail of a neutral translation, but Friel insists on two recognitions: that English usage as it prevails is 'foreign' and that 'we must make them [English words] distinctive and unique to us'. [56] He insists on this because he knows that that which cannot be translated cannot be communicated, and that survival depends on communication.

Since 1972, however, we have seen no sustained treatment of 'the schizophrenia of that city' nor of the ubiquitous urban problems in the Irish theatre, nor any attempts to present rural man to urban man in the sense Friel intends. (It is, of course, possible, by some oblique conceit, to see *Translations* as a parable of modern Derry, a civilisation evicted from historic dignity by the power of a lexicon.) Friel's private belief, partially expressed in *The Mundy Scheme*, is that

Ireland is becoming a shabby imitation of a third-rate American state...We are rapidly losing our identity as a people and because of this, that special quality an Irish writer should have will be lost. A writer is the voice of his people and if the people are no longer individuals I cannot see that the writer will have much currency. [57]

The chief obstacle to the development of such views, and to their effective expression in theatre, is the conservatism of Irish society and, by implication, of its moral and aesthetic codes. In Irish society 'neutrality', not only in external relations but in MacNeice's sense ('the neutral island in the heart of man'), the difficulty in commencing with oneself, is an acute problem for the Irish intellectual. The two types of mentality are connected, of course, just as the dichotomy of psychological experiences separates the discrete and public lives, the intuitive and the rational. The basis of Ireland's political and defensive strategy has been much discussed; but the fact is clear that, besides its economic dependence on other systems, its cultural and social and scientific modes (those by which we know and judge and organise our perceptions and our lives) are interdependent with other cultures. Irish society communicates and therefore must have codes common both to itself and to those other societies. If Tim Gallagher's dry exposition of 'discourse analysis' in *The Communication Cord* has any symbolic relevance, it is in confirming this aspect of national survival. Consequently, in its commerce with other cultures, Ireland cannot maintain an inviolate neutrality: it must open its heart and mind, it must accept, and offer, both 'dross and gold'.

THE GAP

We are therefore entitled, and obliged, to look at the modern Irish stage not only as a place of psychiatric divination but also as the arena in which political discourse is located and its elements exposed. Friel's approach to this question of political theatre has been characteristically circumspect and discreet: as we have seen, he has taken a particularist view of the elements of politics, resulting in a theatre which appears oblique rather than direct but which is concerned with the psychological basis of political action.

Friel has said that he and a play move together – as if towards a final reckoning, a test of strength like the preordained meeting of Hardy and McGarvey. In the case of *Making History* we can see just how slowly that approach has been made. The initial impact on the young Friel of O'Faolain's study of Hugh O'Neill – a study of psychology, of introspection, of the birth and death of civilisations – sets the scene for Friel's own involvement with the course of Irish history. Furthermore it linked that history with the question of individual destiny, of loyalty, of filiation and affiliation.

The agonies that Hugh O'Neill undergoes in *Making History*, and his eventual defeat by them, are thus the sum of all the doubts Friel has raised in his preceding work. The fact that he has been approaching this play for many years, and that his difficulties in doing so largely contributed to his silence as a playwright from 1982 until 1987, explains how so much of the eventual portrait of Hugh O'Neill finds pre-echoes in (especially) *Faith Healer* and *Translations*.

Making History is once again a problem play: a problem for audiences because it lacks dramatic impact, and for critics because it lacks not only form but, ostensibly, content or matter. There is no story-line as such because the playwright is concerned with how the future will determine the stories of the past: the events of O'Neill's greatness and decline, events which were of significance for the whole imperial world, are interiorised and made the subject of a monologue on the nature of affection. The submissions to Elizabeth, the trials of strength and of dignity, the Battle of Kinsale, and the Flight of the Earls, are all displaced in O'Neill's continual examination of the ways we use and are used. The boyhood recollections of an Irish princeling in the family homes of Leicester and Sidney, the marriage to Mabel Bagenal (whom the historians, including O'Faolain, largely ignore), the years of lurking between defeat and flight, like Sweeney, in the scrub of his madness, and the dimming years of exile, take the centre of O'Neill's stage in a mesmerism which, in its disregard for the other characters, often takes the form of soliloquy.

But O'Neill also has a public function representing the same sort of history lesson we have been given in *Translations*. He is a man of his time, tortured, like Columba, by 'the enemy within', but also acutely aware of his duplicity in the revolution of the public spheres. If there is a form to *Making History* it grows predominantly from its author's determination to understand, encompass and engross the mind and character of Hugh O'Neill, and the psychic effect on that mind and character of his environment, his personal history and the strophic times in which he lived, thought and acted.

Hugh O'Neill, in Friel's play, embodies the death of Gaelic Ireland, but also predicts the mantic and semantic troubles of *Translations*, the gombeenism of *The Mundy Scheme* and the drawn lines of *The Freedom*. Here, as much as in his own *Translations* or

Murphy's *Famine*, is a play for modern Ireland. Friel has implicitly revoked his declaration that the death of God makes modern tragedy impossible. By devising a type of drama which dispenses with both form and content he has come closer to solving the problem of the 'language play'. In *Making History* Friel makes the most serious claims yet for the authority of the playwright in describing the interaction of time and language, as the manipulator of 'history'. In the case of Hugh O'Neill he occupies a *tabula rasa*, firstly because, as O'Faolain observed, 'no intimate details of this great man's character have come down to us...we have nothing to go on except his behaviour...no real evidence as to [his] mind'. [58] Secondly because Friel himself has cleared the decks for this new phase of action by the necessary writing of *Faith Healer* and *Fathers and Sons*. There is both a literal and an intellectual nihilism in *Making History* which takes tragedy beyond the delineation of man caught between opposing forces, and replaces him with doubt and fear themselves: this moves the story so wholeheartedly from the physical into the metaphysical that it no longer belongs to traditional drama. Friel has thereby succeeded in answering Stanislavsky's predicament about the closure of plays by, in effect, not beginning them. The antiphonal incantation with which *Making History* ends can simply be read, and experienced, as the dimming of lights that will shortly be raised on that with which *Faith Healer* begins.

The reader coming fresh to O'Faolain's *The Great O'Neill* will therefore be struck by the frequency and intensity of what appear to be references to *Faith Healer*. Friel had to learn a great deal about being a twin, about being a bastard and about the fickleness of 'the healing word' as both master and mistress, in order to approach the condition of hopeless apostasy which characterises his Hugh O'Neill. He seizes on the statement in O'Faolain's closing pages:

> his fingers touch the Archbishop's manuscript...This is his life, his mind, his soul...And every word that he reads is untrue. Lombard has translated him into a star...He has seen it all as a glorious story that was in every thread a heartbreak. He has made Life into a Myth [59]

and he finally responds to that invitation to make his own 'translation', not merely of the 'facts' woven about Hugh O'Neill and his role in the Irish future, but also about life as a myth: he is answering his own call from *Philadelphia* and *Translations*: 'do your job – translate!'

The 'Ledger' which controls the Butlers in *Living Quarters* has become 'the History', a sinister document which diminishes O'Neill's privacy and inserts him into the public events of his problematic country, and inserts *it* into *him*. Where Frank Butler pleads for the right to object to the harshness of the chronicle, to the limitations to his freedom, O'Neill fights for the bare right to any of those 'intimate details' which the chroniclers have denied him. And whereas 'Sir' is simply the servant and guardian of the Ledger, Peter Lombard is the author of 'the History' which catechetically and inexorably steers O'Neill towards a destiny he is neither able nor willing to encounter.

For those without these *stigmata*, these birth-marks, life can be lived as the simple conflict between siblings and affiliates. As O'Neill acknowledges of one of the Ulster princes:

> Maguire's no fool. Maguire has no choice. Maguire has to rise. History, instinct, his decent passion, the composition of his blood – he has no alternative. So he will fulfil his fate. It's not a tragic fate and it's not a heroic fate. But his open embrace of it has elements of both, I suppose.
>
> (*MH* 30)

Heroism need not be tragic, nor tragedy heroic. Fulfilling fate of one kind or another is making history. Most history is private, uncelebrated, unobserved. Maguire is like the Doaltys and the Lanceys, for whom life is black-and-white, where boundaries are clearly drawn. But there is a more cruel fate for those who are unsure, for whom the 'composition of the blood' creates alternatives, demands that choices be made between impossible futures, whose answer resonates, from Columba's dichotomous loyalties to faith and family to Hugh O'Donnell's 'I have no idea at all' (*Tr.* 67). Contemporary Irish drama begins with Gar O'Donnell's 'I don't know. I–I–I–don't know' (*Ph.* 110). Friel has brought it to the point at which the artist, the actor, the pivotal figure of Irish history and the audience are all saying, in O'Neill's closing words, 'Forgive me...I'm sorry' (*MH* 71).

Those words express the reluctant side of Friel's work to date: the admission of a broken, rather than a triumphant, translator or diviner. On our reading of those words, and of the psychological state of mind which the play has been exploring, will depend very

largely our view of Friel's divination. We are being asked to go back
to the basic questions posed by Friel, albeit subconsciously, when
he set out in search of 'concepts of Irishness'; we are still assessing
whatever targets have been put up for us after Yeats's images for the
affections; we are observing one writer who has been looking for 'a
sense of life that will make the end less frightening' and in doing so
has written a play that not only sums up his own drama and that of
his 'constituency' but also represents many of the concepts exposed
and explored in *Double Cross, The Morning After Optimism* and
Famine.

And Friel's particular success in such a difficult play is due to the
fact that he locates the tragedy precisely between the public and the
private. The 'events' of O'Neill's life are of no more significance
than those of Frank Hardy, and the 'liberties' which Friel has taken
with the 'facts' of Irish history (as indicated in chapter 5) are
necessary liberties if we are to be given a different type of history
lesson: one in which the themes of exile and homecoming illustrate
the deep-seated need of the child to be held. An exile from home is
also an exile from meaning, and folktales are all about the search for
meaning which we call home. In the whole of Friel's canon, from
'The Child' to Columba, Gar, Frank and Ben Butler, Fox, Frank
Hardy and now Hugh O'Neill, the story of this search is both a
public adult return to the hearth and a private, adolescent flight to
the lap, the shoulder, the bosom.

'Sorry' is both an apology and an excuse. It is the codeword of
embarrassment between Maire and Yolland. 'Sorry' is at once
pleading and yet final, the admission of a measurable failure, the
expression of immeasurable hope, and also the extinction of that
hope. It drops the speaker into the depths between two types of
opposing certainties, the modern version of the tragic birthmark. As
Fintan O'Toole has observed, this approximates to 'what Pegeen
Mike calls "the great gap between the gallous story and a dirty
deed", the gulf that separates heroic talk from vicious action'; [60] that
'great gap' is the living space of those who have to live in indecision
because, in Antigone's words, 'my choice destroys me'. [61]

We have already seen, in Frank Hardy, faith healer, one man who
is not at all sorry, who needs to meet his destruction in a final
choice that is made for him. And in the half-brothers of Kilroy's
Double Cross we have the example of how such choices are made;
how loyalties become, like identical egg-cells, divided; how an
identity can become trapped between vicious twins. *Making*

POLITICS

History locates its 'hero', its sparagmatic victim, in this 'great gap', the interstice between love and hate that we call 'fear'. The gap is between the private and public worlds, between past and future, between illusion and reality. [62] But because 'God is dead, and with him the tragic hero', the remaking of tragedy and of heroism becomes a task entirely of man's own devising: in a godless world we have to dig our own graves. Now we realise that Friel has been saying this all the time – that in Gaelic Ireland, as in Elizabethan England, there was no God; that 'logic', 'myth', 'God' are all versions of the stories that children save up against the darkness, the loneliness and the questions of the night, anything to keep the talk going.

As in *Translations*, we have the prospect of two lives destroyed by exogamy, of two souls thrown into the gap. O'Neill says of Mabel 'She has left her people to join me here'; Mabel herself claims 'this is my home'; whereas her sister Mary insists 'No, it's not. This can never be your home (*MH* 14, 24). But ultimately Friel, who has played with the received facts [63] in order to create this empathy between O'Neill and Mabel Bagenal, this approximation at an understanding, a translation between cultures, discards her to die, like Yolland, among strangers. He returns to the local, the native who is yet a betrayer, a traducer, an inadequate symbol of his people's predicament, a spokesman who says the wrong, the unexpected, thing, or who speaks too easily in the tongue of the enemy. The hard focus, the cruel anatomical lesson, is the dismemberment, the failure and perdition of O'Neill.

If there is a controlling word in the whole language of *Making History*, a key to the vocabulary of 'the gap', it is: *or*. O'Neill, referring to Maguire's revolt, asks his scout and touchstone, Mabel 'Do I keep faith with my old friend and ally, Maguire, and indeed with the Gaelic civilisation that he personifies? Or do I march alongside the forces of Her Majesty?' (*MH* 27) We have had this already in *Translations*, when, in his turn, the scout asks the invader: 'Do we scrap Tobair Vree altogether...or do we keep piety with a man long dead, long forgotten, his name 'eroded' beyond recognition?' (*Tr.* 44) The choice is between extinction of the old pieties or ignorance of the new; between observing old history and making new history; between recognising the fact of erosion, accepting the new language in which it is cast, and turning one's back on the future. Such liminality is the 'or': the choice which destroys. The choice for O'Neill lies between Maguire and his brother-in-law, the 'upstart' Bagenal:

> impulse, instinct, capricious genius, brilliant improvisation – *or* calculation, good order, common sense, the cold pragmatism of the Renaissance mind...Pasture [or] husbandry...Do I grasp the Queen's Marshal's hand...*or* do I grip the hand of the Fermanagh rebel?
>
> *(MH* 28)

The choice is at once private and public, pertaining both to the single psyche and to his race and culture. Friel with deliberation enforces this with the spectacle of O'Neill relentlessly asking himself a series of private questions ('Do I...or do I?) in this most public way. Bagenal is 'a symbol of the new order which every aristocratic instinct in my body disdains but which my intelligence comprehends and indeed grudgingly respects' (*MH* 28), whereas siding with Maguire would be to 'bear public and imprudent witness to a way of life that my blood comprehends and indeed loves and that is as old as the Book of Ruth' (*MH* 28). Privately O'Neill is safe because, as O'Faolain observes, we do not know his mind. But publicly, just as it is when Frank Hardy essays the laying on of hands, the noose is immediately put around the neck. Friel in fact moves the discussion away from the public issues explored in *Translations* into the realm that Kilroy has opened up in *Double Cross* (written for Field Day): the way that William Joyce and Brendan Bracken, sourceless Irish adventurers, see with unremitted horror the writing of their past in terms of future history. Like Kilroy's double-crossers, Friel's O'Neill asks 'which hand do I grasp? Because either way I make an enemy. Either way I interfere with that slow sure tide of history... Let's put it another way. Which choice would history approve?' (*MH* 28) He thus shifts the weight of the discussion onto the nature of history itself. The passage of time, the way that events, and non-events, within that time are recounted, the names that are to be reckoned with, the subjective and objective sides of any discourse, become the results rather than the causes of some indefinable kind of casuistry, a crude definition which replaces the subtle divination of emotions, cultures and rites. Hugh O'Neill sums up for Mabel the 'or' of his public and private dilemma thus:

> I have spent my life trying to do two things. I have attempted to hold together a harassed and a confused people by trying to

keep them in touch with the life they knew before they were overrun...I have done that by acknowledging and indeed honouring the rituals and ceremonies and beliefs these people have practised *since before history*...And at the same time I have tried to open these people to the strange new ways of Europe, to ease them into the new assessment of things, to nudge them towards changing revaluations and beliefs. *Two pursuits that can scarcely be followed simultaneously* (*my emphasis*).

(*MH* 40)

Trying to 'keep faith' with something which will expel you if you espouse foreign ideas; admitting that that with which you would keep faith is already the victim of history, however subsequent that history may be; realising that one can make either the impossible attempt to follow both paths simultaneously or the equally impossible attempt to do neither.

O'Neill is destroyed simply because in the outcome he has to satisfy history (and an audience hungry for a tragic victim) by a course, any course, of action, rather than masterly inaction, the device by which he has hitherto defeated, or at least eluded, fate. In addition to referring to O'Neill's 'cautious inaction', O'Faolain says that, of a man who could 'postpone decisions indefinitely... knowing how miraculously long the conspiratorial Irishman can refuse to admit consciously that which his soul intends...we do right to be especially slow to suspect any decision in this most cautious and secretive man'. [64] O'Neill can satisfy history neither in prospect nor in retrospect. History, inexorable story-telling, defeats him. It uses him. Whichever way he turns, out of the silent safety of his 'or', leaving the terrible security of the gap means meeting a destiny for which he knows he has been chosen: a reluctant volunteer. The only kind of satisfaction is that final silence granted to Frank Hardy. As O'Faolain puts it, 'the only joy that can have been in his heart was that the suspense was at an end'. [65]

'If Hugh O'Neill cannot offer them safety and justice under our Brehon law, they'll have to look for protection under the new English law,' (*MH* 3–4) his secretary tells him. It underlines the shifting nature of temporary, local relationships, affairs which reflect the *ad hoc* and *ad hominem* nature of Irish society. Exogamy, we are hardly surprised to learn, is 'a class of treachery', but only one such: thinking about 'the new assessment of things' can be just as treacherous. Counterpointed against the accusations of his secretary

Harry Hoveden (in 'fact', or 'history', his foster-brother) – '*or* are you saying that you're going to take the English side against Maguire? (*MH* 30) – is O'Neill's Ophelian dedication of herbs/flowers: 'Coriander Maguire...ripens suddenly and will fall without warning ...Borage O'Donnell...inclined to induce excessive courage, even recklessness' (*MH* 29–30).

Is O'Neill using, or used by, history? Is he the manipulator or the marionette? Friel is in a sense undermining the status of the central character which he has built up in the Hugh O'Donnell of Ballybeg. He is reinforcing the nihilism – even though it is purposeful nihilism – of Bazarov. In this play the impetuous Hugh O'Donnell, Earl of Tyrconnell, makes the realistic, post-Kinsale statement we had been expecting from Jimmy Jack: 'This is the end of it all, Hugh, isn't it?'(*MH* 45) Concomitant with that 'end' is the fact that there is no end, only a continuation of the 'ruthless Gaelic logic' contrasted with the 'cold pragmatism of the Renaissance mind' (*MH* 28); and here Friel makes a mistake, because 'logic' is the wrong word – the right gesture, perhaps, but in the wrong language. Sacrifice to the word (logic) which dominates is, in Gaelic terms, quite inferior to sacrifice to the idea (myth) which continues to liberate; as O'Neill expresses more accurately the 'ruthless logic' of Maguire, he is 'trapped in the old Gaelic paradigms of thought' (*MH* 27).

The child who was Brian (or Bernard) Friel (or O'Friel) and who was so apprehensive as to write the story 'The Child' has become, in the rabble-rousing words of Peter Lombard, 'because of your birth, education and personal attributes...the natural leader of revolt' (*MH* 8). But he is also the natural traitor, the opposer and traducer of that revolt, the shaman who can see both past and future. He is both 'attack' and 'counter-attack', reformation and counter-reformation, the child of both past *and* history, depending on one's perspective.

As a person, a discrete, single item in history's inventory, O'Neill is wiped out by the gap. Where Synge's active playboy could rise above tragedy to complete a pattern of his own fictive destiny and thereby turn tragedy into comedy, Friel's inactive politician is condemned to become the plaything of other people's fictions. Friel's Archbishop, echoing Doalty, says 'if we can forge ourselves into a cohesive unit...we are not warring, we are a united people...no longer a casual grouping of tribes but a nation state' (*MH* 11, 64): thus the Gaelic kingdom could come into its own, with Hugh

O'Neill as its prince. If only the revenants of Irish history could reform themselves into a cohesive body of acceptable fact, the 'nation state' which continues to bedevil the Irish Constitution [66] would become 'a reality'.

Meanwhile the differences between versions, whether in the Ledger or in the History, or the four gospels which explore the awful privacy of the faith healer, remind us that inflections and nuances can kill. 'Sorry' can be a declaration of war:

O'NEILL: Aw, now, sorry.
MABEL: What does sorry mean?
O'NEILL: That my mistresses stay (*MH* 41)

Or it can be a suing for peace. In the interstices of talk we lose the metaphors:

LOMBARD: I'm no historian, Hugh. I'm not even sure I know what the historian's function is...
O'NEILL: But you'll tell the truth?
LOMBARD: My story will be as accurate as possible, if that's what you mean...But are truth and falsity the proper criteria? I don't know. Maybe when the time comes my responsibility will be to tell the best possible narrative. Maybe when the time comes imagination will be as important as information. Who's to say at this stage? But I promise you; there'll be nothing written for years and years. History has still to be made before it is remade.

(*MH* 8–9)

Within the affect of History writ large is a series of greater and lesser stories. Although O'Neill pleads for the centrality of his relationship with Mabel, the historian, the storyteller, decides that 'all those ladies you chose as your wives – splendid and beautiful and loyal though they undoubtedly were – well, they didn't contribute significantly to...the overall thing...they didn't re-route the course of history.' Lombard argues further: 'I don't believe that a period of history contains within it one 'true' interpretation, one single unambiguous 'meaning' just waiting to be mined. But I do believe that it may contain within it many possible narratives,' (*MH* 15) and that it is his responsibility to tell the best possible narrative, one which in this case disregards Mabel and many other of O'Neill's privacies, simply because it has to satisfy a greater cause, a 'fiction in search of belief'. Friel is once more treading on the corns of his constituency, but for the first time he is seriously (rather than facetiously as in *The Communication Cord*) questioning its shibboleths, not simply its conceits (like the furniture in *Aristocrats*) or its self-deceptions (as in *Cass*), but the very codes by which it discriminates, holds its world together, tells itself stories which are not merely credible but realisable. He asks if a particular 'period of history' – whether it is the sixteenth, nineteenth or twentieth century – is amenable to resolution, to unambiguous interpretation. History has to be both made and remade. Lombard insists 'in the centuries to come the way people live must change – inevitably. As indeed will the modes of writing about how they live'; [67] or as a contemporary Irish historian puts it: 'in a country that has come of age, history need no longer be a matter of guarding sacred mysteries. To say "revisionist" should just be another way of saying "historian".' [68]

Making History suggests that in writing Emmet's epitaph we must engage not only in constructing a future narrative for an age of emergence, but also in reconstructing pieties, the biographies of both the princes and the common men; the will must be retrospective too. But the casualties of such a process will be 'truth' and 'falsity' as criteria. In order to be Irish, it is necessary to reject 'either/or' in favour of 'both/and'; it means to suffer the uncertainties of life in the gap, to allow the life sentences of our conflicting and potentially lethal versions of time to run concurrently. The tragedy of this realisation lies in both the rejection of myth and the acceptance of the various narratives which gain their memorability from absolute but uncomprehended and immemorial phenomena. Myth apprehended as life is replaced with life comprehended as myth. Children become citizens who, in Lombard's argument, 'think they believe in some sort of empirical truth. But what they really want is a story' (*MH* 66). Lombard, like the English sappers, is 'making a pattern... offering a cohesion to that random catalogue of deliberate achievement and sheer accident that constitutes your life' (*MH* 67). And in so doing he is inventing the life of a nation–state, giving cohesion to a catalogue of fictions or half-truths. This is the answer for 'Fox O'Neill' to the question Crystal has asked Fox Melarkey: 'What are you?' It has made possible, and therefore intelligible, a world of controlled madness; it has placed it within the institutes. And, more unequivocally than before, Friel has shown where 'the enemy within' can be found in the public domain.

Map-making, whether it is a biography or the history of conquest, reduces its subject to an arrangement of affects or concepts. History is forecast as predictable fact and received, in Friel's words, as 'acceptable fiction' or 'performance'. [69] The story of a culture divining its enduring truths becomes a story of nihilism: the inevitable failure of metaphor. If, like analogies and emblems, it is, as Steiner suggests, the thread between mind and world, what use can it be in a world where nothing happens, and happens viciously? In submitting to this situation – one of his own choosing and devising – O'Neill has proved that the middle way is not only a way of staying at home, but a necessary way of exile into time as well as space. The 'so damned constant' of *The Gentle Island* becomes a play on words, damnation and constancy being the definitions of the gap. In O'Faolain's words, O'Neill was

> the first step that his people made towards some sort of intellectual self-criticism...In his time the world began that narrowing-in process which has, in our day, finished with the virtual obliteration of all seclusion, removed the word aloofness from the vocabulary of politics, left no corner to the hermit, and condemned to death all the traditions that fail the great modern test of Ubiquity. [70]

Friel, with himself as tympanum, unites the private and public worlds. He shows us the frightened child who, although *doli incapax*, must inevitably break silence and thus, by entering the public world, destroy its integrity. As the child makes itself whole, it betrays the tribe. And Friel's sympathy is with the child. Even when that child is wrong like Manus Sweeney, or as atrocious as Fox Melarkey, Friel mediates its atrocity with compassion and tenderness. And that may be his greatest fault as an artist: O'Neill's soliloquy, in which he recalls, in a Cass-like rhapsody, the 'days without blemish' that he spent in Kent, at Penshurst, in 'a golden and beneficent land' (*MH* 34) (echoes again of 'Mr Sing' and *Faith Healer*) as the house-guest and pupil of the Sidneys, robs O'Neill of some integrity. The soliloquy/rhapsody is about integrity itself, about who makes and who is made:

> I was only a raw boy at the time but I was conscious not only that new ideas and concepts were being explored and fashioned but that I was being explored and fashioned at the same time.
>
> (*MH*34)

Sidney, like Lombard, has told O'Neill that he will 'become a

leader of his people' (*MH*35). But he characterises O'Neill's duplicity, the dual loyalties that have been ingrained in him by his
strange upbringing:

> Those Irishmen who live like subjects play but as the fox
> which when you have him on a chain will seem tame; but if he
> ever gets loose, he will be wild again
>
> (*MH*35)

Concluding his reverie, 'Fox O'Neill' says that

> that trivial little hurt, that single failure in years of courtesy,
> has pulsed relentlessly in a corner of my heart. Until now.
> And now for no reason that pulse is quiet and all my affection
> for Sir Henry returns without qualification. But all that is of
> no interest to anybody but myself
>
> (*MH*35)[71]

At this most public moment when he decides to forsake the gap of
indecision to wreak his own and his country's fate, O'Neill expresses
his love for the colonist and insists on the privacy of his reasons. As
a result, Hugh O'Neill is more problematic than Frank Hardy and
less heroic than Hugh O'Donnell. But he represents a new version
of tragedy because his creator has given him this democratic right to
remake 'history'.

Seamus Deane draws attention to Adorno's point that 'art falsifies
atrocity (and perhaps all history) by rendering it in forms which
afford it a meaning or a spiritual dimension which it does not
have'[72]. He adds, 'perhaps it could be said more accurately that
such meaningfulness as art gives to experience is always by nature
retrospective. Indeed, all our thought and all our art is an interpretation of what is already past, the present is always atrocious'.
This study has been addressed consistently to the affective power of
memory and the pull of the time dimension on the imagination: this
is justified because the trend in modern Irish aesthetics lies toward
an examination of that affective past in relation to *will*.

The Irish present *is* atrocious, in its original sense of being
fundamentally brutal, hideous, yet perfectly comprehensible in its
violence: in its institutions and its culture Ireland today suggests
spastic paralysis, involuntary, discommoded, incommunicable. Irish
writers have traditionally sought their salvation in ecstasy, standing
outside the narrow ground, not only to stamp in their autism on
language, but also to reject any emotional possibility at all because

of that autism. The ultimate act of despair, therefore, is not the blood-sacrifice of the maniac but a pointless violence bred from absolutely pure rage: the madness of looking, without protection, on the face of a savage god.

Friel's Irishmen are abroad, even when they are at home. This important fact helps us to understand what Kearney calls 'the crisis of cultural ambiguity which so indelibly hallmarks the modern Irish psyche'[73]. To be capable of introspection, but to stand in 'a pained ecstasy' (*Tr.* 14,65) is to live beyond ambivalence, to have made of oneself the liminal medium which unites otherwise divergent cultures but which is exiled from both. In the sense that Friel's theatre is psychological drama, therefore, it is epic, classical. We are left asking whether we must always kill our father or our brother, in our play, our Eucharist, as we do in our daily lives.

It is therefore quite natural that among the modern Irish dramatists we find men who might want to believe in nothing: to empty their minds of both prejudice and ambition. As Laing says: 'the experience of being the actual medium for a continual process of creation takes one past all depression or persecution or vain glory, past, even, chaos and emptiness, into the very mystery of that continual flip of nonbeing into being, and can be the occasion of that great liberation when one makes the transition from being afraid of nothing to the realization that there is nothing to fear' [74].

Friel has conferred that kind of nihilism on some of his creations – the winners – and denied not only to many others but also, one assumes, to himself. As he himself might say at times of weakness, through Fox Melarkey:

> I want a dream I think I've had to come true. I want to live like a child. I want to die and wake up in heaven with Crystal. What do I want? Jaysus, man, if I knew the answer to that, I might be content with what I have
>
> (*CF* 36)

The child, even he who has abdicated his ecstasy, is enviable because he is the original ignarus, stultus, rusticus, on whom life, in its violence, inflicts a rude eviction. This child needs a code, whether it is the bedtime story or the fireside talk, a private fabula rather than the public hisotria, to help him meet the dark unknown, to create a language in which he can ask the nighttime visitors to tread softly.

In *Translations* Hugh talks of attempting to fill the unfillable cask of his pupils; but Friel mediates with too great a tenderness because he knows that there are two vessels, the intellectual and the emotional. 'All he had witnessed', says the conclusion to the story 'Aunt Maggie the Strong One', 'could no longer be contained in the intellect alone but was dissolving already and overflowing into the emotions'. The relation between emotion and intellect has been another persistent theme in this book. At times it is hard to tell which is flowing into the other, which is the dominant knowledge.

Magnificence has always seemed in Ireland to reside in pathos. This pseudonym for catastrophe has been the path chosen by most Irish writers. Friel seems prepared to challenge the paradox that in order to be magnificent one must first be pathetic. But such a challenge means that the intellectual cask must be allowed to spill over, back into the emotional. 'I have been educated out of my emotions by my intellectual insight. Now I find it necessary to assert an emotional epiphany out of an intellectual and political grid' [75]. To be filled means to hold the balance between yesterday (when the intellect was distilling the emotional lessons) and tomorrow (when it spills over into time future). In order to be full one must have the courage *to be*: to love, to be free, to communicate, to speak the inexpressible 'I am'. That is a state of homecoming, the nunc stans, but further courage is needed for tomorrow, to spill over once again into another exile, a necessary leavetaking.

AFTERWORD

Plays of love, plays of freedom, plays of language: the divisions are not good enough. We are left, especially with Friel's most recent original play, *Dancing at Lughnasa*, with the simple problem of the 'problem play', and all his plays are problems in two senses: first, that of his stagecraft, the way in which he relishes the demands that he places on his interpreters, whether they be directors, actors or audience; and second, that of his increasing maturity as both writer and citizen, which shows us his best work as flawed masterpieces to which the lesser works often supply the keys. But all masterpieces are flawed, because fine drama always succeeds in establishing the *déjà vu* but with all the unfamiliarity and consequent disorientation of the *déjà reçu*. Friel manages this not only at each dramatic interstice but also throughout the whole corpus of his work to date: *Making History* is a problem because it reveals the playwright caught in the gap between romance and didactisism, sorting out, in his claim for the heroic privacy, the same loose ends that bedevilled his faith healer: a marriage, a partnership, an artistry, a gift, a sense of fate, which can satisfy neither the claims of his constituency nor, ultimately, the inner demands of the artist himself, underlining the existence of new disturbances, a further need for departure.

In *Dancing at Lughnasa* (1990) Friel has pushed this claim to artistic freedom further than ever before, underpinning his resolute determination not to write another 'national epic' with the implied claims of *Translations*. Here he writes more directly in the autobiographical mode than he has since *Philadelphia*, both in the description of the household of his own aunts – the giveaway lies in the dedication of the printed text: 'In memory of those five brave Glenties women' – and in the technical construction of a 'memory

224

play'. Moreover, at this stage of his development he appears to be changing the ground rules, at least as far as the framework of the present study is concerned, since, in the sequence of plays which have opened a new cycle in his work (in temperament if not in theme) – *Fathers and Sons, Making History* and *Dancing at Lughnasa* – he is no longer concentrating so steadfastly on a single facet of experience, whether we call it 'love', 'freedom' or 'language', so much as creating layers of experience, addressing several of these ideas with equal priority, piling various kinds of emotion (fear, love, greed), various kinds of association (families, political genres, conscientious objects and objections) and various speeds of action (retrospect, immediacy and divination) into the same dramatic moulds.

Dancing at Lughnasa is Friel's most problematic play to date, partly because, with the novel dramatic experiences it offers, it suggests that we might reconsider *Making History*, seeing it now almost entirely as a family play, a private occasion, rather than as an historical fiction with a public address like *Translations*. It throws into doubt all our previous classifications: which is the symphony and which the chamber music? What is family, and when is a family drama necessarily a public as well as a private occasion? When must we overlay a private grief or hilarity with public connotations, and when must we refuse to do so? The access that we are here granted to Friel's own privacy (through the device of the narrator/participant of-and-in the 'memory play') is at the same time un-remittingly public, just as the ruminant address of his faith healer came from the open confessional: it is at once the exploration of 'the dark and private places of individual souls' and the laying bare of our won, severally and collectively. It hurts us, and yet we tolerate it because Friel lets his audience off the hook, making his plays accessible to Irish audiences who might otherwise have been more difficult to please, to entertain, to mesmerise, than inter-national ones.

I mention hurt, and in the context of the 'memory play' this is of monumental significance because, as Friel reminds us in the closing monologue of *Dancing at Lughnasa*, 'in that memory... the air is nostalgic with the music' (*DL* 31): nostalgic, that is, in the sense in which the entire play has been conceived, both publicly and privately, in the meaning of a word that is both intimate and blatant; *nostos*, home, and *algos*, pain. Memory, therefore, as the painful transitus into time past, into the scenes of childhood which, on the evidence of this play, continue to constitute both Friel's personal quest for meaning and identity and his means of setting his audience on their own independent quests. In this light the play is a homecoming not, as we are ostensibly shown, for the missionary Fr Jack (redolent of the 'disgrace', the lack of 'dignity' of the *The Blind Mice*), but for Michael, the narrator, whom the play facilitates in this return journey with its stage directions as surely as those of *Philadelphia*: *'no dialogue with the BOY MICHAEL must ever be addressed directly to adult MICHAEL,* the narrator' (*DL* 7). In a certain sense Friel has written *Dancing at Lughnasa* more as a self-imposed exercise, taking stock (as does novelist John McGahern in his latest, summary work, *Amongst Women*) of his compulsions, responsibilities and ghosts, making a grab at his receding freedoms and investing them with a significance which some of his constituents might discount.

Dancing at Lughnasa is retrospective – and perhaps retrogressive – in that it does provide a summary of these themes of homecoming: nothing in his previous work is allowed to escape the scrutiny of this most honest of Friel's plays, and thus he gives us an utterly theatrical drama which, like *Aristocrats*, is a more self-contained spectacle than much of his more recent work in 'language play'. There is even evidence – as there was in the 'disavowed'[1] 1972 interview with Smith and Hickey – that his thoughts and emotions as a writer might tend once more towards the short story: the play opens and closes with the monologal lines, 'When I cast my mind back to that summer of 1936 different kinds of memories offer themselves to me' (*DL* 171). In finding our way into Friel's private family history we are thus entering our own privacy, the same access which was Hugh O'Neill's ultimate achievement in addressing a life which public history had defiled.

In terms of the dramatist's progress, we have to observe that in one sense, like Columba, he is 'chained irrevocably' to mother Ireland, but in an elastic sense that permits the essential laughter; in another, that he is demonstrating, as in *Fathers and Sons*, the capacity for self-liberation, for traitorous freedom. 'Inbred, claustrophobic Ireland' has provided – and continues to provide – him socially, morally, politically, emotionally, with the 'concepts' of meaning and identity of which it has been his inspired function to be the diviner. Two great 'memories' dominate this progress: privately, the story 'The Child', and publicly the ambiguous legend of Hugh O'Neill, so provocatively foretold by Sean O'Faolain. Such memories provide copious, enervating draughts of pain and fear, but they also stimulate, energise, because they indicate, for the playwright himself and for audiences, whether they be Irish, English, American or African, routes towards certain types of greater freedom than we had previously imagined: freedoms which are illuminated by truths told and acknowledged rather than truths known but hidden. In this sense, even when taking a holiday from Ireland, from Cathleen ni Houlihan, from Derry, from Glenties, from Ballybeg, Friel has borne witness and done the job of Chekhov's landscape painter: he has translated.

Dancing at Lughnasa provides a self-description: 'dream music that is both heard and imagined; that seems to be both itself and its own echo' (*DL* 71). It is a summary and yet at the same time a prediction; it sets in motion – especially in the pagan dance that provides the climax of the first act and in Fr Jack's description of the 'Ryangans' (borrowed from Victor Turner's Ndembu[2]) – energies that have never previously been quarried in his plays. It is ironic that his Private and Public Gar, so subversive when first introduced in 1964, should today be accepted almost as clichés, as a readily recognisable handle to the twin problems of self-regard and utterance. It also makes him simultaneously local and international. Thus we find a contemporary Arts Council report (on the significance of participation in community arts) accepting Gar as a modern Irish phenomenon, referring to him as a paradigm of 'this tension between the public and the private, between what one says and what one thinks [which] resonates in the working of most people who write with the hope of influencing something'.[3] At the same time it is salutary that Friel's work bears affinity with so many post-colonial *and* post-imperial literatures: not only, as we have noted, those of Africa (Ngugi and Soyinka in particular) but also of Europe: again, we have noted the parallel with the work of Andraz Szuto, to which we might add that of Milan Kundera who, in work such as *Life is Elsewhere*, reflects, as does Friel, on the mutuality of the public and private in artistic growth. This constant reflection – on the loneliness and isolation of the private artist juxtaposed with his immersion in, and engagement with, the public issues and distractions of his age – emphasises that the multiple (rather than singular) homecomings which characterise Friel's most recent work have a ritualistic nature, and it underpins his concern with a destiny that is as much concerned with the future of the will – its freedom – as with its imprisonment in, and defeat by, the past.[4]

In both a technical and an aesthetic sense, therefore, *Dancing at*

Lughnasa represents a merging (as I have discussed them earlier) of the 'aboutness' of the play with the author's intentions: here, then, he seems, by sheer weight of circumstantial force – the unremitting description by Michael, as both narrator and participant, of the quotidian lives of 'those five brave Glenties women' for whom Friel himself has the most transparent affection and for whom he sings the most eloquent and yet unapologetic threnody – to solve the problem identified above by Seamus Deane, of knowing when to develop the dramatic transitus from private to public. Within the acoustic of the Mundy household of Ballybeg, he publishes the daily dealings of womenfolk as he has never previously; their sexuality, their poverty, their sheer sense of fun and hope in the face of extinction. I have mentioned Kundera because, in the closing monologue of this play whose title, and metaphor, is *dancing*, Friel typically oscillates – or perhaps the term is 'vacillates'? – between life being ineradicably and inexorably *here*, at what Heaney would call the *omphalos*, and life being *elsewhere*, part of a floating world which, like the music which provides the core of the play's stage directions (as it does in *Aristocrats*), we can never finally identify, pin down to specifics: like the Irish language and culture of 'Ballybeg', that metaphysical and metaphorical present, it will always, in the terms of the external observer, elude us. Friel achieves this by juxtaposing the idea of *ritual*, 'this wordless ceremony...to be in touch with some otherness' with dancing into 'the very heart of life' (*DL* 71), and thereby provides the audience's transitus from the magic of the stage to the reality of the auditorium, and their own knowledge of 'home'.

This merging of description and intention is, of course, typical of a memory play, and in the sense that *Dancing at Lughnasa* is a 'memory play' it is a play 'about' the nature of home and what happens there: it describes the life of a house which becomes, and is recognised as, a 'home' because everything is both rehearsed and enacted there: a place where memory is shaped hourly, weekly, monthly, a place where fear, hope, tragedy and honesty are as essential ingredients for the family mix as the chickenfeed and the cornflour. It concentrates, as did *Making History*, on forms of truth, on different kinds of memory, and it also continues to ask Lévi-Strauss's question: 'what does "to mean" mean?' The fact that there is no central fact in Friel's own biography – none, that is, more powerful nor more significant than the twin influences evidenced in the compulsive writing of those two memories', 'The

Child' and *Making History* – is testimony not only to the route that he has privately taken towards his own political and aesthetic involvement with the fate of modern Ireland, but also to the public trajectory of this septic isle. Once again, he bears out the sociologist quoted above who finds Gar so compelling a metaphor for modern Ireland: 'the difficulty lies not with the reality of differences, great or small, between artists and the rest; it lies with the assertion of discrete, discontinuous types. If we must use the language of mystery in talking of art and artists, then let us address the real mysteries, and not the relics of another age'.[5] The 'real mysteries', we discover from Friel, are those of painful memory: as we have encountered them in *Living Quarters, Faith Healer* and *The Freedom of the City*. But now Friel is emphasising the *gap* (as I have described it in terms of *Making History*) as the location of the drama between 'both' and 'and', the place where we behave 'as if'. *Dancing at Lughnasa* concludes: 'Dancing as if language had surrendered to movement ... Dancing as if language no longer existed because words were no longer necessary' (*DL* 71): the consummation devoutly to be wished in almost every play by Brian Friel – a silent freedom from the maddening torment of noise, of questions, of words which destroy by their capacity for love and betrayal – is almost, but not quite, within earshot. In this novel dramatic experience we are poised between music and vertigo, exploring the meaning of home as a place constantly defined by the presence of exile, in a way that makes of reverie and reminiscence merely a potently and frighteningly unsatisfactory bridge between privacies and between the public and private worlds, between time privately recollected and history publicly recorded. As usual, this causes Friel to take appalling risks, making new challenges that excite us technically and aesthetically by asking us to review the difficulty of apprehending not just the meaning of both public and private truth but of their very idea.[6]

But beyond this 'play for dancers' as we might call it in Yeatsian terms – and let us not forget that Yeats referred to his plays of that name as 'the struggle of a dream with the world'[7] – we still encounter, because of Friel's own unrelenting rendezvous with destiny, the compulsive even if playful affair with language which finds him, in his latest theatrical venture (the version of Macklin's *The True-born Irishman* as *The London Vertigo*), echoing himself in underlining the semantic and cultural differences between the ostensibly similar languages of the two islands: 'she has brought back...a new language with her...a new kind of London English that is no more like our Irish English than...a fine gilded carriage is like a Carrickmore cart'.[8] After the poise of *Dancing at Lughnasa* we are back amidst the civilian/barbarian debate, once more political, once more potentially and actually brutal. Here again, obliquely but with characteristic force, he takes up the burden with which he has most recently teased us in *Dancing at Lughnasa*, of underlining the capacity of any 'civilised' society to carry within itself a subsisting stratum of 'barbarianism', once more highlighting that problematic line which makes *Translations* so worthwhile: 'back here with you..."civilised" people'.

Ultimately, all Friel's work revolves around the crucial connection between map-making and communication, and this is especially important for an 'extraterritorial' like myself who is intensely conscious that as an Englishman I do indeed speak a *different language* from Brian Friel, one that, as a post-colonialist, he is intent on annexing and subverting. In my case this has only been partly tempered by over twenty years' residence in Ireland, which has also served to create an awareness of self as a displaced consciousness. This book is a public document, but it has also been an intensely private experience. In recent years I have been involved, both as a public servant and as a private citizen, in examining many of the issues which have been discussed in this book and are addressed further in my essays entitled *Homecomings*. In doing so I have tried to reconcile my absence from post-imperial England with my strangeness in post-colonial Ireland: and to develop a voice which might adequately serve that predicament. To quote Yeats, I believe 'I have found all myself'. The right gesture in the right language – perhaps.

This has meant a psychological discovery also. There is a George Yolland and an Owen O'Donnell in each of us. Usually, for the Englishman in Ireland, conscience is dominated by the former. But great chunks of awareness, certainty, sensibility, can start to fall around and become as violent as Frank Hardy's innermost tensions. To be free of these 'thugs' of one's psyche one must recover the power of laughter. One is continually aggravated by the fear of losing and the chance of winning, until ultimately one finds that the qualitative difference between winners and losers is a certain kind of *freedom*; that even when one is powered by a lie, the exhilaration of knowing that no brake can be put on it, that, even though the leap into the dark will be the hour of one's death, one is liberated by the natural fact of the gesture, carries one beyond the logical point of control, to contain and overwhelm the mythos of eternity itself. This is where dream meets reality.

Brian Friel is particularly concerned with the question of loyalty: to one's friends, to one's folk, to one's country, to one's art. This engagement with community, circumstance or context may be difficult to gauge at times of particular tension. Public crises have, up to now, elicited little direct response from a man who nevertheless displays an immense capacity for caring, but all his work is a divining of his constituency, a marking of depths and shallows and a testing of its capacity, against another day of fate. Especially, of its capacity for laughter. And that has also meant a testing of self, a divining of the inner landscape. Studying his work, and knowing him, has helped me to learn that to live, however briefly or disastrously, within our own fictive world, enables us to know that the ultimate necessity is not even betrayal of one's country, but of one's self, and that the ultimate freedom is a self-deriding laughter.

NOTES

INTRODUCTION

1 G. Steiner, *After Babel* (Oxford: Oxford University Press, 1975), p.21: 'a civilisation is imprisoned in a linguistic contour which no longer matches, or matches only at certain ritual, arbitrary points, the changing landscape of fact'. Friel's adaptation of Steiner's arguments – often, as in this case, almost literal transcription – is discussed by Richard Kearney: 'Language play: Brian Friel and Ireland's verbal theatre', *Studies*, Spring 1983; and by Anthony Roche: 'Ireland's *Antigones*: tragedy north and south', in *Cultural Contexts and Literary Idioms in Contemporary Irish Literature*, ed. M. Kenneally (Gerrards Cross: Colin Smythe, 1988).

2 Seamus Deane's reference to Field Day Theatre Company, in a programme note for *Translations*, 1980.

3 *The Seagull*, Act 2: *Plays by Anton Chekhov: translated and with an Introduction by Elisaveta Fen* (Harmondsworth: Penguin, 1954), p.150.

4 G. Steiner, *Language and Silence* (London: Faber and Faber, 1985) p.47.

5 First in chapter 9 of *The Death of Tragedy*; then in his Exeter University lecture 'Antigones', and in the extended treatment of that theme, *Antigones* (Oxford: Oxford University Press, 1984); cf. also *After Babel*, p. 23: 'we have histories of massacre and deception, but none of metaphor. We cannot accurately conceive what it must have been like to be the first to compare the colour of the sea with the dark of wine or to see autumn in a man's face. Such figures are new mappings of the world, they reorganize our habitation in reality.'

6 Brian Friel, 'Extracts from a sporadic diary', in *The Writers: A Sense of Ireland*, eds. Andrew Carpenter and Peter Fallon (Dublin: O'Brien Press, 1980), p. 39. Friel also published further 'Extracts...' relating to the writing of *Translations* in Tim Pat Coogan (ed.), *Ireland and the Arts* (London: Quartet Books, n.d. [1982].) My references to Friel's diaries will therefore be cited as *The Writers* or as Coogan (ed.) as appropriate.

7 V.W.Turner, *Dramas, Fields and Metaphors* (New York: Cornell University Press, 1974), p.23.

8 B.Friel, *The Writers*.

9 ibid., p.39.

10 In conversation with the author.

11 Tyrone Guthrie, *A New Theatre* (New York: McGraw Hill, 1964), p.33.

12 B.Friel, 'Plays peasant and unpeasant', *Times Literary Supplement*, 17 March 1972.

13 B.Friel, 'The theatre of hope and despair', *Everyman*, no.1, 1968.

14 Fintan O'Toole, 'The man from God knows where', *In Dublin*, 28 October 1982.

15 Ngugi wa'Thiongo, *Decolonising the Mind: the politics of language in African literature* (London: James Currey, 1986), p.15. The similarities and reverberations between the work of Friel and Ngugi would repay analysis: see my forthcoming *Homecomings: Ireland and the Post-Colonial World*. Ngugi, for example, has described a similar linguistic illusion to that in *Translations*: 'it is understood that the characters [in his play *The Trial of Dedan Kimathi*] are speaking an African language. But...they are conceived in English and they speak directly in English' (*Decolonising the Mind*, p.43).

16 ibid., pp. 12, 15, 17 ff.

17 Lady Gregory, *Our Irish Theatre* (London: Putnam, 1913), p.20.

18 O'Toole, 'The man'.

19 Hannah Arendt, *The Life of the Mind* (New York: Harcourt Brace Jovanovich, 1978), vol.1, p.191.

1 THE LANDSCAPE PAINTER

1 Seamus Heaney, *Preoccupations* (London: Faber and Faber, 1980), p.56.

2 In *The Saucer of Larks*.

3 In *The Gold in the Sea* and subsequently reprinted in *The Diviner* (Dublin: O'Brien Press, 1983).

4 B.Friel, 'A fine day at Glenties', *Holiday*, April 1963.

5 Communication to the author.

6 Letter to the author. See also a discussion of the documentary evidence in Ulf Dantanus, *Brian Friel, A Study* (London: Faber and Faber, 1988) p. 220, where he elicits the fact that in the parish register Friel's name at baptism is recorded as *Brian Patrick O'Friel* (hereafter referred to as Dantanus (1988)).

7 This device is not altogether original. In *Ubu Cocu* (1893) Alfred Jarry provided Ubu with an unwelcome and troublesome 'Conscience', while, nearer home, Lennox Robinson's *Church Street* (1934) splits the main character into 'Hugh' and 'Evoked Hugh'. Eugene O'Neill also provides us with a split character in *Days Without End*: John Loving becomes 'John' and 'Loving'. The comparison of O'Neill and Friel is discussed in Dantanus (1988), pp. 90–2; and by R.Niel, 'Non-realistic techniques in the plays of Brian Friel: the debt to international drama', in Wolfgang Zack and Heinz Kosok (eds.), *Literary Interrelations: Ireland, England and the World* (Tubingen: Gunter Nar Verlag, 1987), where attention is also drawn to Giles Cooper's radio play *The Disagreeable Oyster* (1957). And Maurice Valency points out that Pirandello, in *Il peacere dell'onesta* (The Pleasure of Honesty), 1912, shows his hero, Angelo Baldovino, distinguishing between his two selves, the public and the private: 'Behind the jealousies and pretences, there remain hidden our most secret

thoughts, our most intimate feelings, everything, in short, that we are for ourselves alone, outside the relationships that we desire to establish.' M.Valency, *The End of the World* (Oxford: Oxford University Press, 1980), p.111.

8 James Forsyth, *Tyrone Guthrie* (London: Hamish Hamilton, 1976), p.25.
9 M.H. Heslinga, *The Irish Border as a Cultural Divide* (Amsterdam: van Gorcum, 1979), p.37.
10 Dervla Murphy, *A Place Apart* (London: John Murray, 1978), p.1.
11 cf. Fergus O'Ferrall, *Daniel O'Connell and Catholic Emancipation* (Dublin: Gill and Macmillan, 1985), pp.97–8.
12 Steiner, *Language and Silence*, p.11.
13 Fintan O'Toole, 'The man from God knows where', *In Dublin*, 28 October 1982.
14 ibid.
15 Friel, 'Self-Portrait', *Aquarius*, no.5, 1972.
16 ibid.
17 ibid.
18 ibid. Seamus Heaney has recounted a similar 'non-event' in recalling his childhood at Mossbawn: 'I do not know what age I was when I got lost in the pea-drills in a field behind the house, but it is a half dream to me, and I've heard about it so often that I may even be imagining it' (*Preoccupations*, p.17); and Beckett's 'Unnamable' declares 'enough of acting the infant who has been told so often how he was found under a cabbage that in the end he remembers the exact spot in the garden and the kind of life he led there before joining the family circle', *Trilogy*, London: Picador, 1979, p.297.
19 Seamus Heaney, *The Times*, 5 December 1988.
20 Sean O'Faolain, *The Great O'Neill* (London: Longman, Green & Co., 1942), p.vi.
21 in conversation with the author.
22 Friel, 'Self-Portrait'.
23 In an address to an Arts Council conference, 'Partnership – local authorities and the arts', University College, Galway, 18 September 1987.
24 Friel, 'Self-Portrait'.
25 Heaney, *Preoccupations*, pp.47 and 43.
26 Heaney, *The Times*, 5 December 1988.
27 Blake Morrison, *Seamus Heaney* (London: Methuen, 1982), p.15.
28 Heaney, *Preoccupations*, p.20.
29 Morrison, op.cit., p.27. Heaney has also written: 'I have maintained a notion of myself as Irish in a province that insists that it is British' (*Preoccupations*, p.35); he sees different characteristics in the two tongues: 'I think of the personal and Irish pieties as vowels and the literary awarenesses nourished on English as consonants' (ibid., p.37).
30 Heaney, *North* (London: Faber and Faber, 1975), p.57.
31 Heaney, *The Times*, 5 December 1988.
32 O'Faolain, op.cit., p.31.
33 ibid., p.30.
34 As Augustine called it: cf. Arendt, op.cit., vol. 2, pp.99–100: 'The Will tells the memory what to retain and what to forget; it tells the intellect

what to choose for its understanding. Memory and Intellect are both
contemplative and, as such, passive; it is the Will that makes them
function and eventually "binds them together". And only when by
virtue of one of them, namely, the Will, the three are "forced into one do
we speak of *thought*" – *cogitatio*, which Augustine, playing with
etymology, derives from *cogere* (*coactum*), to force together, to unite
forcefully.'

35 Steiner, *After Babel*, p.220.
36 Dantanus (1988), p.67.
37 Coogan, (ed.), p.60; Friel's diary entry for 6 July 1979.
38 Steiner, *After Babel*.
39 ibid., p.29.
40 The line comes from Ovid, *Tristium Liber* V, Elegia X, a reference to his
own exile in Pontus where his Latin and Greek were not understood; cf.
Beckett, *Trilogy*, p.135: 'his accent was that of a foreigner, or of one who
had lost the habit of speech'.
41 *Consuetudo nominationum*: 'a figure of speech whereby a thing
which has no name, or an unsuitable one, receives an appropriate name':
Rhetorica Ad Cornificius Herennium, 4.31.
42 cf. Steiner, *After Babel*, pp. 58–9: 'the vulgate of Eden
contained...a divine syntax – powers of statement and designation
analogous to God's own diction, in which the mere naming of a thing
was the necessary and sufficient cause of its leap into reality...There was
a complete, point-to-point mapping of language onto the true substance
and shape of things. Each name, each proposition was an equation, with
uniquely and perfectly defined roots, between human perception and the
facts of the case.'
43 ibid., p.225.
44 cf. O'Faolain, op.cit., p.181. See also J.I. Prattis, 'Industrialisation and
minority language loyalty', in J.Hansen *et al.* (eds.), *Core-Periphery
Theory and Practice* (Bergen: Institute for the Study of Sparsely Populated
Areas, 1983): 'naming practices in Lewis – the use of Gaelic nicknames
(Iain Nogaidh) and patronymics (Murchadh ic Niall ic Dhohmnaill) –
are traditionally an important linguistic reinforcer of community solidarity...The use of Gaelic naming systems has the function of identifying
individuals but within a unique cultural style, and as such patronymics
are an indicator of speech continuity boundaries' (p.253).
45 R.D. Laing, *The Politics of Experience* (Harmondsworth: Penguin, 1967),
p.95.
46 Quoted in Ezra Pound (ed.), *Instigations* (Freeport, New York, 1967).
47 André Brink, *Mapmakers: Writing in a State of Siege* (London: Faber
and Faber, 1983), p.169.
48 Tim Robinson, *On Setting Foot on the Shores of Connemara* (Giggins-
town: Lilliput Press, 1984) p.9.
49 Brink, op.cit., p.163.
50 Turner, op.cit., p. 253.
51 Hegel, *Phenomenology of Mind*.
52 Turner, op.cit., pp.13–14.
53 V. Crapanzano, 'Liminal recreations', review of V.W.Turner, *From*

Ritual to Theatre: the human seriousness of play (New York: *Performing Arts Journal*, 1983), in *Times Literary Supplement*, 27 April 1984.

54 Quoted in Dantanus (1988), p.87.
55 Tyrone Guthrie, *In Various Directions* (London: Joseph, 1966) pp. 32 and 38–9.
56 Samuel Beckett, *Film* in *Collected Shorter Plays* (London: Faber and Faber, 1984) p.163.
57 W.B. Yeats, *Synge and the Ireland of his Time* (Dublin: Cuala Press, 1911), p.3.
58 Heaney, *Preoccupations*, p.135.
59 Richard Kearney, Introduction in R.Kearney (ed.), *The Irish Mind* (Dublin: Wolfhound Press, 1984), p.9.
60 Brendan Purcell, 'In search of Newgrange: Long Night's Journey Into Day', in Kearney (ed.), *The Irish Mind*, p.44.
61 Mark Patrick Hederman, 'Poetry and the Fifth Province', *The Crane Bag*, vol.9, no.1, 1985.
62 S. Heaney, *An Open Letter* (Derry: Field Day Pamphlets no.2, 1983).
63 Heaney, *Preoccupations*, pp.132, 145.
64 ibid., p.17.
65 O'Faolain, op.cit., p.14.
66 Speaking at the opening of an exhibition of work by John Behan, Kenny Gallery, Galway, 18 September 1987.
67 Steiner, *Language and Silence*, pp.12 and 39.
68 ibid., p.33.
69 E.Estyn Evans, *The Personality of Ireland* (Belfast: Blackstaff Press, 1973) pp. 26–27.
70 A.T.Q. Stewart, *The Narrow Ground: Aspects of Ulster, 1609–1939* (London: Faber and Faber, 1977) p.181.
71 F.S.L. Lyons, *Culture and Anarchy in Ireland 1890–1939* (Oxford: Oxford University Press, 1978) p.145.
72 Crapanzano, 'Liminal recreations'.
73 *Butcher's Dozen*, originally published Dublin: Peppercanister Press, 1972; reprinted in Thomas Kinsella, *Fifteen Dead* (Mountrath: Dolmen Press, 1979).
74 Friel, in 'The Future of Irish Drama', *The Irish Times*, 12 February 1970.
75 cf. Eavan Boland, 'The Northern writer and the Troubles', *The Irish Times*, 13 August 1972.
76 Quoted by D.E.S. Maxwell, *Brian Friel* (Bucknell: Bucknell University Press, 1973), p.29.
77 Friel, 'Plays peasant and unpeasant'.
78 Brink, op.cit., p.192.
79 In conversation with the author.
80 Thomas Kilroy, 'The Irish writer, self and society 1950–1980', in Peter Connolly (ed.), *Literature and the Changing Ireland* (Gerrards Cross: Colin Smythe, 1982).
81 A. Brink, *An Instant in the Wind* (London: Flamingo, 1976), p.138.
82 *The Writers*, pp.40–1.

83 Thomas Kinsella, 'The divided mind', in S.Lucy (ed.) *Irish Poets in English* (Cork: Mercier Press, 1972), pp.209, 213.

84 O'Toole, 'The man'.

85 cf. also the story 'Kelly's Hall'.

86 *The Irish Times*, 12 August 1972.

87 *Henry the Fifth*, Act lll, scene 1.

88 Declan Kiberd, 'Inventing Irelands', *The Crane Bag*, vol.8, no.1, 1984.

89 Francis Peabody Magown, Jr, *Kalevala* (Cambridge, Mass: Harvard University Press, 1963).

90 W.B. Yeats, 'Literature and the living voice', quoted by Denis Donoghue, 'The problem of being Irish', *Times Literary Supplement*, 17 March 1972.

91 Friel's diary entry for 15 May 1979, first published as a preface to the programme for *Translations* and reprinted in Coogan (ed.).

92 S. Deane, 'Irish poetry and Irish nationalism', in Douglas Dunn (ed.), *Two Decades of Irish Writing* (Cheadle: Carcanet Press, 1975), pp. 5, 7.

93 T. Kilroy, preface to *The Enemy Within*.

94 S. Heaney, interview with Seamus Deane, in *The Crane Bag Book of Irish Studies* (Dublin: Blackwater Press, 1982), p. 66.

95 Beckett, *Trilogy*, pp. 26, 267.

2 THE SHORT STORIES

1 Beckett, *Trilogy*, p.336.

2 S. Deane, introduction to *The Diviner*, p. 9.

3 Dantanus (1988), pp. 84, 128, 132, 152, 202.

4 Interview with D.E.S. Maxwell, *Images: Arts and the People in Northern Ireland* (Belfast: Northern Ireland Information Office/Arts Council of Northern Ireland, n.d.).

5 ibid.

6 Ulf Dantanus, *Brian Friel: the Growth of an Irish Dramatist* (Goteborg: Gothenburg Studies in English 59, Acta Universitatis Gotheburgensis, 1985) p. 174: hereafter referred to as Dantanus (1985).

7 A.N. Jeffares, 'Place, space and personality and the Irish writer', in A. Carpenter (ed.), *Place, Personality and the Irish Writer* (Gerrards Cross: Colin Smythe, 1977), p.167.

8 Quoted in Heaney, *Preoccupations*, p.139.

9 Friel, 'Plays peasant and unpeasant'.

10 B.Friel, 'The child', *The Bell*, vol.18, no.4, July 1952.

11 Dantanus (1988), p.23.

12 B. Friel, 'A challenge to *Acorn*', *Acorn*, no. 14, 1970.

13 Robert Lacy, *Canadian Journal of Irish Studies*, vol.7, no.2, December 1981.

14 S. O'Faolain, *The Irish* (Harmondsworth: Penguin Books, 1969), p. 143.

15 O'Faolain, *The Great O'Neill*, pp. 7, 23.

16 cf. Deane, 'Irish poetry and Irish nationalism', and 'Remembering the Irish future', *The Crane Bag*, vol.8, no.l, 1984.

17 *Diviner*, pp.15–16.

18 Meg Enright's mistaken perceptions about time future in 'Winners' provide a similar example of physical sense becoming metaphysically damaging.

19 *Diviner*, pp. 9–10.

20 ibid., p. 13.

21 Dantanus (1988) p.57.

22 In conversation with the author.

23 *Diviner*, pp. 15–16.

24 ibid., p. 12.

25 Northrop Frye, *Anatomy of Criticism* (New York: Cornell University Press, 1957), p. 151.

26 Chekhov, *The Cherry Orchard*, Act 2, pp. 354, 355; Act 3, p. 375, in *Plays by Anton Chekhov* (Harmondsworth: Penguin, 1954).

27 Maxwell, *Brian Friel*, pp. 38, 46; cf. also Maxwell's comments, ibid., pp. 17–18, 31, 46–7.

28 Raymond Williams, *The Country and the City* (London: Chatto and Windus, 1973), p.62.

3 PLAYS OF LOVE

1 Friel, *Living Quarters*, p.44.

2 In Peter Lewis (ed.) *Radio Drama* (London: Longman, 1981), p.52.

3 Frye, op.cit., p. 134.

4 Ian Rodger, *Radio Drama* (Basingstoke: Macmillan, 1982), p.18.

5 ibid., pp. 18–19.

6 Ronald Mason in conversation with the author. In addition to the early radio plays, the following have been produced by the BBC: *The Enemy Within*, 1963; *The Blind Mice*, 1963; *The Founder Members*, 1964; *Philadelphia, Here I Come!*, 1965; *The Gentle Island*, 1973; *Faith Healer*, 1980; *Translations*, 1982; *Aristocrats* and *Making History*, 1989; and the short story 'The potato gatherers', 1985 (information supplied by BBC Radio Drama department). cf. also Dantanus (1988), pp. 75–7.

7 'A sort of freedom', typescript, p. 48.

8 'To this hard house', typescript, p. 53.

9 'A doubtful paradise', typescript, p. 48.

10 'A sort of freedom', p. 38; the text of the typescript (from the archives of BBC Northern Ireland) which I have quoted, clearly differs from that read, and quoted, by Ulf Dantanus: cf. Dantanus (1985), p.84.

11 ibid.

12 'To this hard house', p. 22.

13 'A doubtful paradise', p. 38.

14 'A sort of freedom', p. 43.

15 ibid., p. 8.

16 'To this hard house', p. 22.

17 William Molyneux, *Dioptrica Nova* (London: 1692).

18 'A sort of freedom', p. 3.
19 Although, as Ronald Mason pointed out to the author, a radio version of *Philadelphia* depends on *one* voice speaking Gar's *two* roles.
20 Edmund Burke, *Reflections on the Revolution in France*, ed. Conor Cruise O'Brien (Harmondsworth: Penguin Books, 1968), p.169.
21 Guthrie, *In Various Directions*, p. 25.
22 ibid., pp. 28–9.
23 'The blind mice', typescript, p. 30.
24 Interview in *The Guardian*, 8 October 1964.
25 ibid.
26 ibid.
27 'The blind mice', p. 26.
28 ibid., p.34.
29 ibid.; on the Irish proclivity for abandoning God (*deus absconditus*), see R.Pine, *Rough Edges: Commitment in Contemporary Irish Drama* (Dublin: Arts Ireland, 1989).
30 ibid., p.37.
31 ibid., p.48.
32 W.B.Yeats, *Wheels and Butterflies*, 1934, p.6.
33 cf. Arendt, op.cit., vol.1, pp. 202–12.
34 W.B. Yeats, *The Poems*, ed. R. Finneran (Dublin: Gill and Macmillan, 1984), p. 73.
35 Arendt, op.cit., vol.1, p.75.
36 James Simmons, 'Brian Friel, Catholic playwright', *The Honest Ulsterman*, no.79, Autumn 1985, p. 62.
37 cf. Dantanus (1985), p.215.
38 Christopher Murray, 'The rough and holy theatre of Tom Murphy', *Irish University Review*, Spring 1987, vol.17, no.1.
39 I owe this point to Colm Toibin, 'Tom Murphy's volcanic Ireland', *Irish University Review*, vol.17, no.1.
40 See my chapter, 'Tom Murphy's theatre of madness and despair' in my forthcoming *Homecomings*.
41 Programme note for *Famine*, Druid Theatre, Galway, 1984.
42 Thomas Murphy, *Bailegangaire* (Dublin: Gallery Press, 1986), p.71.
43 Fintan O'Toole makes the case for Murphy in 'Homo absconditus, the apocalyptic imagination in *The Gigli Concert*', *Irish University Review*, vol.17, no.1.
44 Preface to E. O'Neill, *Long Day's Journey Into Night* (London: Cape, 1976).
45 Interview with John Waters, 'The frontiersman', *In Dublin*, 15 May 1986.
46 G.B. Shaw, *John Bull's Other Island*, in *The Bodley Head Bernard Shaw* (London: The Bodley Head, 1971), vol. 2: Act 1, pp. 913, 919.
47 ibid., Act 4, p. 1016.
48 Steiner, *After Babel*, p. 47.
49 Friel's diary entry for 6 July 1979 (Coogan, ed.).
50 Quoted in Arendt, op.cit., vol. 2, p.4.
51 Friel also somewhat ineptly attempts the same comparison in *The Blind Mice*.
52 Beckett, *Trilogy*, p.352.

53 cf. Arendt, op.cit., vol.2, pp.99, 164.
54 Steiner, *In Bluebeard's Castle* (London: Faber and Faber, 1971), p.13.
55 Quoted by G. Poulet, *Studies in Human Time: Valéry* (Baltimore, Md.: Johns Hopkins Press, 1956), p.280.
56 cf. Arendt, op.cit., vol.1, p. 192.
57 ibid., vol.2, p. 193.

4 PLAYS OF FREEDOM

1 Chekhov, *Uncle Vanya*, Act 2, p. 209.
2 Descartes, *Philosophical Works* (Cambridge: Cambridge University Press, 1970), vol. 2, p.75.
3 MacNeice, op.cit., p.69.
4 John Hewitt, *The Selected Poems of John Hewitt* (Belfast: Blackstaff Press, 1981), p.20.
5 cf. Thomas Kinsella and Sean O'Tuama (eds.), introduction to *An Duanaire: poems of the dispossessed* (Mountrath: Dolmen Press, 1981), pp. xxvii–xxix.
6 Heaney, *An Open Letter*.
7 Kinsella and O' Tuama, op.cit., p.195.
8 John Milton, *Paradise Lost*, book 1, lines 1-6.
9 O'Neill, p. 61.
10 cf. Beckett, *Trilogy*, p. 167: 'that is what reason counsels. But reason has not much hold on me just now...I intend to take the risk.'
11 Beckett, *That Time* (1974–5), in *Collected Shorter Plays* (London: Faber and Faber, 1984), p.228.
12 Beckett, *Endgame* (London: Faber and Faber, 1958), p.21.
13 T.S.Eliot, *The Family Reunion*, in *The Complete Poems and Plays* (London: Faber and Faber, 1969), p.307.
14 Lewis, op.cit., p.100.
15 ibid., p. xlvi.
16 quoted in Laing, op.cit., p 118.
17 Friel, 'The theatre of hope and despair'.
18 ibid.
19 *The Irish Times*, 14 August 1972.
20 Eamonn McCann, *War and an Irish Town* (London: Pluto Press, 1980, second edition), p.13.
21 ibid., p. 9.
22 ibid., p 118.
23 O'Neill, p. 147.
24 Gus Smith and Des Hickey (eds.), *A Paler Shade of Green* (London: Frewin, 1972), p.221.
25 ibid.
26 *The Irish Times*, 13 August 1972.
27 Smith and Hickey, *Paler Shade of Green*, p. 222.
28 The late Stewart Parker latterly followed a rather ambivalent path: he wrote a six-part series *Lost Belongings* for BBC Northern Ireland television in which 'the myth of "The Exile of the Sons of Uisliu" or

"Deirdre of the Sorrows" tied together the multi-layered tragedies of ancient and modern Ireland' (Helena Sheehan, *Irish Television Drama: A Society and its Stories*, Dublin: Radio Telefís Éireann, 1987, p. 22). He also wrote a more unequivocal confrontation between Catholic and Protestant beliefs, traditions and communities in *Pentecost* written for Field Day (also 1987). The title of the television series *Lost Belongings* in itself ambiguously draws together the idea of displaced tradition and the fact of present dislocation or dispossession.

29 James Simmons, 'Brian Friel, Catholic playwright', *The Honest Ulsterman*, no. 79, Autumn 1985, p.61.

30 Deane, Introduction to *Selected Plays of Brian Friel*, p.16.

31 cf. Smith and Hickey, *Paler Shade of Green*, p.224.

32 Joseph Mary Plunkett, 'I see his blood upon the rose', in *The 1916 Poets*, ed. Desmond Ryan (Dublin: Figgis, 1963), p.192.

33 Seamus Deane in conversation with the author.

34 in a letter to Seamus Deane, quoted by Deane in conversation with the author.

35 Seamus Deane, ('The writer and the Troubles'), *Threshold*, no.25, Summer 1974.

36 ibid.

37 ibid.

38 Conor Cruise O'Brien, *Herod: Reflections on Political Violence* (London: Hutchinson, 1978), p.19.

39 Kinsella, *Fifteen Dead*, p.57.

40 Interview with D.E.S. Maxwell, in *Images*.

41 O'Brien, op.cit., p.20.

42 Simmons, 'Brian Friel, Catholic playwright', p.63.

43 Kinsella, *Fifteen Dead*, p.57.

44 ibid.

45 *Report of the Tribunal appointed to inquire into the events on Sunday, 30th. January 1972 which led to loss of life in connection with the procession in Londonderry on that day by the Rt Hon. Lord Widgery OBE TD* (London: Her Majesty's Stationery Office, 1972).

46 Elizabeth Hale Winkler, 'Reflections of Derry's Bloody Sunday in literature', in Heinz Kosok (ed.), *Studies in Anglo-Irish Literature* (Bonn: Bouvier Verlag Herbert Grundmann, 1982), p.421.

47 Lewis, p.xliii.

48 ibid.

49 Bernadette Devlin (now Devlin McAliskey), politician, who has stood for election in both Northern Ireland and the Republic. Born 1947, elected MP at the age of 21 in 1969. Founded the Irish Republican Socialist Party in 1971. Author of the autobiography *The Price of My Soul*.

50 Simon Winchester, *In Holy Terror* (London: Faber and Faber, 1974), p.202.

51 McCann, op.cit., p.28.

52 Ulick O'Connor, 'Brian Friel: crisis and commitment. The writer and Northern Ireland' (Dublin: Elo Publications, 1989: text of a lecture to Yeats International School, Sligo, 20 August 1987). Reference in this

context should also be made to T.G. Fitzgibbon, 'Some overt and covert political implications in Brian Friel's *The Freedom of the City, Volunteers* and *Aristocrats*', paper read to the American Conference of Irish Studies, Boston, 1986.

53 Abbey Theatre programme, 1 February 1988.
54 Sean O'Casey, *Three Plays* (London: Pan, 1980), p.130.
55 ibid.,p.107.
56 Turner, op.cit., pp.259–60.
57 Beckett, *Trilogy*, pp.166, 274, 295, 379.
58 Heaney, *Preoccupations*, pp.214–15.
59 ibid.
60 ibid.
61 'The theatre of hope and despair'.
62 *Hamlet*, Act 3, scene 2.
63 In conversation with the author.
64 *Selected Plays of Brian Friel*, p.353: these lines were omitted from the text as originally published.
65 Simmons, p.66.
66 From a radio broadcast quoted on the dustjacket of the first edition of *Lovers*.
67 Michael Longley, interview with Dillon Johnston, *Irish Literary Supplement*, vol.5, no.2, Autumn 1986.
68 Friel's diary entry for 10 September 1977, *The Writers*, p.42.
69 Turner, op.cit., p.255.
70 Like the commentators in 'Winners' (*Lovers*) and the Stage Manager in Thornton Wilder's *Our Town*. Ruth Niel also draws attention to Wilder's *Pullman Car Hiawatha* in this respect.
71 Thomas Kilroy, op. cit.
72 In conversation with the author.
73 Friel's diary entry for 7 December 1976, in *The Writers*, p.40.
74 cf. Dantanus (1988) pp.85–6.
75 Friel's diary entry for 5 November 1979, in Coogan (ed.), p.61.
76 Friel's diary entry for 16 December 1977, *The Writers*, p.43.
77 Tyrone Guthrie, quoted in Sam Hanna Bell, 'Theatre', Michael Longley (ed.) *Causeway: The Arts in Ulster* (Belfast: Arts Council of Northern Ireland, 1971), p.89.
78 Friel's diary entry for 8 January 1977, *The Writers*, p.41.
79 cf. F.Ormsby, 'Brian Friel's plays', *The Honest Ulsterman*, 1970, no.23.
80 Vivian Mercier, *Beckett/Beckett* (Oxford: Oxford University Press, 1977), p.xii.
81 I am reminded of the attitude of Nikolai Vasilievich in Gerhardie's *Futility* (1922) which Friel had not read at that time: Nikolai single-mindedly pursues a young girl, whose love offers him a once-in-a-lifetime freedom, to the neglect of his own family. His wife says: 'I had to realize that indeed nothing could shame him. So good and wise and indeed well versed was he in his wickedness, that there could be no crime, no sin, of which we others could accuse him of which he had not already in his goodness and wisdom accused himself', William Gerhardie, *Futility* (New York: St Martin's Press, 1971), pp.34–5. Once again the

similarity between the saintliness of the Russian *staretsi* and the Irish bewitched, both of them disengaged from moral society, is striking.

82 *The Seagull produced by K.S.Stanislavsky*, edited with an introduction by S.D. Balukhaty, translated by David Magarshack (London: Dobson, 1952).

83 Friel's diary entry for 10 September 1976, *The Writers*, p.40.

84 Reference should be made to an unpublished monograph, 'Filiation and affiliation in the work of Brian Friel', Anthony Bradley, University of Vermont.

85 cf.Dantanus (1988) p.99 and Dantanus (1985) p.221.

86 For example, the question of Yolland's age: the stage directions refer to Yolland as being in his late twenties or early thirties. The really vexing question, for those who want to be vexed, is: what age was Yolland *père* when George was conceived? The year is now 1833, and Yolland senior was born in 1789; he is now 44. Allowing George to be anything from 28 to 32, his father engendered him when he himself was anything from 12 to 16 years old. 'There were no longer any frontiers to man's potential!' Similarly in *Fathers and Sons* Vassily Bazarov notes that his son 'usually brings someone home with him every holiday' (*FS* 39) despite the fact that this is Bazarov's *first* visit home. And those with a flawless knack for map-reading can indulge in locating the actual 'Ballybeg', using the information supplied by Friel (*Tr.* 67) that by walking from Ballybeg for twenty-three miles one may arrive in Glenties. But this is to indulge too much in the 'how many children had Lady Macbeth' school of criticism.

87 As D.E.S. Maxwell says in respect of *Philadelphia, Cass* and *Crystal and Fox*, 'he looks on these…as inspections of the diversities of love, undertaken in the way that a sculptor views his work from different angles', D.E.S. Maxwell, *Brian Friel* (Lewisburg Pa.: Bucknell University Press, 1973), p.78.

88 W.J. Cloonan, *Racine's Theatre: The Politics of Love* (Mississippi University Press, 1977), pp. 113–16.

89 George Steiner, *Antigones* (Oxford: Oxford University Press, 1986).

90 In conversation with the author.

91 Flann O'Brien, *At Swim-Two-Birds* (Harmondsworth: Penguin, 1967), p. 25: 'it was undemocratic to compel characters to be uniformly good or bad, or poor or rich. Each should be allowed a private life, self-determination and a decent standard of living.' It is ironic to note that in *Making History*, history, fate, or the historian, deny all three to the ailing Hugh O'Neill.

92 Steiner, *After Babel*, p. 454.

93 C.W.E. Bigsby points out the significant number of plays employing the device of the mental hospital in contemporary drama: Durrenmatt's *The Scientists* (1962); Weiss's *Marat/Sade* (1963); Kesey's *One Flew Over The Cuckoo's Nest* (1963); Albee's *Listening* (1960); Storey's *Home* (1970); Orton's *What the Butler Saw* (1968); Shaffer's *Equus* (1973) Edgar's *Mary Barnes* (1977); Stoppard's *Every Good Boy Deserves Favour* (1977); Mary O'Malley's *Look Out...Here Comes Trouble* (1970): 'The language of Crisis in British theatre', *Contemporary English Drama*, p.19.

94 Eugene McCabe, in conversation with the author, remarked that he feels considerable pity for S.B.O' Donnell, a point very well drawn out by Joe Dowling's 1986 production of *Philadelphia* at the Gaiety Theatre, Dublin, with Seamus Forde as S.B. In this production, however, the gesture was omitted, and the author's stage directions were ignored; instead, S.B. picked up, and scrutinised, his son's passport.
95 Fergus Linehan, *Hibernia*, September 1967, p. 26.
96 Frye, op.cit., p. 285.

5 PLAYS OF LANGUAGE

1 Steiner, *After Babel*, p.73.
2 cf. the Cornish proverb, collected in 1790: 'Bes den hab tavas a golhas e dir' (a man without a tongue has lost his land), Myrna Combellack Harris, 'Cornish bilingualism in the coming decades', *Bulletin of the European Bureau for Lesser Used Languages* , 1989, and Csilla Bertha, 'Tragedies of national fate; a comparison between Brian Friel's *Translations* and its Hungarian counterpart, Andras Suto's *A szugai menyegzo*', *Irish University Review*, vol. 17, no. 2, Autumn 1987.
3 Tom Paulin, *A new look at the language question* (Derry: Field Day Theatre Company, 1983 *Field Day Pamphlets* no.l).
4 Friel's diary entries for 29 May and 1 June 1979, in Coogan, p.58.
5 Friel's diary entry for 6 July 1979, p.60.
6 cf. Ronald Hayman, *British Theatre since 1955* (Oxford: Oxford University Press, 1979), p. 9.
7 Quoted by Hayman, *British Theatre*, p.8.
8 Friel's diary entry for 22 May 1979, in Coogan (ed.), p.58.
9 D.E.S. Maxwell in Connolly, op.cit., p.173.
10 Information from Heslinga, op.cit., p.194.
11 ibid., p. 161.
12 ibid.
13 ibid.
14 Larcom, quoted by Kevin Barry, *The Crane Bag*, vol.7, no.2, p. 119.
15 P.J. Dowling, *The Hedge-Schools of Ireland* (Cork: Mercier Press, 1968); John O'Donovan, *Letters Containing Information relative to the Antiquities collected during the progress of the Ordnance Survey* (1927); T.Colby, *Ordnance Survey of the County of Londonderry*, 1837.
16 John Andrews, *The Crane Bag*, vol.7, no.2, pp.118–24; just as Baudelaire commented at the Salon of 1846, 'there are two ways of understanding portraiture, either as history or as fiction', Charles Baudelaire, 'The Salon of 1846' in Baudelaire, *Art in Paris 1845–62* (London: Phaidon, 1981), p.88.
17 Sean Connolly, 'Dreaming history: Brian Friel's *Translations*', *Theatre Ireland*, no.13, 1987, p.42.
18 B. Friel, John Andrews and K. Barry, 'Translations and paper landscape: between fiction and history', *The Crane Bag*, vol.7, no.2, p.122.
19 ibid., p.123.
20 Sean Connolly, 'Dreaming history', p.43.

21 *The Crane Bag*, vol.7, no.2, pp.122–4.
22 cf. Richard Kearney, 'The creativity of language', *Dialogues with Contemporary Continental Thinkers: the phenomenological heritage* (Manchester: Manchester University Press, 1984), pp.20, 23, 28.
23 cf. Tom Dunne, 'A polemical introduction', to T.Dunne (ed.), *The Writer as Witness* (Cork: Cork University Press, 1987).
24 Kearney, *Dialogues*, p.44.
25 *The Sunday Times*, 28 September 1980.
26 Carpenter, op.cit., p.181.
27 cf. *Annals of the Four Masters*, ed. John O'Donovan (Dublin: Figgis, 1856), vol.6, p. 2285. It is ironic also to note O'Donovan's wry comment about differing chronologies: 'the Irish were defeated at Kinsale on the 24th. of December, 1601, according to the old style then observed by the English, but on the 3rd. of January 1602, according to the Irish and Spaniards' (ibid. p.2290).
28 'Making History', typescript, p.58. The words are omitted in the printed text (*MH* 44).
29 Interview with Paddy Agnew, *Magill*, December 1980.
30 cf. also O'Faolain, op.cit., p.12.
31 'The required declaration is not an oath...the signing of it implies no contractual obligation, and...it has no binding significance in conscience or in law...It is merely an empty political formula, which deputies could conscientiously sign without becoming involved, or without involving their nation, in obligations of loyalty to the English Crown', *Speeches and Statements by Eamon de Valera 1917–1973*, ed. M. Moynihan (Dublin: Gill and Macmillan, 1980), p.150.
32 In a lecture at Trinity College, Dublin, 28 April 1987.
33 Ibid., quoted by Dan H.Laurence.
34 Steiner, *After Babel*, p.161.
35 Heidegger in 'Poetry, language, thought', quoted in the programme note to the original production of *Translations*. The passage continues: 'in fact it is language that speaks. Man begins speaking and man only speaks to the extent that he responds to, that he corresponds with, language, and only in so far as he hears language addressing, concurring with, him.' Steiner also prefaces *After Babel* with this passage.
36 Richard Kearney, 'Language play: Brian Friel and Ireland's verbal theatre', *Studies*, Spring 1983 (reprinted, with additional material, in Kearney, *Transitions: Narratives in Modern Irish Culture* (Dublin: Wolfhound, 1987), p.29).
37 Claude Lévi-Strauss, *Myth and Meaning* (London: Routledge and Kegan Paul, 1978), p.12.
38 cf. Seamus Deane, 'An example of tradition', *Crane Bag Book of Irish Studies* (Dublin: Blackwater Press, 1982) vol. 1, p. 373. Deane also observes 'the Irish idea of tradition was naturally more inclined towards the notion of continuity betrayed than of continuity retained' (ibid. p.374).
39 Lawrence Durrell, *The Key to Modern Poetry* (London: Peter Nevill, 1952), p.158.

40 Kearney, 'Language play'. For this reason Kearney has placed considerable emphasis on what I have called Friel's 'dramatisation' of Steiner's text. In the Appendix to his essay he lists the main points in the first chapter of *After Babel* which Friel has 'translated'. Two further significant statements by Steiner also require to be noted: firstly, that from p.58 of *After Babel* which becomes the core of the map-making exercise in *Translations*; secondly, *In Bluebeard's Castle* (London: Faber and Faber, 1971), p.21: 'Hegel could argue, with rigorous logic of feeling, that history itself was passing into a new state of being, that ancient time was at an end', which becomes the philosophy of Yolland *père* (*Tr.* 40).

41 Introduction to the programme for *The Communication Cord*.

42 Robert Hogan, *Since O'Casey and other essays* (Gerrards Cross: Colin Smythe, 1983), p.131.

43 ibid.

44 Friel's diary, 1 June 1979, Coogan (ed.), p.59.

45 Beckett, *Trilogy*, p.177.

46 Laing, op.cit., pp.108–9.

47 Bigsby, 'The language of crisis in British Theatre', *Contemporary English Drama*, p. 25.

48 See a collection of reviews of *The Communication Cord* in *Theatre Ireland*, no.2, January–May 1983, by (among others) Gerald Dawe, James Simmons and Emelie Fitzgibbon.

49 Kearney, 'Language play'.

50 cf. Friel's diary for 7 January 1977 and 2 June 1977, *The Writers*, pp.41–2.

51 Seamus Heaney, *North* (London: Faber and Faber, 1975), p.60.

52 In conversation with the author.

53 Dowling, pp.38, 210.

54 John O'Donovan, in a letter quoted in the programme for *Translations*: 'The men only, who go to markets and fairs, speak a little English.' Cf. also Michael Hartnett, *A Farewell to English* (Dublin: Gallery Press, 1975), p.67: 'a fit language for selling pigs'.

55 Dowling, op.cit., p.59.

56 ibid. p. 82.

57 ibid., pp. 84–5.

58 Proinnsias MacCana, 'Early Irish ideology and the concept of unity', in R. Kearney (ed.), *The Irish Mind*, p.60.

59 ibid.

60 Andrews, *The Crane Bag*, loc.cit, p.121.

61 ibid. p. 122.

62 Beckett, *Trilogy*, p.303.

63 Kearney, 'Language play', p.34.

64 'Everything unreal...all served up in that polite, dead language. No roots. No contact with nature, with people', Thomas Kilroy, *The Seagull* (London: Methuen, 1981), p.10.

65 Virgil, *Aeneid*, Book 1, line 16.

66 Steiner, *In Bluebeard's Castle*, p.21.

67 O'Faolain, op. cit., p.94.

68 cf. Mahler's pathetic insistence on the permanent in the concluding lines

of *Das Lied von der erde*: 'everywhere and eternally the distance shines bright and blue. Eternally, eternally.'

69 O'Faolain, op. cit., pp. 1, 148.
70 ibid., p.15.
71 Friel originally discovered this fragment, attributed to Ovid, in a collection which it has since proved impossible to trace.
72 In conversation with the author. The point is also made strongly in an interview with Fintan O'Toole, *In Dublin*, 28 October 1982.
73 Brian Friel, *American Welcome, Best Short Plays of 1981*, ed. Stanley Richards (Radnor, Pa: Chilton, 1982).
74 Kearney, 'Language play'.
75 In conversation with the author, and in the interview with O'Toole, *In Dublin*.
76 Steiner, *Language and Silence*, p.109.
77 Laing, op.cit., p.162.
78 Goffman, op.cit., p.5.
79 ibid. p.73.
80 ibid., pp. 99, 116. It should furthermore be noted that Tim's 'discourse analysis', especially the way he promotes the Steinerian problem of inter-personal and inter-cultural translation, owes something to Denis Donoghue: 'The addresser wants to send a message to the addressee. This message needs a context which both parties can share, a code common to them in encoding and decoding the message... The source selects three sub-acts: reception, decoding and development', Denis Donoghue, 'Communication, communion, conversation', *Ferocious Alphabets* (London: Faber and Faber, 1981), pp.42–3.

6 A FIELD DAY

1 Tom Stoppard, *Rosencrantz and Guildenstern Are Dead* (London: Faber and Faber, 1967), p.31.
2 Brian Friel, 'This doubtful paradise', typescript, p.31.
3 O'Faolain, op. cit.
4 In P.Connolly (ed.), op.cit., p.203.
5 It may be helpful to elaborate the intention behind this *regard* in further consideration of the 'Judas-hole': in this case, in the sense used by Jerome Bruner in his 'essays in autobiography' *In Search of Mind* (New York: Harper & Row, 1983), Bruner asks 'How could people *know* that something was potentially threatening unless they could first *see* it?' He speaks of 'something passing through a Judas Eye, letting a perceiver decide whether to open the portal of perception to let it in' (p.80). The Judas-hole thus becomes not only a gimmick in *Aristocrats* (etcetera) but also an integral part of the 'aesthetic security system' outlined above.
6 I employ the neologism 'anatonic' as the preliminary (and antithesis) to 'catatonic', meaning 'toning up': anabasis as opposed to katabasis.
7 Gus Smith and Des Hickey (eds.), *A Paler Shade of Green* (London: Frewin, 1972), pp.224–5.
8 In a lecture to the Royal Dublin Society, November 1984.

9 *Everyman*, no.1, 1968.
10 'Plays peasant and unpeasant'
11. *Magill.*
12 *The Irish Times*, 27 April 1987. His membership, as a direct personal appointee of the Taoiseach (Prime Minister) was taken to indicate his support for the Fianna Fail party. But despite the fact that he was photographed entering the House on the first day in the company of the Taoiseach's son (also a Senator) and that he inadvertently sat during the opening session on the government benches (see *The Irish Times*, 7 May 1987) until removing himself to the seats for Independents, he displayed no automatic loyalty to any party or group.
13 Tom Paulin, *The Riot Act: a Version of* Antigone *by Sophocles* (London: Faber and Faber, 1985).
14 Derek Mahon, *High Time* (Dublin: Gallery Press, 1985).
15 Thomas Kilroy, *Double Cross* (London: Faber and Faber, 1986).
16 Stewart Parker, *Pentecost*, in *Three Plays for Ireland*, Oberon Books, 1989.
17 Terry Eagleton, *Saint Oscar* (Derry: Field Day Theatre Company, 1989).
18 Seamus Heaney, *Sweeney Astray: a version from the Irish* (Derry: Field Day Theatre Company, 1983).
19 Field Day Pamphlets, no.1: Tom Paulin, 'A new look at the language question'; no.2: Seamus Heaney, 'An open letter'; no.3: Seamus Deane, 'Civilians and barbarians'; no.4: Seamus Deane, 'Heroic styles'; no.5: Richard Kearney, 'Myth and motherland'; no.6: Declan Kiberd, 'Anglo-Irish attitudes'; no.7: Terence Brown, 'The whole Protestant community'; no.8: Marianne Elliott, 'Watchmen in Sion'; no.9: Robert McCartney, 'Liberty and authority in Ireland'; no.10: Eanna Mulloy, 'Dynamics of coercion'; no.11: Michael Farrell, 'The apparatus of repression'; no.12: Patrick J.McGrory, 'Law and the constitution: present discontents'; no.13: Terry Eagleton, 'Nationalism: irony and commitment'; no.14: Fredric Jameson, 'Modernism and imperialism'; no.15: Edward Said, 'Yeats and colonialism'.
20 *Field Day Anthology of Irish Writing*, ed. Seamus Deane (Derry: Field Day Theatre Company, 1990).
21 Smith and Hickey, *A Paler Shade of Green*, p.223.
22 Programme note for *Translations*.
23 Programme note for *Three Sisters*.
24 In a speech at University College, Dublin, 21 September 1987.
25 Seamus Deane, programme note for *Three Sisters*.
26 *The Seagull produced by K.S.Stanislavsky.*
27 Programme note for *The Communication Cord*.
28 Colm Kelly, 'Homecomings and diversions: cultural nationalism and the recent drama of Brian Friel', *Studies*, Winter 1987
29 Programme note for *The Communication Cord*.
30 Kelly, 'Homecomings and diversions'.
31 cf. Mitchell Harris, 'Friel and Heaney: Field Day and the Voice of the Fifth Province', MLA conference paper, 1984.
32 cf. Dantanus (1988), pp.184–5.

33 In a letter to the author.

34 Olwen Fouéré, quoted in Kearney, 'Language play'.

35 Discussed by Martin Esslin in a lecture on Beckett's latest work, Trinity College, Dublin, December 1984.

36 Interview with Diana Taplin, *The Guardian*, 1 December 1986.

37 cf. D.E.S. Maxwell, 'The honour of naming: Samuel Beckett and Brian Friel', *A Critical History of Modern Irish Drama 1891–1980* (Cambridge: Cambridge University Press, 1984).

38 I am indebted to Vincent Mahon for this observation.

39 In *Rough for Theatre l*, dating from the 1950s, Beckett anticipates Friel on the alter ego: 'what does my soul look like?'(*Collected Shorter Plays*, p.71). There is of course an even earlier example of an Irish writer exploring this theme: Flann O'Brien's *At Swim-Two-Birds* (1939) says 'he was consumed with doubts as to his own identity, as to the nature of his body and to the cast of his countenance' (p.42). Beckett also engages in a Chekhovian ideal of freedom: 'Tomorrow, who knows, we may be free' (*Rough for Radio ll*, p.124). In *Endgame* Hamm answers Clov's question 'Do you believe in the life to come?' with 'Mine was always that' (*Endgame*, London: Faber and Faber, 1958 p.35). Furthermore, both writers allude to time past as a door into time future: Winnie's 'the old style' in *Happy Days* (London: Faber and Faber, 1963), p.16, and Nell's 'yesterday' in *Endgame* correspond closely to Trilbe's 'yesterday' in *Cass*.

40 Fintan O'Toole, 'Contemporary Irish Theatre: the illusion of tradition', in Coogan (ed.), p.132.

41 Thomas Murphy, *The Morning After Optimism* (Cork: Mercier Press, 1973), pp. 46 and 68; cf. Act 2 of *The Seagull* (Chekhov, op.cit. p.141): 'your "I" becomes blurred and you begin to think of yourself as if you were someone quite different – as "he" '.

42 In the filmscript of Richard Attenborough's *Gandhi*.

43 'Plays peasant and unpeasant'.

44 'Self-portrait'.

45 Interview with Maxwell, *Images*,

46 *Sunday Independent*, 19 July 1987.

47 'Fathers and Sons', typescript draft, p.22.

48 McNally wrote (among many other plays, ballads and musicals) *The Apotheosis of Punch* (1789), *Tristram Shandy* (1783) and *Critic Upon Critic* (1792).

49 'Fathers and Sons', typescript draft, pp.77–9.

50 Or, as Eliot puts it, 'The man who returns will have to meet/The boy who left', *The Family Reunion*, part 1, scene 1, *Complete Poems and Plays*, p.288.

51 'Fathers and Sons', typescript draft, p.152.

52 ibid., pp.180–1.

53 *The Irish Times*, 14 September 1982.

54 In conversation with the author.

55 *Images*.

56 *Magill*.

57 Smith and Hickey, *A Paler Shade of Green*, p.230.

58 O'Faolain, op. cit., pp. vi, 143.

59 ibid., pp 280–1.

60 Fintan O'Toole, *The Politics of Magic: the Life and Work of Tom Murphy* (Dublin: Raven Arts Press, 1987), p.15.

61 Tom Paulin, *The Riot Act*, p.332.

62 cf. O'Toole, *Politics of Magic*, pp. 97–8, 131, 137.

63 In respect of Mabel Bagenal, particularly the little we know of her, and of her leaving O'Neill, cf. O'Faolain, pp.62 and 121–2.

64 O'Faolain, op. cit., pp. 85, 129, 128.

65 ibid. p. 149.

66 cf. Justice Donal Barrington, Thomas Davis Lecture, 'The North and the Constitution', broadcast by Radio Telefís Eireann, 31 January 1988: published in Brian Farrell (ed.), *De Valera's Constitution and Ours* (Dublin: Gill and Macmillan, 1988).

67 'Making History', typescript draft, p.84.

68 Roy Foster, 'We are all revisionists now', *The Irish Review*, no.1, 1986, p.5.

69 In conversation with the author.

70 O'Faolain, op. cit., p.278.

71 Friel has adopted the description of 'Fox O'Neill' from a letter from Andrew Trollope to Walsingham, 12 September 1585, included in *The Life of Hugh O'Donnell* by Luadhaidh [Louis] O'Cleary, trans. D. Murphy, 1893.)

72 Discussing Adorno's 'Engagement' in *Crane Bag Book of Irish Studies*, vol.1, p.512.

73 Kearney, 'Language play'.

74 Laing, op.cit., p.36.

75 In conversation with the author.

AFTERWORD

1 'disavowed': in the sense that Friel has disclaimed, in conversation with the author, any recollection of participating in the conversation recorded in Gus Smith and Des Hickey (eds.), *A Paler Shade of Green* (London: Frewin, 1972), pp. 224–5.

2 in addition to his work cited above, reference should be made here to Turner's *From Ritual to Theatre* (1983) and *The Ritual Process* (1969/74). Michael Etherton makes valuable connections between anthropological work of this genre and *Dancing at Lughnasa* in his programme note on the play (Abbey Theatre, Dublin, 1990) and hints at it in his otherwise disappointing account of Friel in his *Contemporary Irish Dramatists* (Basingstoke: Macmillan, 1989).

3 Ciaran Benson, 'Art and the Ordinary: reflections on art, non-artists, and policy-making in Ireland', in *Art and the Ordinary: the ACE Report*, ed. C. Benson (Dublin: The Arts Council, 1990).

4 I discuss this further in 'Map-Making', a comparison of Friel's *Translations* and Brink's *An Instant In the Wind*, and in 'The decentralisation of literature', both in my *Homecomings*.

5 C. Benson, 'Art and the ordinary'.
6 George O'Brien refers to this as 'the discovery of an alternative emotional language' in his study *Brian Friel* (Dublin: Gill and Macmillan, 1990, p.59) which appeared too late for consideration in this volume; O'Brien also makes the valuable point (p. 123) that 'it is his persistent attempts to reveal images of the human, images that articulate an innate emotional power through their unsuccessful resistance to cultural and institutional impositions, that give Friel's work its depth and consistency'.
7 W.B. Yeats, quoted by Liam Miller, *The Noble Drama of W. B. Yeats* (Dublin: Dolmen Press, 1977), p. 195.
8 'The London vertigo', typescript, p. 4.

BIBLIOGRAPHY

Arendt, Hannah, *The Life of the Mind*, New York: Harcourt Brace Jovanovich, 2 vols, 1978.

Beckett, Samuel, *Trilogy [Molloy, Malone Dies, The Unnamable]*, London: Picador, 1979.

Brink, André, Mapmakers: Writing in a State of Siege, London: Faber and Faber, 1983.

Carpenter, Andrew (ed.), *Place, Personality and the Irish Writer*, Gerrards Cross: Colin Smythe, 1977.

Connolly, Peter (ed.), *Literature and the Changing Ireland*, Gerrards Cross: Colin Smythe, 1982.

Dantanus, Ulf, *Brian Friel, A Study*, London: Faber and Faber, 1988.

Dowling, P.J., *The Hedge-Schools of Ireland*, Cork: Mercier Press, 1968.

Evans, E.Estyn, *The Personality of Ireland*, Belfast: Blackstaff Press, 1973.

Forsyth, James, *Tyrone Guthrie*, London: Hamish Hamilton, 1976.

Frye, Northrop, *Anatomy of Criticism*, New York: Cornell University Press, 1957.

Guthrie, Tyrone, *In Various Directions*, London: Joseph, 1966.

Heaney Seamus, *Preoccupations: Selected Prose 1968–1978*, London: Faber and Faber, 1980.

Hederman, M.P. and Kearney, R. (eds), *The Crane Bag Book of Irish Studies*, vol.1, Dublin: Blackwater Press, 1982. Vol.2, Dublin: Wolfhound Press, 1987.

Heslinga, M.W., *The Irish Border as a Cultural Divide*, Amsterdam: van Gorcum, 1979.

Hogan, Robert, *Since O'Casey and Other Essays*, Gerrards Cross: Colin Smythe, 1983.

Kearney, Richard (ed.), *The Irish Mind: Exploring Intellectual Traditions*, Dublin: Wolfhound Press, 1984. *Transitions: Narratives in Modern Irish, Culture*, Dublin: Wolfhound Press, 1987.

Kinsella, Thomas, *Fifteen Dead*, Mountrath: Dolmen Press, 1979.

Kinsella, Thomas and O'Tuama, Sean, eds., *An Duanaire: poems of the Dispossessed*, Mountrath: Dolmen Press, 1981.

Laing, R.D., *The Politics of Experience*, Harmondsworth: Penguin, 1967.

Lewis, Peter (ed.), *Radio Drama*, London: Longman, 1981.

BIBLIOGRAPHY

Lyons, F.S.L., *Culture and Anarchy in Ireland 1890–1939*, Oxford: Oxford University Press, 1978.

McCann, Eamonn, *War and an Irish Town*, London: Pluto Press, 1980 (second edn).

Maxwell, D.E.S., *Brian Friel*, Bucknell: Bucknell University Press, 1973.
A Critical History of Modern Irish Drama, 1891–1980, Cambridge: Cambridge University Press, 1984.

Morrison, Blake, *Seamus Heaney*, London: Methuen, 1982.

Ngugi wa'Thiongo, *Decolonising the Mind: The Politics of Language in African Literature*, London: James Currey, 1986.

O'Faolain, Sean, *The Great O'Neill*, London: Longman, Green, 1942.

O'Toole, Fintan, *The Politics of Magic: The Life and Work of Tom Murphy*, Dublin: Raven Arts Press, 1987.

Steiner, George, *After Babel*, Oxford: Oxford University Press, 1975. *In Bluebeard's Castle: notes towards the Redefinition of Culture*, London: Faber and Faber, 1971.

Turner, V.W., *Dramas, Fields and Metaphors*, New York: Cornell University Press, 1974.

Zach, Wolfgang and Kosok, Heinz (eds), *Literary Interrelations: Ireland, England and the World*, Tübingen: Gunter Narr Verlag, 1987.

INDEX